NBO
Ellis

ARKINSAW COUSINS

A Story of the Ozarks

BY

J. BRECKENRIDGE ELLIS

NEW YORK
HENRY HOLT AND COMPANY
1908

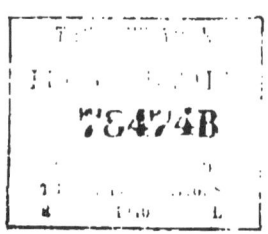

COPYRIGHT, 1908,
BY
HENRY HOLT AND COMPANY

Published February, 1908

TO
MY THREE—
Mother, Father, Brother

ARKINSAW COUSINS

CHAPTER I

IN many a small American town of older growth, families, perhaps half a dozen, are to be found bearing the same name. They are all more or less closely connected by ties of blood, though this may be unknown. The passage of years and the marriage into other families have produced great apparent diversity in character and temperament. In one town, the Clarks and Thompsons represent the extremes of social position; in another, the Davises or Porters fight each other over political or religious differences. And yet, if one could probe beneath the crust of prejudice, he might find that in some distinctive quality, every Clark is a Clark, and every Davis a Davis.

In Core City, Arkansas, lived the Thornberrys. Of all the men of the county, Winthrop Thornberry was the richest; whereas Hodgins Thornberry, if not the poorest, was perhaps the most worthless. Old Timothy Thornberry and his grandson, Will, owned the grocery on the corner; another grandson, Peter, was cashier in the National Bank; while a third, Oscar, conducted a restaurant. Nor were the annals of crime in Core City destitute of a Thornberry; for, while George Nicodemus, a Thornberry's son, was not in the penitentiary at the time of this story, it is because he had already served *his just sentence.*

One evening in April, while the rain was doing its utmost to undermine the reputation Core City sought to build up for its climate, a bright lamp appeared at Mrs. Eden's front window. It threw a shaft of cheer down the red footpath of pure native earth that ran to the front gate. It was time for Mary to return, and the mother smiled to herself as she placed the light. Not so her uncle Groner Thornberry, who at a distant table, had been perusing a novel by the aid of that very lamp. But Groner, a widower boarder of fifty or more, spoke not a word. With one hand clutching his crutch, and the other gripping the word he had last seen, he hobbled to the window; and, holding the book close to the blaze, and his bullet-shaped head close to the fine print, read on with moving lips. His face, which was creased with many lines, the results of rheumatic limbs and a discontented spirit, was clean-shaven, as if its owner would not suffer a single hair to conceal its permanent expression of dissatisfaction.

"Now," said Mrs. Eden cheerfully, "Mary can find her way without splashing into the pool." The light revealed, in the middle of the path, a slight depression filled with reddish water. It had been the intention, and, indeed, was even yet the intention, to fill up the depression, but somehow, one never thought of it except while it was raining.

"Yes," said Uncle Groner, looking up, "never mind *me;* I can balance here on my crutch and read when I *have* to." Then for fear he might hear a rejoinder, he dived into his book with an air that intimated his intention of staying under a very long time.

Mrs. Eden stepped to his side. The light revealed almost as many lines upon her face as upon his, but *they were the lines* of care and service. A homely face, one would have thought, seeing it for the first time; a hard, weather-beaten brow; a twisted mouth; a broad, uncompromising chin; a stunted nose; an eye without distinctive color—maybe gray.

"Lean on my arm, Uncle Groner," said Mrs. Eden helpfully.

"No," said the other, who was of precisely the same stuff of which martyrs are made, "if I must be taken out of my easy-chair every time Mary leaves the house, just say so; let's be frank about it and not try to gloss over matters. No, I'm much obliged, but I'll just prop myself up with my crutch." Again he dived to the remotest depths that his novel afforded. Mrs. Eden would never have taken the light from any man to light her own feet; but she was a mother, and her chin grew firmer as she turned away.

Soon after, Mary came. She, of course, went around the cottage to the kitchen-door; and, having set her umbrella to dry on the steps, she came in like a fragrant breath of the spring night. In her dark brown hair seemed to linger the perfume breath of the apple blossoms which give fame and beauty to the Ozarks. All the air was thrilling with delicious perfume from the fruit trees; the warm rain splashed the odors upon the edge of the little porch, and poured them down the complaining waterpipes, and washed them against the old-fashioned windowpanes.

"How sweet everything smells," said Mrs. Eden, who, somehow, had not thought of it until she saw her daughter.

Mary smiled sympathetically as she placed a large empty basket in its wonted place. She was about nineteen, some twenty years younger than her mother, although there seemed a wider chasm of time between them. Both were dressed as became women who must work hard and live frugally; but the plain attire of the girl graced the full curves and suited the stately height, and became a setting of small importance when one looked upon the serene and refined face. Mary's dark eyes were those of one who lives in dreams; and the placid brow, shaded by silken hair, was smoothed by the fair fingers of youth's ideals. Mrs. Eden, rugged and angular, seemed to have weathered more storms than commonly smite the waters of forty years. Yet the widow reflected in the clear, honest eye and in the peaceful, if creased brow, kinship to her daughter's spirit.

They were in the kitchen now, and Uncle Groner had possession of the front room.

"I ought to change this dress," said Mary, looking down at the bespattered skirt. "The walks are all torn up, and I had a pretty hard time getting to Mrs. Tripe's. But I would like to save that other skirt to wear the first time to church."

"Don't brush it," said her mother, "you'll just make it worse. *I* wouldn't change it. It's so rainy to-night—" her voice took on a sleepy, comfortable tone like that of a lazy waterpipe murmuring at the corner, "so ra-ainy and ba-a-ad, that I don't believe company *can* come."

"I've known them to come on very unlikely nights," said Mary doubtfully, "but I do want to save that fresh skirt. Anyway, I'll clean up the supper dishes first." Her voice suddenly grew half-hopeful. "They aren't cleaned up—are they?"

"Well," said Mrs. Eden regretfully, "no, Mary, they are not. While you were gone with the bread, Mrs. *Fimbleton's* baby got to crying so that they couldn't do a thing with it, so they came after me, and I had a time with it."

"Poor darling," murmured Mary, "I'm afraid they will lose the baby, yet."

Mrs. Eden's eyes filled with ready tears. "I'm afraid so," she said, as she removed a cloth thrown hastily over the soiled dishes. "Mary, if you say so, we will put off these dishes till morning, and do them before breakfast."

Mary hesitated. She was tempted. "No," she said suddenly, "don't you remember how it always hurries us when we do that? And if we're late, somebody always comes. And you know a team of horses couldn't hold Uncle Groner from getting up at five o'clock. No, let's do it now, mother."

Presently the rattle of dishes mingled with the dripping of the rain. Mary's sleeves, rolled above the elbows, showed the white, firm arms of youth and health, as her hands, glistening with soapsuds, washed the cups and saucers. Mrs. Eden's hands, wielding the tea-towel, showed red and hard and thin. For a time, there was no sound of voices in the cottage. In the next room, Uncle Groner perused the mystery of hidden hands, his blue thin lips moving ceaselessly, but without sound. In the kitchen, the little, round, nickel clock, standing upon its three shiny pegs, slipped noiselessly toward eight. Mary, tall and lithe, looked beyond the work of her hands, upon visions far different from the interior of a kitchen; while Mrs. Eden, low and heavy in build, stood near the dishpan, seeing nothing less beautiful, less divine, than her own dreamy maidenhood reframed in a picture of innocence and grace.

"I am trying to *think*," said Mrs. Eden suddenly,

"of the lines about the sadness of the days that are gone, 'When unto dying eyes'—do you remember?"

Mary answered softly:

> "'When unto dying eyes
> The casement slowly grows a glimmering square;
> So sad, so strange the days that are no more.'"

"That's it," said Mrs. Eden, slowly polishing a plate, and forgetting to take up the next.

"Are you thinking of days that are no more, mother?" asked Mary gently. The other looked at her with solemn eyes, seeing the daughter through the husband's memory.

But Mrs. Eden was one who combined the practical with the poetical.—"I suppose I thought of that," she said, "from noticing how dark the window is getting—and everything. Mary, I fear that lamp is going out."

"Yes, we said we would fill it to-day," said Mary, starting and looking at the lamp, which held its pale watch upon the mantle beside the glimmering-faced clock. "Do you think it will hold out till we have finished?"

Mrs. Eden turned up the wick to get more of it into the open. "Maybe so," she said hopefully, "but we'll have to hurry."

Mary had now come to the forks and knives. She rattled them briskly. "It is strange," she said, "that at the very time you spoke, I was thinking of Tennyson, too. It was his lines about Fortune, and they seemed so true, just as if written for us. And that's the only kind of poetry I like. Most of everything that's written seems meant for other people!"

"Now, I'll venture to say I know the very lines you

mean," cried her mother triumphantly. Still polishing the glistening plate, she looked up at the ever-darkening ceiling and declaimed:

> " ' Turn, Fortune, turn your wheel with smile or frown;
> With that wild wheel we go not up or down ';——

Goodness! I'm letting those other dishes get cold."

Mary turned up the wick higher and quoted:

> " ' Smile and we smile, the lords of many lands;
> Frown and we smile, the lords of our own hands;
> For man is man——' "

Mrs. Eden eagerly interrupted with

> " '—And master of his fate.' "

"That's splendid!" cried Mary, with enthusiasm. "Oh, mother, let's work that for a motto, and put it in our room before Ruth comes home!" Ruth was Mary's sister, who had spent the past year with a wealthy uncle.

"It would be fine," said Mrs. Eden, "and there's plenty of that red worsted. And I could draw enough blue out of an old stocking to give relief to the eye."

The lamp went out.

"Oh!" said Mrs. Eden, in the utmost surprise.

Uncle Groner's voice came to them in an angry undertone: "Somebody is a-knocking at the front door." His growl boded no good to friend or stranger.

"Oh!" whispered Mary, hastily seizing a towel, "who would have thought anybody could get out on such a wet night?"

"I would never have dreamed it," answered Mrs. Eden, hastily feeling about and overturning a chair.

Uncle Groner's voice came in sepulchral reproof: "*Polly Thornberry!*" *Mrs. Eden, some twenty years* ago, had been Polly Thornberry; and as Uncle Groner never approved of anybody who married a Thornberry, he made nothing of the intruding Eden, either when alive, or deceased.

"I am coming," called Mrs. Eden cheerily. "Mary, pick up the chair, if you can find it in this gloom."

"'Turn, Fortune, turn your wheel,'" murmured Mary as she groped in the darkness. Her mother hastened toward the white slit showing under the bottom of the partition door. As she turned the knob to go in to her uncle, she murmured over her shoulder to Mary:

"'Frown and we smile, the lords of our own hands!'"

CHAPTER II

Mrs. Eden emerged from the darkness of the kitchen. The cottage had two front doors, each opening into a front room; the kitchen with its porch formed the "el." Although somebody was knocking at the front door, near which sat Uncle Groner Thornberry, Mrs. Eden deemed it wisest to admit the visitor into the other front room. Accordingly, she caught up the lamp, leaving the widower and his lady novelist in semi-gloom, and hastened into the parlor proper.

Upon the narrow porch which ran before both front doors, stood two figures; that of a man attired in rubber overalls, a whip in his hand, with a certain breath of the stables about him, and a woman, insufficiently protected from the driving rain. At the gate shone the bright eye of the night hack.

"Howd'y, Cousin Polly, howd'y?" said the hackman heartily. "I heerd as you said the other day to Cousin Tim that you didn't know but as you would like to have a boarder. So here's one that wants boarding, and I thought I might be doing both of you a good turn to bring you together. That's all I've got to think of now, just to do other folks a good turn, for my own affairs is done got past any thought of *them* a-turning—for the *good,* leastwise; yes, mo'm."

"Come in," said Mrs. Eden to the woman, "you are getting so wet. Cousin Hodgins, can't you come in?"

"Nope, Cousin Polly, I must go and meet that other train. It's been *due some time,* but I reckon it'll show up within the next half-hour. If it don't, *I'm* goin' to bed. Well, lady, if you decide to board with Cousin Polly, I'll bring your trunk around some time tomorrow, I don't know just when; it's depending on the weather a good deal, and how I feel too; I ain't nigh as strong as I look, which has always got me into disfavor, people expecting more of me than they could git. Good-night, Cousin Polly, I hope I've did you a good turn, for I meant to." Hodgins Thornberry splashed his way back to the vehicle, shouted at the livery horses in a prodigious voice, and rolled away through the rain.

Mrs. Eden, being wholly unprepared for such a turn of events, nevertheless conducted the lady into the parlor, and sought to make her comfortable. While she administered to the needs of the dripping visitor, she talked to her in a motherly voice: "I just happened to say in Cousin Hodgins's hearing that if Mary and I had a boarder, we could do better; but I had no idea of seeking one. I am afraid we couldn't take care of you as you would have a right to expect. We are not very regular here—except about getting up early in the morning—and our fare, though wholesome, is quite plain. I am sure Cousin Hodgins thought he was doing something fine for us both, but his judgment is often at fault. There's a lodging-house on the next street about four blocks away, and when the rain has stopped, I'll go there with you."

"Oh, please don't," said the other earnestly. *"Won't you let me stay here?"* Mrs. Eden regarded her thoughtfully. She saw a girl of perhaps twenty or twenty-five or, possibly, twenty-eight; yes, probably twenty-eight. She was slight of form, with black hair, *black eyes,* and creamy-white, drooping lids. The face was almost pretty; perhaps it was pretty. It showed culture and restraint, and seemed to conceal more than it revealed. There was a reserve so profound that it amounted almost to secrecy; and a quietness so evident that it suggested sleepiness.

"My name is Pickens," said the stranger, looking up swiftly; "Goldie Pickens." After all, it was incorrect to say that her eyes were black, for while one was black, the other was blue. The view of both orbs gave an odd expression to the face, not an unpleasant one, but sphinx-like.

"Oh," said Mrs. Eden, smiling, "the music-teacher?"

"Yes," said Miss Pickens softly as she lowered her lids. "I suppose you knew I was coming here to spend five or six months for my health. And as I am not wealthy, I would like to pay my expenses as I go, Mrs. Eden. Is Mr. Winthrop Thornberry a relative of yours?"

"He is a cousin."

"His daughter is going to take lessons from me—twice a week. Perhaps *your* daughter—Miss Mary—would like to take; if so, I could partly pay my board in that way."

Mrs. Eden sighed. "Mary was saying a few days ago how she would love to take lessons; but we never felt that we could afford it; we have no piano."

"Oh, I will rent a piano," said Miss Pickens softly.

"There is a widower uncle who lives with us," said Mrs. Eden doubtfully. "He pays his board. I feel quite sure he would object to a piano in the house."

"Oh, no, he will not object," said Miss Pickens, drooping her lids.

Mrs. Eden was surprised. "You have never met Uncle Groner, *have you?*"

"No," said the lady simply, "but I feel sure he will not object. I will talk to him. Then you will let me stay?"

"I shall be glad for you to stay," said Mrs. Eden, "if you can be satisfied. You may try it upon that condition. My daughter and I are very busy people, and we cannot take much extra work upon ourselves."

"I'm sure everything will be satisfactory," murmured the other.

"That's more than I am," said Mrs. Eden, "but you may take chances with us."

In the meantime, Uncle Groner, outraged at having his lamp swiftly removed from under his very eyes, had stumbled to the kitchen, hoping to continue his novel without a great interval of suspense. He found the room in darkness, while Mary's cautious whisper warned him that there was no use to light the kitchen-lamp, since the oil was out. The elderly widower stood this state of affairs as long as he could, then marched upon the parlor door just as Mrs. Eden opened it to come out.

"I will come in there," Uncle Groner announced, advancing his crutch over the threshold, "for light I must have."

"Do so," said Mrs. Eden; then to her prospective boarder, "This is my uncle, Mr. Thornberry."

Uncle Groner looked severely at the valise at Miss Pickens's feet, and said tentatively, "A canvasser?"

"Uncle Groner, you heard Cousin Winthrop speak of the lady who was coming to make up a music class in Core City. This is the lady—Miss Pickens."

"How do you do, Miss Pickens?" said the established boarder, making for the stand-table whereon the lamp rested. "I do not like music. I never cared for it. I trust you will not object, if I go on with the work I am reading."

"I pray you to do so," said Miss Pickens softly. "Nothing is so distasteful as to be interrupted in the midst of a stirring tale."

"Why, you are right there," said Uncle Groner, seating himself at the table, but neglecting to open his book.

"I see you are reading one of my favorite books," said Miss Pickens gently.

When Mrs. Eden went to the kitchen, she found Mary crouching like a rabbit in a burrow. Mary made not the slightest noise, but alas! her mother knew she was there.

"Mary!" called Mrs. Eden cautiously.

"Mother," came a voice from the darkness, "my dress is so stained! I could not possibly see company as I am. I will just crouch here till they go away."

"But they are not going away," said Mrs. Eden firmly.

"Oh, mother!"

"No. Besides there is only one of them. You have heard of the Miss Pickens who is coming here to work up a music class? Her health failed her, where she was teaching in one of the largest conservatories of the East. Well, *she* is the 'company'; and she wants to board here and give you lessons."

Mary's voice came in ecstatic tones: "Oh mercy, mother, don't let her get away!" There was a scramble in the darkness.

"Come right in as you are," said Mrs. Eden. "I don't propose turning one hand's breadth out of the way for any boarder *on earth*. She might just as well get used to seeing you in your work-clothes. Your Uncle Groner is with her this moment."

Mary wailed: "Then all is lost! You know how he fought the very suggestion of our helping out our poor income with another boarder."

"Let's hurry," said Mrs. Eden; "maybe we can circumvent your Uncle G."

Mary stifled something like an undignified giggle, as they sped to the parlor door. They opened it. Uncle Groner had left his seat beside the lamp and now he occupied a chair near Miss Goldie Pickens. His crutch lay across his knees, and he was listening to her soft voice with evident interest.

"And then," said Miss Pickens, evidently continuing their conversation, "I will read aloud to you some choice work of fiction. I have been told that my voice is not disagreeable; I can assure you it wears well. In this way, you and I, Mr. Thornberry, might pass many delightful hours."

"Yes, yes," said Uncle Groner, nodding his bullet head in emphatic approval.

A discussion of terms followed the entrance of the ladies. Miss Pickens was shown a room upstairs with which she professed herself charmed. She was definitely accepted as a boarder with Uncle Groner's full approbation. When they were once more settled in the parlor, the old widower made a pretense of reading his novel, but many a glance slipped off the edge of the page and encompassed the demure, saint-like face of the music-teacher. The drooping of Miss Pickens's lids and the slightly convex curve of the mouth gave an effect to the entire countenance, of separation, as it were, from the material elements of daily life. In *the presence* of that serious face and mellow, sometimes half-audible voice, the higher functions of human affairs seemed commonplace, and the commonplace, vulgar. Moreover, the very slightness, not to say thinness, of the graceful form, suggested an existence entirely apart from the domain of bread and meat, while the changes of position, the slight advancement of one little foot before the other, the bend of the elbow, and the crook of the white fingers, seemed to be done to some fairy music too ethereal and remote for others' perception.

In contrast with this grave, half-appealing demeanor, Mary Eden cannot be said to have appeared at her best. In the homely surroundings of the kitchen, her dreamy brown eyes and pure brow had presented a delicate fineness like the quaintness of a white angel painted into a background of yellow brown, deepening to black. But Miss Goldie Pickens was so much more angelic against any background, that Mary's more masculine qualities were thrown into relief. The honesty of her spirit gave a curious effect of ruggedness to her expression, similar to the physical ruggedness of her mother. She became less the soft, yielding, fascinating woman, and more the unvexed soul of courage, patience, and will. Mrs. Eden perceived the difference, and felt intuitively that, to a man, the Pickens saintliness would more readily appeal. The mother-heart naturally felt resentment against the innocent boarder, but the Christian foot trampled this resentment in the dust.

"It would be of great help to me," said Miss Pickens, looking at Mrs. Eden as at a mother, then at Mary as at a sister, and then at Uncle Groner as at a person of immeasurable superiority, "if you could suggest any *one likely to take* lessons from me. You say Mr. Winthrop Thornberry is your cousin; his daughter has engaged my services; perhaps you have other relatives in Core City?"

"I'm sorry to say that we have," said Uncle Groner, closing his book with a vicious snap. "The hackman who drove you here is one of 'em—Hodgins Thornberry."

"Is there any one in his family who wishes to pursue a musical education?"

Groner Thornberry snorted. "I wish you could teach him the tune the old cow died on; then maybe he'd go off and do it."

Miss Pickens looked pained, and her lids drooped.

"Cousin Hodgins is very poor," said Mrs. Eden. "They couldn't afford it."

"Isn't it dreadful to be poor!" exclaimed Mary, with energy. "It's like walking down a beautiful country lane with your hands and feet tied; you can not reach out to gather the roses, and you can take but a short step at a time."

"It is sad," said Miss Pickens, her voice almost whispering like a soft breeze among autumn leaves.

"I think it's a disgrace," said Uncle Groner. "And to my mind, it's more like a man at a rockpile with an iron ball to his leg."

Mrs. Eden looked at Mary and said, with a subtle lightening of her pliant face, "But we may smell the roses; and for every short step we take toward God, He comes a long way toward us."

"Well," said Uncle Groner, shying off from this lead, "Winthrop Thornberry's rich enough; he's the richest man in the county; five hundred thousand dollars at the least, and only two children. But it's nothing to *him if his kinfol*ks die in the poorhouse."

Miss Pickens clasped her hands. "I shall be so timid when I go there to instruct his daughter; I shall be afraid of committing some breach of etiquette. I have never been used to the homes of the rich."

"When I go into a rich man's house," said Uncle Groner loudly, "I just dig my heel into his carpet, the same as if it was a rag carpet like this one; and when I shut the door, I slam it, if I want to. I suppose it's a continual feast to Winthrop Thornberry that he's a rich man; but he don't get any of his pleasure out of me; I don't feed anybody's pride."

"Cousin Winthrop is as good a man as ever lived," said Mrs. Eden, with energy. "Miss Pickens," she added, reproof in her eye, "you ought to feel complimented, for I haven't known Uncle Groner to take so much time from his novels for many a day."

Miss Pickens cast a respectful, yet gracious, look at the old widower, who immediately betook himself to cover. "I think," said Miss Pickens, who had a wonderful memory for names, "I heard the hack-driver—Mr. Hodgins Thornberry—speak of a Mr. Timothy Thornberry. Has that gentleman any children?"

"No," said Mrs. Eden, "but his three grandchildren live with him. They are all grown young men. Mr. Timothy Thornberry is my half-uncle."

"Do you think any of the young gentlemen would like to take music lessons?" asked the young lady softly.

Uncle Groner came out of his book. "Will is in the grocery-store with his grandfather," he said; "Oscar runs a restaurant; and Peter is in the bank. I don't see any gap in their activities for music to come in. The fact is, *Miss Pickens*——"

"I wish you would call me 'Miss Goldie,'" said the lady, with shy appeal.

"Why, thank you," said Uncle Groner, his dried and wrinkled face showing a slight color of pleasure, not unlike a water-soaked apple touched by frost, "I was about to say that the Thornberrys will be of little service to you, Miss—er—Miss Goldie. The Thornberrys have never made what they should have made out of themselves. I don't know any tribe so capable and at the same time of so little account. Just think of one Thornberry running a restaurant, and another the town-hack, and all the kin nearly ready to die of joy because the last one I speak of is willing to *be* a hackman. If there wasn't such a business as driving a hack back and forth and moving houses—Hodgins is also a house-mover—I reckon nothing on earth could have been found that he'd 'a' been willing to do."

"Oh, do listen!" said Mary suddenly, as above the pouring of the rain, footsteps sounded upon the front porch; "and I have neglected to change my dress!"

Other footsteps followed the first. The porch fairly shook with the invasion. "Well," said Uncle Groner, turning desperately to the music-teacher, "how do you like that tune?"

A loud knocking sounded at the door. Mrs. Eden went to open it and confronted once more her cousin Hodgins Thornberry, the hackman. Over his broad shoulders she caught a glimpse of what appeared to be innumerable faces, while the white eye of the hack glared at her from the yard gate.

"Howd'y, Cousin Polly, howd'y?" cried Hodgins, in gusty welcome. "I've brought quite a bunch this time, hey? Come on the late train, just in. All of *'em strangers, every one* of 'em."

"But——" said Mrs. Eden weakly.

"Is this Mrs. Eden?" said a tall, dignified gentleman, stepping forward.

"Yap, it's her," said Hodgins cheerfully. "Well, good-night, everybody."

"Wait," said Mrs. Eden, in distress. "Wait, Cousin Hodgins, there is some mistake."

"No, they ain't no mistake," said Hodgins loudly. "I done my best to take 'em to the hotel. I told 'em you didn't have no extry rooms with your new boarder on your hands. They wouldn't listen to me. Come they would, and go they won't, so it's good-night to one and all." Hodgins Thornberry splashed away, his rubber cape glimmering in the pale lamplight.

"Mrs. Eden," said the tall gentleman, gently making his way into the parlor, "I am Sylvester Mulkey. This is Mrs. Mulkey. This is my daughter, Gladys Lucile. This is my father."

"Where are the others?" asked Uncle Groner, propping his rheumatic limbs by means of the crutch and glaring with a hostile eye.

"There are no more," said Mr. Mulkey, with impressive gravity. "Mrs. Eden, we have often read your poems in our religious journals. We feel as if we had known you always. Our minister, brother Waitewhile—are you acquainted with brother Waitewhile?"

"Yes, indeed," said Mrs. Eden. "He always spends the night here when he goes to his appointment in central Arkansas."

"Ah, yes. Well, brother Waitewhile told us to be sure and see you when we came to Core City—we are moving here to live—our furniture now stands in the car on the track. I *said*, 'What! is Mrs. Eden in Core

City? Surely not the author of the religious poems we have read so often.' Brother Waitewhile assured me it was none other. Then I said we would come and stop with you until our house could be made ready for us."

"Now, Polly Thornberry," muttered Uncle Groner, "you see what comes of poetry."

"I'm glad to see any of brother Waitewhile's friends," said Mrs. Eden, "but I am sorry to say, Mr. Mulkey——"

"That is all right, that is all right," Mr. Mulkey interposed, noting the rag carpet, the handmade couch, the footstool composed of tomato cans, the mottoes upon the wall that served as pictures, and, in brief, the aspect of simple yet dignified poverty. "Pray make no excuse to us. We are glad to be with friends and to find shelter from the elements."

"But, Mr. Mulkey, we have only six rooms in the house, and Miss Pickens has taken one of them."

"That is all right," said Mr. Mulkey, waving his hand and looking down upon everybody from his superior height. "We can put up with any sort of inconvenience. My wife and daughter can sleep in one bed, and I will share some couch with my father. In this land of strangers, we knew not where else to go. We could not turn aside from *Mrs. Eden's* door," he added with gentle dignity.

Mrs. Eden looked at them with a speculating eye. They seemed a great many. Indeed, the little parlor had the appearance of a packed committee-room. Mr. Mulkey himself, with his head dodging the chain from which a swinging-lamp used to depend, brought out by contrast the very wide circumference of his wife. *Gladys Lucile* Mulkey was a beautiful girl of about

Mary's age, not quite so tall, but rounder and more solid. Old Mr. Mulkey, a gentleman of about seventy, leaned upon his cane and seemed to be appealing for a chair to rest his thin and feeble frame.

"Do sit down," said Mrs. Eden, taking compassion upon the venerable Mulkey—upon him of the cane and long, flowing, white whiskers.

"Thank you very kindly," said the old man, "for I'm nearly tired to death. Come and set me, Sylvester."

"Yes, father," said Mr. Mulkey, going up to the old man and putting an arm about the spare form. He did something to one of the venerable legs, and the elder Mulkey was seated. "I can get up of myself," he said, looking about with content, "but when up, I can not get down. So I make it a custom to stay down, except when Sylvester is about. Sylvester understands my legs as nobody else does."

"You are fortunate," said Mrs. Eden gently, "to have a son ready to minister to you. We have a folding-bed in the other front room—a room we use as our dining-room, when we do not eat in the kitchen."

"Now that is all right," said Mr. Mulkey kindly, "the folding-bed will do very nicely. We will not object to staying in the dining-room at night. Of course, you couldn't have known we were coming, and when one moves, he prepares his spirit to undergo all sorts of inconvenience."

"Mrs. Mulkey," said Mrs. Eden, "you and your daughter can have my bed upstairs, in the room next to Miss Pickens."

"And what will you do?" asked Gladys Lucile doubtfully.

"I am sure I do not know," said Mrs. Eden.

"We must all *do just the* best we can," said fleshy

Mrs. Mulkey. "Mrs. Eden is a mother, and she knows how I feel. We must all do just the best that we can under the circumstances."

"That is it," said Mr. Mulkey, seizing the word eagerly. "Under the circumstances, yes. We must all do the very best we can, and do it with cheerful hearts."

"As for *me*," Uncle Groner spoke up abruptly, "it is my bedtime, and I allow to get into my room before somebody takes it. So, as Cousin Hodgins says, 'goodnight, one and all!'" Uncle Groner stumped upstairs and slammed himself into his room. Mrs. Eden was somewhat discomposed by this conduct; but Mr. Mulkey waved his hand, saying, "I take no offense, madam, at the invalid's impatience. Doubtless he is suffering."

Mrs. Eden still stood bewildered. "Mother," said Mary, suddenly coming to her rescue, "I have it! Everything will be all right. I will explain when we are alone."

"In that case," said Mr. Mulkey, "I trust we may retire early. We would like to sit and visit with you, but we have been on the Texarkana train all day, and are quite exhausted."

A scene of varied activity ensued. In the course of time, bed-clothing had been arranged, revealing still farther the poverty of the Eden household. Mrs. Mulkey and her beautiful daughter reigned in Mrs. Eden's bedroom, thus taking the last available room upstairs. Mr. Mulkey and his father were turned at large in the dining-room, thus forcing Mrs. Eden and Mary into the kitchen, where they now stood on their last foot of ground.

"Now, Mary," whispered Mrs. Eden, panting from *labor and* excitement, "what is your plan? We can't sleep on the bare kitchen floor. If we sit up all night, we couldn't read to each other, for that would keep our guests awake."

"No, that isn't it," said Mary, as she lit a roll of paper and held it up to make a light. "Let's slip over to Uncle Timothy's and stay there till morning; then we can creep back here just before day and make the kitchen fire and nobody will be the wiser."

"Why, what a lark!" cried Mrs. Eden. "Hold that paper higher while I find my cloak—don't burn your fingers—where *did* I leave my cloak?"

"You were cutting wood, in the woodshed, this afternoon," suggested Mary.

"Maybe it's there," said Mrs. Eden, with bright hopefulness. "If it isn't, I am sure I don't know where it is."

"Anyway," said her daughter cheerfully, "it has almost stopped raining. Maybe it will stop in a minute."

"Yes, maybe it will," said the mother joyously. The paper went out. The rain came on with renewed violence.

"Mother," Mary whispered, "would you mind to wait here while I go to Uncle Tim's? I will have Will come back with me, and we will bring you an overall. My umbrella is there on the back porch. I'm not afraid. What do you say?"

"I say do it!" said Mrs. Eden eagerly.

CHAPTER III

MARY left the kitchen door wide open. For a moment there was a faint gleam upon her cloak and umbrella from some far-away, insufficient street light; then she was swallowed up in the darkness, and the driving rain obliterated her footsteps. She knew the way well—through the back lot, across a street, down a narrow alley for several blocks, to Timothy Thornberry's back gate. She was brave, and though she could not see her hand before her, there was little hesitation in the swift, springy step. It was not until she had traversed the back lot and gained the street that she remembered the torn-up condition of the walks. Core City was in a fever of granitoid enthusiasm. Go where you might, you found planks on end, and cones of concrete and cinders. Sometimes a red lantern gave a warning wink; sometimes you were expected to use your own judgment. With her skirts held closely about her, Mary Eden felt her way, hopeful at last of reaching firm ground.

At last, she came to a crossing. Her extended hand found the head of the alley and she plunged into it, though it did not seem familiar. Fortunately, the ground could no more be made muddy by rains than a slab of granite can be softened by a summer shower; so on she went, her umbrella in one hand, her skirts in the other. When she had gone some distance, she began to feel about with the umbrella, scraping it *against high board* fences, and thrusting it into little barn windows. Having presently assured herself that she was in the wrong alley, it was necessary to cross over to the next. This was rendered difficult by not knowing exactly where she was. However, feeling no uneasiness, Mary took the first turn to the right that her prying umbrella discovered, and began a detour. Up to this time, an occasional faint radiance had spasmodically appeared in the upper air, indicating that the city lights were about to die out, according to their wont on intensely dark nights. A uniform black overhead now told her that they had done their worst.

Suddenly she stumbled into a shallow ditch which had been left unguarded, from a feeling on the part of the contractor that everybody ought to know about it. She was uninjured, but her fall made a splash just as she became aware of a man's footsteps. It was useless to think of escaping an encounter, so Mary said in a clear, but slightly tremulous accent, "This is a very dark night, sir."

She was answered by a man's slow, soft voice, whose suggestion of easy comfort did not conceal a distinct note of surprise. "Yes, too dark to be out alone. Why on earth, Mary, are you wandering about behind these barns and stables?"

"Oh, Will!" Mary exclaimed, delighted at recognizing her cousin. "You are the very one I wanted. Where is your hand?"

"It's looking for yours," said the young man, in an accent of profound enjoyment. The nearness of Mary always made everything seem different to Will Thornberry, and the difference was nearly always enchanting. He found her hand and held it in a firm, if wet, clasp. It was no longer *of moment to* him why she was there.

The only problem that presented itself to his mind was how to extend this delightful companionship indefinitely. As he held her hand, there were communicated to his thirsty soul the graces and charms and sunny homelike qualities from the fount of her being.

"I'm on my way to your house," Mary exclaimed, squeezing his hand in enjoyment of his protecting presence. "Who would ever have thought you could be so useful!" she added, with a gurgle of fun in her tones.

"I don't know how useful I'll be," remarked the other, "for home is hard to find." He laughed boyishly. "Cousin Hodgins stopped and told us he'd taken you a houseload of folks, and grandpa 'lowed I'd better go see if we couldn't help you somehow; but the walks are so torn up, I got to exploring, till now I don't know where I am. One thing that sorter handicaps me is being run after by dawgs."

"We must hurry to find your house," said the other, with decision. "Let's prowl along this way. You go first."

"Now you be very careful," said the young man. "I'll hold your hand. It's no trouble. This is an adventure, isn't it! Mary, this is what I call life."

"But adventures aren't life," said Mary seriously. "You mustn't think of life in that way. This is just a sort of a—a—recess."

"At any rate," he rejoined, "we may enjoy it until school takes up." He felt she was drifting around to her didactic standpoint, not because she was naturally serious, but because she felt his lack of purpose. He liked her best when she forgot to seek to improve him; but, even at her scholastic worst, he adored her. "I believe," he added, "that this is Buck Smith's place."

"*I wish you* realized deeper what life means," she

said, with thrilling earnestness. "To live is to feel the throb of the great world as it turns heavily in daily stress."

He might have replied that, to his perception, to live was to feel her hand in his, and her voice falling like gracious music upon his ear. But it would not do to say anything like that—no, it would never do. "Never" is a hard word for the heart to construe.

Will sighed; and as his boot struck something that made a clatter, he said abruptly: "Now I *know* this is Buck Smith's, for that old tin lard-can has been lying up against this worm-eaten fence ever since I was a boy. So we know that we're on the wrong road. That's *one* point gained, anyway."

Mary silently allowed herself to be turned about and led forward by her passive hand. Upon this girl Will had many claims of interest. The mere fact that he was a human being was sufficient to engage her philanthropy. Their long comradeship, from the days of hobbyhorses and mud pies to those of lengthened skirts, derby hats, and the church choir, counted more to her mind than their distant kinship; but more than all, he was Peter's brother.

As Peter's brother, it was not enough for Will to be handsome, indolent, good-natured, and haphazard; he ought to be something greater, something to set him apart from the unaspiring. She was thinking of this as she followed, rather than of the rain, or of the hand that guided her.

Presently her feeling found abrupt utterance: "You're so young and strong! And you're a man. Oh, what you could do if you would!"

"I suppose so," said Will lazily. "One trouble I've found is to keep *from doing* more than I wanted to.

But I'm not complaining, Mary. I've managed, pretty generally, to keep out of more than my share." (He pronounced it "shur.")

"Your education is——" Mary sighed.

"Yes," said the kind, slow, mellow Southern voice, "sadly neglected. But yonder's the light from Oscar's window. We're at home now. Oscar is studying. I reckon it was too rainy to keep the restaurant open. Oscar will load himself with enough education to ballast the whole family. And Peter——" He checked himself abruptly, then chuckled. "Peter, he'll hold up the family dignity."

"Your brother Peter," said Mary, with distinct emphasis, "has always tried to make the most of himself."

"And he's done it, too," Will said promptly; "what you see is all there is."

Mary drew her hand away as she asked, with cool aloofness, "What do you mean by that?"

Now, Will had a motto which was often of great solace. It ran, "Best way's to say nothing." He was sorry he had forgotten it. He knew that Peter was something of an idol to Mary Eden, and while himself convinced that the oldest brother was formed of ordinary clay, with a dulled nostril for the incense which burned before him, it was not for Will to prove himself an iconoclast. So they reached Timothy Thornberry's side door with a little cloud between them.

It was Peter Thornberry who opened the door while Will paused to drain the umbrella. Mary's eyes brightened shyly as she looked into the long, narrow, purposeful face of the oldest brother.

"Mary!" he exclaimed, "how wet you are! and muddy!" She could not tell if he were glad to see her, and, indeed, Peter himself did not know. Since he had taken upon himself the office of mentor to all the Thornberry connection, he was careful to reward no deflection of duty. Duty, as Peter conceived it, was to live like a polite person in a book. He felt that Mary liked him, at least to the uttermost borderlands of cousinship; whether farther, he had not inquired, and, possibly, Mary did not know. He liked Mary Eden better than any other maiden, cousin or not, but in her present plight, she did not present the appearance of one who had been conducting herself as a polite person in a book.

The lamp from the high mantel above the fireplace brought out plainly the difference between the handsome, rather shaggy-haired, slightly lounging, and stockily built Will Thornberry, with his kindly brown eyes, and Peter—slim, tall, graceful, serious, almost magisterial, and very dark, with lean cheeks, high, narrow forehead, and thin retreating hair above it.

Old Timothy Thornberry, who had been seated near his wife at the open fireplace, rose at Mary's entrance.

"Why, howd'ye, Mary?" he called heartily; "come right up to the fire. When Hodgins told us about all that company, your Aunt Polly"—indicating his round-faced, smiling wife, who gazed fondly at Mary from under her old-fashioned lace cap—"she 'lowed you-all would be ran out of house and home. Will went projecting over there to find what he could do, but I see he's come back like a drowned rat."

Timothy Thornberry, the grandfather of Peter, Oscar, and Will, and the half-uncle of Mary's mother, was past seventy. His hair, perfectly white, was cut short over the round head. His snowy beard came to a point some eight inches from his chin. His cheeks were red, healthy, and smooth; seemingly, the bird of time had slipped from his face, unable to gain a foothold long enough to leave an impression of its claws. He had the kindly, luminous brown eyes of Will, and the same gentle, leisurely voice. He spoke, too, with the same soft slurring of letters and melting together of words, too euphonious and easy to be dressed up in an unnatural garb of dialectic spelling. His garments indicated careful economy. The long black coat shone in the back like a pale moon, and the trousers, brown and glossy, were hairy at the extremities.

Mary explained that her mother was waiting for some one to bring a protecting garment, that she might come through the rain to spend the night. "My own cloak will do fine," said Mary, "but if Will takes it, he ought to have a lantern." She spoke with a faint flush in her cheeks, knowing that Peter was waiting to see if she could clear herself from his possible displeasure. Apparently the family oracle was appeased, for he made her comfortable in a low rocking-chair near the hearth.

"Sure," said Timothy Thornberry, resuming his own seat when he found that the visitor was installed. "Sure," he repeated in his comfortable drawl. "William, where is that lantern?"

"I don't know," said Will; "but you know the old thing got so that it acted crazy; anyhow."

"I reckon you could find your way with it, son. Call Oscar. See if he knows anything about it. We've got to get communicated with Polly somehow. She can't spend the night over yonder in the kitchen."

Oscar, next to the oldest brother, was called downstairs. He came, carrying his open book. He greeted *Mary* with cousinly heartiness.

"I don't know a thing about that lantern," he said, rumpling his hair in a disturbed way, and taking off his spectacles to rub them. "I wish I did know where it is. I think Joe Claybourn borrowed it."

"And didn't he bring it back?" asked the old man hopefully.

"Who, *Jim?*" interposed Will; "Jim never brought back nothing!"

Oscar, finding the conversation diverted from himself, slyly peeped into his book, and gained at least a paragraph before he felt driven out into society again. Even then he utilized the time by memorizing what he had just read.

"Wife," said the old man helplessly.

"I'll go look for it," said the old lady, "though it's like lookin' for a rich man in the eye of a needle." She went out; but the fact that she was presently two rooms removed from the others did not debar her from maintaining a brisk conversation. As she was pretty hard of hearing, she had much difficulty in catching the words that were shouted to her from the sitting-room.

"I wish," said Peter, frowning, "that the family would quit screaming from one end of the house to the other. I know it must bother the neighbors. It isn't respectable."

"Well, son," said Timothy, lighting his pipe, "your grandmother has so much to say and so little strength to travel back and forth to say it, that, barring telephones, I don't know anything for it but lung power."

From the distant kitchen came a long murmuring sound, perfectly unintelligible, except that it ended in a tone of marked *inquiry.*

"She's asking something," said Will, balancing himself on the hind legs of his chair.

"Wife," called the grandfather, "we can't hear one word you are a-saying."

Oscar, finding himself forgotten, dived again into his volume; it was a Latin grammar. He had engaged with the deponent verbs.

"Maybe she has found it," said Mary hopefully; "I'll go and see."

"No," said Peter, "you stay by the fire, Mary; your hand is still cold." He took it and held it up. The color slowly crept to her face. He laid the hand gently upon her lap and added, "I will go for you." Mary brushed back her hair with the hand Peter had held. She felt deeply the subtle deference, the refined voice that found a note, all its own, in addressing her—in brief, Peter's whole air of protection, which indicated that she belonged to him rather than to Will or Oscar. Will, too, was aware of Peter's polished show of proprietorship. During the delightful walk through the darkness, Mary's hand had all the time lain in the youngest brother's, without any consciousness upon her part; and yet, when Peter drew her fingers through his, to find if they were cold, the glow of the hearth seemed to set her cheeks afire. Will stared thoughtfully at the flickering flames, his brown hair standing over his brow and turning down their edges toward his eyes. Even when the lantern was found, and brought, palely a-light, he seemed lost in his own reflections. He rose and took it without seeming to know exactly where he was, and went out silently.

Peter drew up a chair beside Mary and smiled at her. "You are a brave soldier," he said. "I do hope *you won't take cold.*"

Mary happily assured him that there was no danger. As they talked, Peter bore himself with that elegant ease and dignity that naturally belonged to the only Thornberry "in a bank." The young man was entertaining. He was inspired to be at his best by the charming picture his young cousin presented. As Mary sat before the fire, with the lamplight touching the side of the back of her head, and the firelight painting her smooth, pure brow and speaking face, the plainness of her attire and the travel-stained condition of the skirts seemed to add piquancy to her charm; just as in a real picture, it is not the new house against the field of grain that gives greatest charm, but an old building, partly in ruins. It is only by use that an object becomes homelike, and homelikeness was one of Mary's characteristics, because her fine dresses were pitiably few.

Will adored her for this everyday air; and Peter liked her in spite of it. He tried, now, to forget her plain clothes, and that was not difficult when he rested his eyes upon her face. He had three good, serviceable jokes and one conundrum which he had gleaned from the week's papers; he knew of a member of the church who was thinking of moving down into the cotton belt below Little Rock, and he had been to Fayetteville to witness a game of football between the university and Rolla. He was, consequently, rich in resources, and time seemed to gallop, while old Timothy and his wife sat looking on in easy content, smoking and knitting respectively; and Oscar, with eyes fixed, smiled absently when the others laughed aloud, and moved his lips silently over his surreptitious acquisition of learning.

All too soon Will Thornberry returned, bringing Mrs. Eden. They came in a little whirlwind of motion and excitement, and the old people immediately broke into exclamations of uneasiness over the wet condition of the widow, and of pleasure over her coming, that wrought fearful havoc with Peter's sonorous, carefully laid conversation. He withdrew within himself as they swept up to the fire. Oscar, jostled out of his Latin grammar, looked wildly about as if wondering what it was all about. Will picked up a guitar and, sitting apart, idly strummed with one finger, his face turned so he could not see Mary.

"And so you have a new boarder, Polly," said old Timothy, smoking leisurely; so leisurely, indeed, that he was frequently obliged to draw hard to prevent his pipe from going out. "That's going to bring you considerable trouble, considerable. I never knew a satisfied boarder. I reckon if Job had went to boarding, we'd a-heard complaints from him that boils couldn't wring out. And I judge a young woman is more unwieldy still."

"I've told her," said Mrs. Eden, smiling, "that we are not going out of our way for her. She'll have to put up with what we have. And you know Uncle Groner just naturally won't let us get *clear down* to bed-rock on saving. And our income is not enough, Uncle Tim; it must be increased somehow."

"Looks like you ought to have enough to live on, Polly," said the other, considering. "How much do you make out of that bread-baking?"

"We bake fifty loaves, three times a week."

"That's considerable money," mused the old man. "Polly, how much did you give on the church debt this spring?"

"Now, Uncle Tim, you know how hard it was to *raise that*——"

"How much, Polly?"

"I gave fifty, and Mary twenty-five; it was little enough. You know we are better off than most of the members. Oh, they are *so* poor!"

"That's seventy-five dollars," said Timothy Thornberry, nodding and rubbing his white beard. "Polly, how much do you pay on the preacher's salary?"

"Only twenty-five," said Mrs. Eden apologetically.

"That's a hundred. Polly, how much of that bread do you give away?"

Mrs. Eden laughed.

"Timothy," spoke up the old lady, "you leave Polly alone. Everybody that knows her, knows you can't give her nothing she won't give away when your back's turned. Maybe she'll get her reward for it some day, but it's certain she ain't got it yet."

"But I have!" cried Mrs. Eden, her eyes shining so bright and her bearing so confident that one forgot the hard, heavily-cut face and the shapeless, toil-swayed form. "Every dollar I give away buys me a pound of happiness. Giving is *life;* and you know a tree," she went on, her voice vibrant with enthusiasm, "bears its fruit, not for the good of the tree, oh, no!—it is for the world."

"Cousin Polly," spoke up Peter, in an admonitory voice, "you are getting excited." Peter regarded excitement as almost vulgar.

"Yes; I forget myself," said Mrs. Eden, dropping her voice. "I don't want to preach. And I know we are keeping you up, Aunt Polly. Do you-all remember those lines—I think they are by Celia Thaxter?—

"'Dark skies *must* clear, and when the clouds are *past*
One golden day redeems a dreary *year*.'"

"It's a long time to wait," said Mary softly.

"Yes, it *is* long," said Mrs. Eden, her eyes still shining, "but when a golden day really comes, you forget all the waiting. I know, for I have seen—a few——"

Her voice faltered, as there flashed upon her mind the memory of her wedding-day. But she cleared her throat and laughed at her own faltering, and throwing back her head, cried bravely:

> " '*One* golden day redeems a dreary *year*.
> Then let me be.
> I *must* be glad and grateful to the *end*.'

I've lost the rhyme somehow," she added, "but you know what I mean. So every time when I get discouraged, I go and do some good, strong, hard work, and turn my sorrow into labor."

"Why, Polly," said Timothy Thornberry, stroking her hair, "*you* don't get discouraged, do you? I never knew anybody as bright and full of business."

"No wonder she gets discouraged," spoke up Will, striking his guitar a vicious blow. "Having a sorrow is bad enough; but turning it into labor is just to make bad worse."

Mrs. Eden laughed. "I know you, Will, better than you know yourself," she said affectionately. "You are true blue, and you will do things when they need to be done."

Will tucked his guitar under one arm and, going over to Mrs. Eden, put the other around her neck. There was an instant's pause, then he said abruptly, "Good-night, everybody."

CHAPTER IV

TIMOTHY THORNBERRY sat before the open door of his "grocery store." It was a two-story building, facing the public square. The upper floor was devoted to the mystic rites of masonry, odd-fellowship, and woodman's craft, according to whose turn it might be to guard the sacred portals. The lower floor, rented by Timothy and his grandson, Will, in partnership, was so crowded with boxes and pyramids of cans and barrels that a lane of the narrowest extent was afforded from back to rear. The single front window was decorated with jars of olives, nuts, and apples, and packages of various breakfast foods. At one place the aisle, down the length of the building, had opened up as if to give the customer room in which to turn around; but the large iron platform of the scales had been crowded into the clearing.

Timothy lounged in his split-bottomed chair on the uneven brick pavement. Will's head appeared at the show-window, and his grandfather hailed him lazily, "Lookin' for somethin', hey?"

Will nodded abstractedly. A good deal of his time was spent in searching for their various possessions; but he realized that little help was to be expected from his grandfather. It had been said that many boxes and kits had been in the shop for years, and that both partners had forgotten their very existence.

The old man smoked his pipe and looked with interest down the street. A wagon was drawing near, loaded down with household furniture.

"Who's movin'?" Timothy inquired of the merchant who sat upon the doorstep of the next frame building. The merchant, not knowing, propounded the question to the proprietor of the next business house, who happened to be standing in his doorway, idly whittling. The inquiry was thus passed from house to house till it reached the corner, unanswered.

In the meantime, the moving wagon had come to a sudden, almost disastrous standstill in front of Timothy's door. In laying the new stone crossing, a gap had been left open just wide enough to catch a wagon wheel, and narrow enough to hold it when caught. This was the cause of the present stoppage. The pieces of furniture, shaken into convulsions by the sudden wrench, quivered in their ropes, and the tall headpiece of a bed had an air of shuddering at its close proximity to the kitchen-cabinet. The owner of the household goods, a tall, solemn-looking gentleman of forty-five, with a prodigious black mustache, leaped to the ground at the shock; but the driver, Hodgins Thornberry, not only retained his seat with admirable equipoise, but maintained an uninterrupted working of the jaw that bespoke a plentiful supply of "natural leaf."

The owner of the furniture was Mr. Mulkey, the newcomer to Core City. He looked inquiringly at the driver of the dray. "Well," he said impatiently, "what are we to do? Remember we must get that car unloaded before the accommodation comes down from Van Buren."

"I don't know," said Hodgins Thornberry, shaking his head; "we're in a bad fix, *I* call it. It will be a powerful job to get that wheel out of that crack—now you know it will."

Old Timothy Thornberry slowly rose from his

split-bottomed chair, and leisurely started across the street to the scene of misfortune.

"The wheel must be prized out," said Mr. Mulkey fiercely. "Man, we are in a hurry. Get a crowbar; call in some of your fellows to help." His brow was dark with commanding will, and his tone coercive.

Hodgins crossed his legs. "I reckon we *will* have to prize her out," he agreed, "but don't you worry about that train a-comin'. It don't never come on time, and if it did, it would just switch around your car, or wait for some of the boys to shove it down on the side-track. They ain't no hurry, you might say. That ain't the way *we* do, in Core City. We take things *easy*. And when you look at it philosophical, that's the only way to take things. Just consider the subject of Death. Some take death hard, some take it easy. But does that make any difference to Death? It does not, and I'll tell you why: because we must all die, some sooner than others, and few as soon as they ought."

The look which Mr. Mulkey cast upward at the logician plainly indicated that he regarded him as coming under the "few" just specified. But Mr. Mulkey was nothing if not portentously dignified. Accordingly, turning to old Timothy:

"Sir," he said, "I am Mulkey—Sylvester Mulkey."

"Mighty glad to meet you," said Timothy heartily, shaking his hand. "I'm Captain Thornberry. You seem sorter handicapped here. You must be the gentleman staying at my niece's; Mrs. Eden is my great-niece, and the best woman in town, as anybody will tell you."

"I find her," said Mr. Mulkey solemnly, "a worthy woman. In her—ah—*condition* of—of life, her spirits keep up remarkably well. Yes, I'm in a strait. I've tried to persuade my man to proceed, but he—er—ah——"

The patronizing words just used referring to Mrs. Eden, the voice of ownership when alluding to Hodgins Thornberry, and the superior manner vouchsafed Captain Timothy Thornberry, were the admiration of the little crowd of men who had assembled to gaze at the lodged wheel. If the wheel could have been lifted out of the crevice by inquisitive eyes, the wagon would instantly have rolled on in triumph. But the wheel cried, almost in an audible voice, for a pole or bar, and the exertion of seeking such an instrument appealed no more to those spectators than the average manuscript to the average publisher.

"Captain Thornberry," said Mr. Mulkey, plainly surprised that the shabbily-dressed old man in the broken straw hat should bear a title, "can you advise me what to do?"

"Now, I'll tell you," said Hodgins, lazily crawling down from his high seat. "I'm going to my dinner. And when I get fed and rested, I'll hunt up some hands to help. So I'll just unhitch these horses and take 'em along with me." He began to unharness.

Timothy nodded with approval, and said to Mr. Mulkey, "You've got the best part of the day before you."

Mr. Mulkey looked at his watch and sighed. "It's an hour past the time Mrs. Eden told me to come to dinner. Surely they will not dine till I come?"

"Yes," said the captain, "they sit down to table punctual to the minute. Groner would see to that."

"You mean the positive gentleman?"

"*Groner Thornberry's* positive enough when it's a

matter of his own comfort," said Timothy. "He would not allow them to keep a meal waiting for the President; and I allow there's very little left when he lays down his knife!"

"I see you're a grocer," observed Mr. Mulkey, as his eyes caught the sign, "THORNBERRY GROCERY." "Let's cross to the shop. I'll get a light lunch. You have good, fresh cheese?"

"It's fresh enough," said Timothy, sinking back into his split-bottomed chair. He raised his voice: "Come out here, William, and wait on Mr. Mulkey. Mr. Mulkey, this is my grandson, Will Thornberry. What about that cheese, son? Didn't it seem mighty insipid to you—sorter sickenin' like?"

"Yes, it did," said Will, nodding his shaggy head. "I didn't like the taste of the stuff, one bit. I wouldn't advise nobody to buy that cheese; it's not tasteable."

Mr. Mulkey stared in surprise at the handsome young man whose frank, open face beamed upon him in all sincerity, while the broad shoulder propped restfully against the wall. "Well," he said doubtfully, "suppose you give me a nickel's worth of crackers." Mr. Mulkey, in truth, supported his overwhelming dignity upon the most rigid economy.

"I'll give you the crackers, if you say so," drawled Will, "but they are not fit to eat. The last rains have made everything mighty damp, and the crackers—well, you can pretty near bend 'em double without making a single crumb; ain't that so, grandpa?"

"Sure," said Timothy, nodding his snowy head. "Yes, I wouldn't advise you to buy no crackers in the bulk; and we're just out of boxed crackers. You can get 'em next door, and cheese, too, I reckon."

"I should like *to deal with* you," said Mr. Mulkey,

with a tolerant smile for these peculiarities. "For the sake of the little woman who received us as strangers, your niece, Mrs. Eden, in brief. I should like to make you my grocer while I live in Core City. Come, come, Mr. Thornberry—ah, pardon me," he added, with an amused wave of the hand, *"Captain,* I should say; suggest something that you know you have."

"William, where are them dates and raisins?" inquired Timothy.

"That's just what I've been looking for," said Will, shaking his head. "Now as to those apples, you can have all you can eat for nothing; and I'll treat you to bananas."

Mr. Mulkey hesitated. Dignity seemed to forbid him sitting down to a free board of apples and bananas for his dinner; but, after all, was it worth sacrificing his purse to impress these simple rustics with his high position? Society must look up to him, but no society was here; simply a seedy old man and an uneducated young fellow, evidently of no degree. Mr. Mulkey drew his pocketknife, ready for paring.

Presently Will sauntered down the street to the restaurant, a cheap framework, covered with wire gauze, having at the rear a wire-gauze kitchen, alluring to the passerby and tantalizing to the cloud of flies. The lunch counter thus, as it were, thrust boldly upon the public eye, was now occupied by the dinners and the elbows of a line of customers who perched upon high stools with their legs drawn up to inconvenient rounds.

Oscar Thornberry, the proprietor of this open-air resort, having served the last comer with chile and crackers, stood at the entrance of the kitchen with one eye on the coffee urn, and the other on his Grote's

History of Greece, which, however appropriate the title to surrounding conditions, was in little sympathy, textually, with odorous hamburger, viciously hot tamali, and unctuous chile. Will slyly called his brother to the screen door.

"Come out here," he whispered, "I want to show you a sight."

Oscar obeyed abstractedly, his eye still filled with gods and goddesses. Will nodded up-street. There stood the moving van, heaped wth furniture, immovable in the crevice, and horseless, while across the street stood the tall, funereal Mr. Mulkey, keeping a watch upon his possessions, and dining off Arkansas apples. Oscar doubled up in sudden appreciation and clapped Will upon the back.

"Is he from up north?" queried Oscar. (He pronounced it "nawth.")

Will made no reply. His brown eyes had suddenly descried a young lady coming down the street; it was Mary Eden. Will abruptly deserted his brother in order to reach the grocery first; to miss one opportunity of meeting Mary would have seemed to him a real calamity. Oscar, thus deserted, hastily opened his history at the place his finger was keeping warm, and instantly found himself in the Peloponnesus. A cry of "Pie!" from within recalled him rudely to the United States.

As it was neither a court day, nor a Saturday, there were few people upon the principal street of Core City. There was nothing to obscure the vision of Mary, moving along the rough brick pavement, serene and intent upon her own affairs, unaware of the fact that she had become the center of observation. Peter Thornberry saw her from the bank-window, and thoughtfully lit his pipe. There was a girl, he reflected, who would make a creditable wife; she liked him as much as he liked her, and that was an eminently satisfactory condition of hearts. Mr. Mulkey saw her, and mused that she had recently come from the table under which he felt his own long legs should have been stretched. Will thrilled as she drew near, but showed his customary passive indifference. Timothy hailed her genially.

She returned his hearty call with unwonted seriousness. "Uncle Tim," she said, "I would like to see you alone for a few minutes."

"Certainly," said the captain, who had already risen with courtly grace. "William, go along with yourself."

Mary smiled at the young man with cousinly kindness. "No, you may come too, Will, if you like."

Will's alacrity in following to the rear of the store showed that he "liked." They scrambled over the iron platform of the scales and came to rest upon some barrels at a safe distance from Mr. Mulkey.

"Uncle Tim," said Mary, looking into his kindly face with disturbed eyes, "I'm in trouble. You know we took Miss Goldie Pickens to board with us; well, the Mulkeys are on our hands, all four of them, and Cousin Winthrop has just come for mother. His wife has typhoid fever, and he can't find anybody else who is willing to nurse her; so mother had to go. And I have *so* much to do in keeping our customers supplied with fresh baked bread, and 'tending to the chickens and the garden, and the rest of it, that I can't cook for all of these strangers. Really, Uncle Tim, they ought to feel that, themselves. But I can't tell them to go. *What shall I do?*"

"Won't Groner settle their case for them?"

"I asked Uncle Groner; but, no—I think he wants them to stay, because while they are there, we have extra good meals, and you know Uncle Groner. So he won't do a thing to get them to leave."

"Mr. Mulkey is standing out in front," said Timothy, nervously pulling his white beard, "but I never asked a man in my life to go away from the abode of a Thornberry. He ought to be ashamed of himself. But I don't feel that I could tell him, Mary. I really don't."

"I'll tell him!" snapped Will.

"No," said Mary, looking at Will with a judicial eye, "it will be hard to get him to leave, and whoever accomplishes it will have to be very firm. I'm sure Mr. Mulkey will object; Will would be strong enough for him at the first, but would soon give in."

Will made no reply; either because he was offended at this charge, or was silently admitting its truth.

Timothy asked: "What about Miss Pickens? Is Groner satisfied to have her stay with Polly?"

"Oh, yes, he is delighted with her. She takes great trouble to read to him, and when I left home she was singing him a song."

"She must sing uncommonly well to charm Groner Thornberry," commented Timothy, tugging at his beard.

"But she doesn't, Uncle Tim. It isn't her voice, nor what she says. I don't know where her strength lies. She has made slaves of every one of the four Mulkeys; they think her an angel."

"What do you think?" Will frowned.

"She is almost no trouble," Mary evaded. "But what shall I do about clearing out the house? Sister

Ruth is coming home right away—we look for her any day. Oh, what am I to do, with mother gone? She can't come back and forth. She'll have to stay out at Cousin Winthrop's till his wife has recovered, for everybody considers the disease contagious."

"I've been thinking," said Timothy, drumming upon the barrel with idle heels. "There is Marietta Thornberry." (Marietta was the wife of Hodgins Thornberry, the hackman.)

"Yes," said Will, brightening, "there is Cousin Marietta.

"You know," added Timothy, gaining confidence, "whenever anything unpleasant in the family must be said, Marietta is always the one to say it. And what with harping at Hodgins from year in to year out, for his laziness and shiftlessness, she keeps herself in constant practice. Let's go for your Cousin Marietta."

"I believe," murmured Mary, brightening, "that you have struck it."

"Yes," said the captain, becoming better pleased with his suggestion, "I think this is the pure ore. Very well. I'll go over there some time this evening and project with your Cousin Marietta."

"You had better go now, Uncle Tim," said his niece anxiously. "The longer the Mulkeys stay the deeper their roots will fasten."

"Honey," the old gentleman feebly objected, "they ain't any *rail* hurry, is they? I'll put it off till about four o'clock. You run along, child; it will all be 'tended to."

Mary rested her hand upon the barrel-head and looked suspiciously at the other. Lights of mischief began to play in the dark brown eyes, and a smile crept about the mobile mouth. In the homely surroundings, her fine brown hair and tall, fully developed form appeared more than usually gracious. Beyond her, soap-boxes stacked one upon the other, and jugs and jars, and a flour-smeared blue kit of mackerel, stood forth like a dingy framing to a picture of rare purity and throbbing health. Will gazed, and turned away with a thrust in his heart, as he thought of his brother. But Mary, all unconscious of Will's hidden wound, and equally unconscious of her own attractiveness, kept her eye relentlessly upon Timothy Thornberry.

"Uncle Tim," she said, leveling her finger at him, "four o'clock won't do. Please come with me right now."

"And who will take care of the store?"

Inasmuch as Will's bodily presence answered this futile query, Mary honored it with no word. "Here is your hat, Uncle Tim," she said gently, but firmly.

It was not that he dreaded facing Marietta Thornberry, but any sudden plan or undertaking was repugnant to his inmost being. However, he followed passively, and as they emerged from the front of the store they found Mr. Mulkey hopefully eyeing Hodgins Thornberry, who was coming down the street leading his team. The loose harness jingled as the horses walked as if triumphant music were proclaiming that the moving-van would soon be rescued from the crevice at the crossing. It occurred to Timothy that he might speak to Mr. Mulkey on the matter in hand, and save himself this walk to his cousin's. He looked at Mr. Mulkey and thought he would do so. Even when he had passed on, he did not know but he might turn around and accost him. But, as he would himself have explained it, "Somehow, he didn't."

The home of *Hodgins* Thornberry was on the outskirts of Core City, in the poorer districts surrounding the canning factory. It was a small cottage, with chickens in the front yard, a cow in the back, and a pig or so in the lot, to say nothing of Mrs. Thornberry, who more than occupied the remainder of her territory with outdoor washing. In order to reach the mistress of this estate it was necessary to lower one's rigging in voyaging under two suspension-bridges of freshly-washed linen. Having thus arrived at port, the captain and his niece found Mrs. Hodgins Thornberry with her arms in the washtub, after the old approved fashion, vigorously rubbing a garment of unmistakable identity upon the washboard. About her sturdy legs was a lad of three, who manifested an unerring instinct in getting where he would be very much in the way; insomuch that his mother made the complete circuit of her tub in the effort to avoid treading upon him with a foot none of the lightest.

Mrs. Hodgins Thornberry was, indeed, solidly built and shortened to sail close to the earth; nor were her shoulders too broad or her limbs too thick and muscular for the burdens that had, by matrimony, been thrust upon her. On the birth of her first child, Hodgins had vanished from the surface of the earth, so far as Core City knew to the contrary. He had remained a myth and mystery three years, to return one day, as calmly and genially as if he had stepped out but an hour before. He had offered no explanation, save that he had found peace and infancy incompatible. Two years passed by, when, unluckily, another child made its appearance with as loud a whoop as tiny lungs could produce. Exit Hodgins. In the words of romance, "three years pass by." Then the wandering sire re-*turned, as un*dismayed, as kind, and as indolent as ever,

To the bitterest censure of his more intimate acquaintances, he had offered in mild self-defense, "I can't stand 'em under three year." But to his wife, who felt it her duty, and possibly her pleasure, to upbraid him about this and minor matters when he was in earshot, Hodgins had never offered the least palliation, nor could he be coaxed or driven to reply to her many reproaches by so much as a word.

"The best way, I find," he once confided to his cousin, George Nicodemus, "is to leave every word lie where my wife puts it; for, to pick up one would make two spring out of the ground. I couldn't say nothing of the innocentest nature that wouldn't furnish her material for a book. Ain't I tried it? In ever' word that falls from my mouth, she sees a hour-sermon with a dozen divisions all neat an' regular. She's got a genius that way; but I don't want no such genius expended upon *my* head."

Mrs. Hodgins Thornberry received her visitors in as good a humor as a woman with such a capricious husband and such a large washing upon her hands could be expected to entertain. The difficulty was placed before her; too many Mulkeys, and not sufficient force of character to get rid of them.

"Yes," said Marietta, "I am your woman. I will go with you at once, for not being a Thornberry, I believe in doing a thing before it grows too big to handle. I will take my arms right out of the washtub and come."

Like an old, familiar song of infancy and childhood, those last words fell upon Mary's ear. As well as she could remember, whenever Cousin Marietta was called upon to "speak up," she had first been obliged to take her "arms out of *the washtub.*" Perhaps this modern condition of woman, half in air and half in water, had been shadowed forth in the old type of the mermaid. They presently set out, Cousin Marietta leading her last child by its pudgy hand.

They came to Mrs. Eden's cottage. On the front porch, in a low rocking-chair, sat Miss Goldie Pickens, reading aloud. Upon the front steps, with his crutch across his lap, and his ears tilted thirstily upward, was Groner Thornberry. The voice of the boarder was mellow, low, and restrained; her face was grave and spirituelle, her eyelids drooping, her lashes almost hiding the narrowed gleam of the busy orbs. Her skirts swept the floor in simple decorum, and her cheek rested upon one slim hand with the shyness of a child. In the doorway stood a large trunk, apparently stuck in the entrance.

Cousin Marietta took in Goldie Pickens with one swift, uncompromising glance. "Is that one of the Mulkeys?" she demanded, starting forward with signal resolution upon her face. On being assured that Miss Pickens was the boarder, she looked disappointed.

"Do you want her?" she demanded.

"Oh, yes, indeed," said Mary hastily.

Marietta looked at the music-teacher, and, with compressed lips, made a curious sound in her throat, very much like a grunt from her own tiny back lot. They came up to the porch, breathing hard. Goldie rose and received them—but, according to her wont, concentrated her attention upon the male member of the party.

"So this is Captain Thornberry," she said, in something like patriotic ecstasy. "I have heard so much about you that I feel honored to be brought thus into personal touch with one of the heroes of the South. *May I take your* hand, captain?"

"I'm no hero," said Timothy, stretching out his hand, and noting for the first time that several ravelings projected from his wristband like cat's whiskers; "just an old man who has tried to do his duty."

Goldie did not protest, in words; but she gave the veteran a look which told him that she cherished him as a gallant officer. Timothy held the frayed cuff behind his back, and slyly plucked at its antennæ with his other hand.

These amenities were lost upon Mrs. Hodgins Thornberry. "Where," she asked abruptly, "are those Mulkeys?" And upon being told that they were within—"And why is the door blocked up with that Mulkey trunk?" It was not left to chance or verbal statement to declare whose trunk it was, for it bore the inscription in large white letters, "COLONEL SYLVESTER MULKEY."

"The trunk," said Groner Thornberry, who was in an ugly humor at having the reading interrupted, "is waiting till it is decided what room to take it to. It was put off here when the wagon went to the rented house with the furniture. The Mulkeys are staying here till they fix up their new place."

"Come!" Mrs. Hodgins Thornberry briefly commanded, as she started for the side door. Mary hastened to follow, but the captain thought best to remain where he was appreciated.

The Mulkeys were found occupying the parlor with the temporary air of camping out. Fleshy Mrs. Mulkey had several large pasteboard boxes upon the floor, within reach, from which she might take such articles as chance required; articles not to be expected in the parlor of one's host. Gladys Lucile Mulkey, always strikingly handsome and impassive, was reading a novel. Old Mr. Mulkey sat stiffly erect, near his daughter-in-law, looking slightly flustered at the energetic entrance. Mrs. Mulkey, red in the face and panting, dived into one of the green boxes, but not quick enough to conceal a red flannel rag from the eye of the newcomer.

Mary, in a shrinking voice, presented her Cousin Marietta. "I would rise to greet you," said the gallant old gentleman, "but when I get up, I can not get down; from a peculiar stiffness of some cartilage or other, I reckon. Anyway, it takes my son to set me after I'm up."

Mrs. Hodgins Thornberry was slightly mollified by this simple but inconvenient infirmity, but she still looked at the box in which the red flannel rag now reposed.

"Yes," pursued the old gentleman, following the direction of her eyes, "my daughter was rubbing me. You doubtless smell the ointment. It is powerful, to some people—offensively so. I have the kindest children in the world," he added, smiling affectionately at the fleshy lady.

"Mrs. Thornberry," said Mrs. Mulkey kindly, "won't you sit down?"

"No," said Mrs. Hodgins Thornberry.

"It is impossible for me to stay warm all over," continued old Mr. Mulkey, "but the greatest trouble are my calves; and I can not get at my calves on account of my constitutional stiffness. Elbows I can rub myself. My elbows and calves can not stay, all four, warm at the same time, because there is not so much caloric in my body. But you have no idea how uncomfortable it becomes to have the *same* elbow or *the same* calf cold for a considerable period of time.

My elbows now being quite warm, my daughter was drawing some of the warmth down to my calf—my left calf. And that is what the red flannel rag was for, madam."

"Yes," said Cousin Marietta briefly. She looked fixedly at Gladys Lucile, who was uninterruptedly pursuing her novel, and then turned to Mrs. Mulkey. "Mrs. Mulkey," she said, "your daughter looks very much like Mary's sister Ruth. What was your maiden name?"

"Thornberry," said Mrs. Mulkey. "I was a Thornberry; but not related to the Arkansas Thornberrys, as far as we can find."

"Your daughter is related to 'em, at all events," said Marietta, with emphasis. "But I came to speak to you on an important matter. You can not stay here any longer, Mrs. Mulkey; neither you nor any of your family. I speak kindly and like a Christian; but it wouldn't matter how I pronounce the words, the fact would be just the same. The fact is, that you must all be out of this house before supper-time. Now, you know Mary's mother has been called to a sick-bed, and that the contagious disease will prevent her coming back and forth. Mary is a busy young woman, and can not entertain guests in her house and sneak off to her uncle's to sleep at night for lack of room. Moreover, her grown sister is coming home—her sister Ruth; and Ruth is a young lady who requires a great deal of room."

"Mrs. Mulkey," gasped Mary, trembling like a little child, "I am so, *so* sorry, but Cousin Marietta is right."

"But we can not go," said Mrs. Mulkey, bewildered. "What can we do? We are to remain here till we have laid our carpets *and arranged* our beds, at least. Mr.

Mulkey so understands it. He is away, watching them prize the wagon out of the fissure in the rock."

"You must all be gone by supper-time," said the other positively. "You have rented a house, and the proper thing is to get into it. Mary can not have this extra burden. It would break down her health."

"I do not see how we can go," said the fleshy lady, shaking her head.

"I see how," remarked Cousin Marietta. "The other hack will be here in an hour, and the man will hoist that trunk up in front. I will see that your father gets up, and Mr. Mulkey can see to it when he reaches his destination that he gets set down."

"Mother," said Gladys Lucile, her face very red, "would you want to stay where you are not wanted?"

It was seldom that Gladys Lucile spoke, and when she did her mother regarded the words as the deliverance of an oracle. She looked at Cousin Marietta, to discover if that redoubtable lady would quail under the keen thrust. But Cousin Marietta did not quail; and when Uncle Groner and Goldie Pickens seated themselves at Mary's supper there was not a Mulkey in the house.

"Well!" said Uncle Groner, laying down his knife and fork, and compressing his lips till a dozen new wrinkles showed upon his round, mottled face. "No biscuits!"

"And no Mulkeys," said Mary gaily. "Poor old Mr. Mulkey, I felt sorry for him, but Mrs. Mulkey is just too fat to stir my compassion."

"You must remember," said Uncle Groner significantly, "that Miss Pickens is still with us."

Goldie, in her softest voice and sweetest manner, *took up the* words. "Forget that I am here, Miss

Mary, if it is ever a question of an added burden. I know too well what life means, to be willing to add one straw to the load that another is carrying. If there is ever a time when I can be of help to you, do let me! I find this light bread delicious."

Mary looked doubtfully at Goldie, a slight puzzled gleam in her honest eyes. But Goldie Pickens was no puzzle to Uncle Groner; she was an angel, and every mellow word that fell from the curved mouth seemed to call for the accompaniment of a golden harp.

CHAPTER V

THE kitchen, in which Mrs. Polly Thornberry reigned supreme, was a small room, connected with the rear of the house by a screened-in porch. The porch was thus walled with wire gauze, to admit the bracing Ozark air to one, who might pass the night upon a cot, free from the contamination of papered walls of plank. The fact that no one had ever slept "out on the porch" did not argue the uselessness of the gauze; for there was no knowing when old Timothy or one of his grandsons would sleep out of the house, and, in fact, they had so long considered this probability that it was customary for them to refer to the enclosure as "the porch where we sleep at night."

Few Core City houses were provided with plastered walls, because during the long, delightful warm season it seemed impossible that a cold winter could come; and even the grip of an uncommonly rigorous winter, though it might put an end to the most sheltered slip of a peach tree, seemed but a prophecy to these hopeful and genial souls that there must necessarily come a warm winter the following year.

Sunday morning, immediately following the seven-thirty or eight-o'clock breakfast, was the period set apart by tradition and custom for the homely service of blacking one's shoes. It was done in the back yard, or upon the porch, according to the weather. It might be called one of the social functions of the family. *Timothy and his* grandsons took turn about at the brush and the old-fashioned blacking, while a brisk conversation enlivened the occasion. Those who had "blacked," or were yet "to black," perched upon the porch-steps—the gauze door was never closed—or upon the well-curbing, and discussed politics, literature, science, and the social life of Core City. On the Sunday morning in question, the four men in their fresh clean shirts, unembarrassed by coat or vest, were thus engaged, Peter at the brush—Will next in line.

As Peter polished in a leisurely and delicate style, he took time to choose his words. He was addressing his grandfather: "It isn't the way to do," he said, with the air of one speaking the last word upon a subject. "You must admit that the Thornberrys have never made what they might out of themselves."

"On general principles, you are right," said the old gentleman, sticking out his freshly polished boots with rather a conscious air, "but I never treat myself on general principles. I made up my mind twenty years ago that I would not be bored. I have gained ten years of good living by sticking to that determination. When a man comes to see me, and sits down and fastens to his chair, having nothing to say, I simply get my hat and ask him if he doesn't want to step downtown. And if he doesn't, he can stick there for me. I like company. I was glad to see Mulkey come, and I was glad to see him go; for he'd talk of nothing but your Cousin George's mines, and just to sit and congeal, a-lookin' at a man that has nothing to tell me, and him a-lookin' at me, fairly sick to get away, but not knowing what ails him—that I can not stand."

"Society demands it," said Peter. "If there is anything that society depends upon, it is politeness, and when you showed Mr. Mulkey that you weren't interested in those mines, you offended him."

"I'll tell you what offended Mr. Mulkey," spoke up Will; "it was because Cousin Polly Eden took him and his family in, crowding herself out, and then couldn't keep him till his carpets were put down in his house."

"Boys," said the old man, "why don't you call him 'Colonel'? That's the title on his trunk." He chuckled and added: "He ran for Congress, 'way up in Indiany, and he had quite a race, to hear *him;* well, 'Colonel' is all he ever got out of it, in my opinion, though he's told about it so often, I think he pretty nearly believes that he was elected. He dates the events in his life by 'before I ran for Congress,' or 'since I ran for Congress,' and once, I don't know but he said 'when I was *in* Congress.' "

At this moment diversion was produced by the muffled voice of Mrs. Polly Thornberry from the "summer kitchen."

"Whoop-pee!" called Timothy, "we can't make you out."

The voice murmured on; at the same time the door rattled violently. "Oh, that doorknob!" exclaimed Timothy, rising. "When *will* I remember to put it on the door? The old lady is losing some of her grip, and it is mighty hard on her to be handicapped that way." He opened the door, which still boasted of a knob on the outside. "Come and join us, wife, we need your being on the top step for queen of the hour. Easy now, lean on me, for your legs—I reckon there's no objection to referring to them at this late day?—are mighty uncertain."

"*I was saying* in the kitchen, but nobody would

answer me," said the old lady, in mild reproof, "that I remembered hearing of a Thornberry in Indiany that married a Munkey. But shorely this Mulkey family can't be the same—though the way Gladys Lucile sits reading when company is present reminds me mightily of Groner Thornberry, to say nothing of *you*, Timothy."

Oscar, who sat on a corner of the well-curbing, his book upon his knee, understood the indirect reproof from his grandmother, and looked up with an air of alert interest.

"Miss Gladys Lucile Mulkey is a remarkably pretty young lady," observed Peter, with the air of a cannoisseur.

"Miss Goldie Pickens is mighty agreeable," said Timothy. "She is so modest."

"I don't care at all for Miss Pickens," said Peter; "she can't compare to Miss Gladys Lucile Mulkey."

"There's no use talking about a Mulkey," Will declared; "they'll never get over the kindness that was shown 'em."

"Will," said his brother—not his brother Oscar, of course, as the latter, while gazing at his grandmother, was thinking of Aphrodite—"are you going to church this morning?"

"I might," said Will, "but I don't think so."

"You ought to go for respectability. The restaurant will keep Oscar away, but you and I have no such excuse."

"Yes, Will," said his grandmother gently, "respectability ought to make you go to church."

"*I'd* go if I could," said Oscar, rubbing his leg with a certain snug air of cheerfulness, "for it's the respectable thing."

"Look a-here," said Timothy, gazing about, "ain't they no religion in this family?"

Oscar, finding his mind too distracted from its work, carried his book into the house.

When he had vanished, Will murmured: "What do you reckon Osk is going to do with all that learning he's storing up?"

Timothy shook his head. "If he was concentratin' on law or medicine he might set somethin' afire. He can't fry ham in Latin, or flavor his ice-cream sody with hist'ry."

"He's concentratin' on Cousin Winthrop's daughter," said Will wisely. "I guess there's no chance for Osk, she is so rich. But as old Uncle Mose used to say, I reckon he's trying to make himself 'fitten.'"

"What!" cried Mrs. Thornberry, her lace cap trembling in surprise. "Do you think Oscar has any notion of that stuck-up limb?"

"I think I know the signs," said Will.

Peter laid aside the brush. "Then that does Oscar great credit," he said didactically, "and I, for once, am proud of him. It is of small moment whether he wins Ethel or not. But it is a satisfaction to know that he has fallen in love with that kind of a girl—Cousin Winthrop is the richest man in the county; Ethel has been to the state university, and she holds herself high."

"So high," remarked Mrs. Thornberry, "that she can't see the people in the street who want to speak to her."

"She's a proud girl," said Peter, "but she has much to be proud of."

Later in the morning, Timothy and his wife, accompanied by Peter and Will, started forth for church.

"We're too early," said the old man, "but I'll stand around outside and chat my old friends, and Polly can gossip with the women till time for religion to begin."

"It's a quarter after eleven," said Peter, "and eleven is the time set."

"That's nothin'," returned his grandfather scornfully. "No time in this town, for any sort of a meetin', was ever set that caught anything. As for me, I never go there soon enough to look at their traps. Yonder comes Mary, and Miss Pickens. We'll join them. My! Miss Pickens looks like an angel. If I was one of you boys—hum! Howdy, Mary, ain't you afraid you'll be late? Miss Pickens, allow an old man to say that you are charming this morning."

Goldie Pickens, all in white, cast down her eyes, seeming to intimate that physical beauty was not so much what she sought as spiritual perfection. There was, moreover, a distinct Sunday air about her which put compliments far away, as something carnal.

"I taught my Sunday-school class," said Mary brightly, "and hurried home, fearing Uncle Groner might be really ill. I think he'll do very well, however."

"He gets worse every Sunday morning, doesn't he?" asked Will. "I think he does it to keep you at home with him."

"I think he'll do fairly well," said Mary, who had a mind of her own, as Uncle Groner often found to his sorrow.

Peter stepped to Mary's side and took possession of her. He had been both surprised and displeased that Will should have thrust his attention upon her when he, Peter, was *present*; for, in a sense, he regarded his distant cousin as belonging to himself. Will fell in step with the music-teacher, but his heart was warmed; Mary had given him the understanding smile of comradeship.

"Why, bless my soul!" exclaimed Timothy, as they came to the church, "they are singing. Well," he added hopefully, "maybe Brother Wells has read his chapter."

As they entered the church, the congregation turned as one man to see who they were. Old Mrs. Thornberry, conscious that they were the center of attention, hastily crowded from sight a depending handkerchief of her husband's, which, in spite of her watchfulness, the captain had brought to church. The seats near the doors were filled, not to say crowded, but there were plenty of benches at the front as bare as if they threatened a contagious disease. The minister, however, had a strong voice, and made nothing of the wide waste over which his words must carry before they could reach the ears of the first dying sinner.

Our little party entered a seat as far back as they could, in this order: Mrs. Polly Thornberry, the captain, Miss Goldie Pickens, Peter, and Mary. As Will was crowded out, he squeezed himself into the seat just behind Mary, taking no note of the legs of the end man, who clung tenaciously to his corner. Peter was thus blessed by being between two fair maidens; but although Will found himself almost in the bosom of a hulky man who breathed hard, and smelled of strong tobacco and a barn, he was more than content; for he could gaze uninterruptedly at the back of Mary's head, and, occasionally, catch a glimpse of a dainty ear, a smooth rounded cheek, and, less often, the sweep *of long lashes.*

"Brethren," said the Rev. Mr. Wells, "I have decided to give you this morning the biography of Balaam; when I entered this pulpit, I had not decided what I should discourse about, but I think I shall speak on Balaam. Yes, I am sure I shall." No one took hopes of a short sermon on being thus advised that the discourse was unprepared. The minister was an elderly gentleman, who, in the course of his life, had picked up a great deal; and if he had known more than he did, he would have told it. Timothy stretched his long, thin legs. "But, in order to understand Balaam," pursued the speaker, "it is necessary to go back of Balaam and regard his ancestry, and, indeed, consider the whole Jewish economy."

Peter disengaged his mind from all this and became subtly aware of the impress, as it were, of Goldie Pickens. She had hardly been upon his mind since her coming to Core City. That very morning he had expressed his preference for Gladys Lucile Mulkey. But he had never been brought into so close a relationship with the young lady. Now he sat by her side, and, in the press of those determined not to go forward to the naked benches, she was even placed in physical contact. There was something in this nearness inexpressibly soothing to Peter's feelings. It had never been so with him on taking Mary's hand. Perhaps it was from the knowledge that Mary thought a great deal of him, and might think more.

Peter found the greatest satisfaction in the closeness of the music-teacher, because she was all a mystery, a spiritual haze, akin to her white fluffy dress. Indeed, the girl and the dress seemed to have been molded out of the same fleecy, indefinite cloud. There were no sensible seams. Her arm was warm, but her soul was a cold, crystal pool with no dangerous reefs, no hidden ledges of rock. Peter mused upon the difference between Mary and Goldie. It was not safe to predict what Mary might do under impulse; but Goldie impressed Peter as being like a "polite person in a book." In the course of the long sermon, it began to grow upon him that it was a credit to the Thornberry connection—of whom Peter was not disposed to think very highly—to board such a modest, reserved maiden—a maiden, moreover, with a face of such distinct attractiveness, with an arm so warm.

The minister had talked long, but he was still dealing with abstractions; Balaam had not yet ridden upon the scene. However, Goldie Pickens was not sitting in fixed expectancy, waiting for the bold rider. Her mind was very busy with characters nearer home. Peter, like every other unmarried gentleman, was a definite possibility to the young lady. And Peter, unlike any of the other Thornberrys in single state, was "in a bank." Therefore, he was interesting on two counts.

Goldie was not a romantic girl; the romance of her life was in the past, and marriage did not conjure up to her imagination a line of flower girls, a circling ring, and carriages in waiting. Marriage had come to mean an escape from poverty and toil. When one is twenty-eight, one will soon be thirty. Her first and only love had embittered her youth. She had been passionately, but discreetly, loved by a young man too poor to wish to double his poverty by the annexation of her own. Long before coming to her twentieth year, she had admitted his wisdom; but by that time, her early disappointment had shaped her personality. *Now, at twenty*-eight, she could view matrimony with a dispassionate eye, and prepare calmly, even shrewdly, for its possibility.

Peter was at least five or six years younger than she, but she did not look so old as she felt; Mary, she reflected, was in love with him—but while Goldie had never made a match of her own, she had broken off matches between other principals. Peter, possibly, imagined himself in love with Mary; but what of that? Peter was "in a bank"; that was enough to say of *him*. Goldie had on several occasions, unpleasant to recall, ruined almost certain prospects by revealing, at an inauspicious moment, a certain craving for money which, at times, it was well-nigh impossible for her to conceal. She could not censure herself for this love of money. Reared amidst dire privations, in a large city, driven to menial service by the necessity of a bedridden mother, she had toiled and craved and despaired.

No wonder she looked forward to a lonely future with dread, and to a life of toil possibly ending in absolute want, with horror. As a music-teacher, depending upon the support of capricious local classes, yet forced to dress with a certain elegance in order to procure "paying pupils," the expense of board and clothes left little for a rainy day.

While Goldie sat with her arm crowded against Peter's wrist, she was forming plans for the campaign. There was the choir; she would take possession of it. She knew from experience that there was dissension in the choir, and, though, apparently, it consisted of but ten persons, it must contain two, possibly three, factions. What they were divided over was of no consequence to Goldie, though doubtless of lifelong importance to the *factions*. The factions—judging from her knowledge of other choirs—were composed of singers who would not yield their position on some certain point—no matter what the particular point in *this* choir, it was, of course, one of *conscience*. Goldie was a newcomer. She was a stranger to all the choristers. She was not related to any one advocating or opposing the Point. They could all agree on her. She would become their organist. She would put Peter in the choir; but in some way—she had no doubt of finding a way—she would keep Mary out. She would help Peter learn his part, lingering beside him after the others were gone. She would, thus, be thrown much in his company.

In the meantime, there would be other acquaintanceships formed. Peter might be set aside for a more worthy man. She must extend her lines, join a certain Literary Club of which she had heard, enter society without sacrificing decorum, and thus march to victory, with the church under one wing, and the world under the other.

"And now," cried the Rev. Mr. Wells, "I come to a closer view of my subject."

Timothy leaned over to his wife, and whispered in her ear, "I'm goin' out."

"Timothy," she whispered, in quick alarm, "are you sick?"

"Nuck," whispered the captain, putting his lips closer to her ear, "but I can't sit listenin' to such a one-sided debate as this; we've been a-hearin' the ass all the time, and not a word from Balaam." He started to rise.

Goldie laid a gentle hand upon his sleeve, and looked at him with beseeching shyness. Timothy sank back into his seat, as if he had been mesmerized, and Peter, *witnessing the* subjugation of his sometimes obdurate grandfather, looked at Goldie and thought, "What an angel."

When the benediction had been regretfully pronounced, the congregation streamed like an escaped flood into the yard. There was much greeting of friends, many inquiries about absent members, and a comparison of opinions relative to the fruit crop.

"Mary," said Mrs. Thornberry, "come, go home with us to dinner."

"Thank you," said Mary, "but our dinner is provided, and you know we couldn't leave Uncle Groner."

"Well, *our* dinner isn't provided for," remarked Timothy, "and I guess we can stand Groner a couple of hours."

"Why, *Timothy!*" expostulated his wife.

"Then do come with me," cried Mary. "I think there's enough for all, and if there isn't, you're just as welcome as if there were."

"William," said his grandmother, "run home and bring that pie, and we'll add it to Mary's dinner."

"I have pie," said Mary. "In fact, that's all I made preparation for. I have two kinds. Do come! It will be so sociable."

"William," said Timothy, "go to Oscar's restaurant, and see if he has anything to send us—something already cooked."

"It had been in my mind," said Mrs. Polly Thornberry, "to knock over a chicken for our dinner; so pie is all we have. I meant to prepare the chicken last night, somehow we never got around to it. Run on, William, forage something for us. Have you any butter, Mary?"

"Oh, oh!" cried Mary. "We had the last for breakfast. But I expect I can borrow some," she added, in cheerful hopefulness.

Will, whose lot it ever chanced, was to be sent away from Mary, hastened to his brother's restaurant. Having reached home, the party separated. Mary and her grandmother went to the kitchen, while Miss Goldie Pickens seated herself in the parlor, having at her feet Peter, Timothy, and Groner. If anything could have compensated Uncle Groner for a delayed dinner, it would have been Goldie's meek, unworldly face; but nothing could, and he sat in restive mood, tapping the floor with his crutch, and wrathfully wondering why Mary had brought all these relations home to dinner.

Goldie sighed. Peter's quick ear detected the soft sound. He looked at the drooping eyelids inquiringly. "I do wish," murmured Goldie, "that Miss Mary would let me help her with her work. It would be a kindness to me, because sometimes I grow so lonely. But she will not. I asked her to let me help with this dinner. I would consider it a—a—a frolic." She hesitated at the word as if fearing it might be too festive for Sunday use.

"Oh, Mary doesn't mind!" said Timothy, trying to console this sensitive heart. "She's been used to hard diggin' all her life."

"So much the more, then," sighed Goldie, "should she let me bear some of her burdens. Do you know, I think good people are usually selfish? Now, Miss Mary is so good—I never knew a girl so conscientious and really *good* as Mary Eden. And I think that makes her a little intolerant of others—don't you think so, Uncle Groner?"

"Course I do," snapped Uncle Groner hungrily.

"But I am afraid this sounds as if I were blaming

Mary," Goldie went on, "and I could not blame her, for she is *so* good. To change the subject—but I am afraid," she paused with a deferential smile at old Timothy, "that the captain thinks I talk a great deal."

"No one could do it better," said the gallant captain.

"Why, Captain Thornberry! I was not expecting that from you! But I was about to discuss your church choir."

"Then please count me out," remarked Timothy drily.

"Do you mean that there is trouble in your choir?"

The captain hesitated, and his eyes twinkled as he recalled the trivial matter that had really brought dissension. His lips parted. Then he checked himself. "No, Miss Goldie, not to my own wife!" he cried resolutely, and his eye indicated that he had already passed through deep waters by being less cautious.

"Captain," said Goldie, in meek reproof, "you who were so valiant in war, is it not your duty to arbitrate this difference, for the good of the church?"

"If I was in a book, I might do that," said the captain grimly, "but being in real life, I guess I'll have to act like an ordinary human."

The old gentleman presently left the room, and Goldie suggested a stroll. Peter rose with pleasure to accompany her, but though Uncle Groner had been included in her gracious smile, he found it impossible to ply his crutch fast enough to keep abreast.

Out under the apple blossoms Goldie, in the most delicate manner, elicited the information that Peter's father and mother were dead, and that his grandfather had taken the three boys to his own home some ten years ago. The sympathy that Goldie knew so well how to express, and which to a degree she really felt, charmed the young man like some strange and delicious music. Leading him to speak of himself,—for thus she was accustomed to afford young gentlemen their greatest enjoyment,—it was not difficult for her to glean that Peter looked upon himself as the one who must raise the Thornberry family to distinction. Having found his keynote, she harmonized her views and utterances thereby. He was amazed to find with what rapidity the influence of this charming, well-bred maiden was taking possession of him. That very morning they had been practically strangers. And now, before dinner, when another man might well have been hungry, he was wondering, with a queer fluttering of the heart, if love were in the air.

It is difficult to lead gently down from such heights to the prosaic statement that Mary was unable to borrow butter of her neighbor, owing to that neighbor being without, yet in a tale of common life it is sometimes difficult to keep love and butter far apart.

"Never mind," said her grandmother, "I expect Will can supply us from the restaurant. I hope he will bring a chicken."

"I think he will," said Mary; "a chicken, nicely baked and browned. I believe I'll not try to cook anything till he comes, for we couldn't possibly know what he will bring."

"Yes, let's wait," said Mrs. Polly Thornberry, sitting down by the cold oven.

Mary seated herself and clasped her hands upon her aproned lap. "Aunt Polly," she said, "I have been very much interested in a church out in Oklahoma. The people are very, very poor, and the building is *about to be* sold. If they could raise two thousand dollars it would save them, because some one has promised to give as much again if that much is collected."

"Whenever," said the old lady, "I hear of a rich man, out of his ease and plenty and daily comforts, giving what he won't miss, provided others will pinch themselves and wear out shoes canvassing in order to raise the balance, I think thoughts to myself that are not Christian thoughts; so, perhaps, it's as well for me to say no more."

Mary laughed. "But," she said, "the fact remains that the building will be sold if we don't lift the mortgage; and after those poor people have worked a dozen years to get a start. And I want to give something. Don't you?"

"Of course I do," cried the old lady. "I was thinking about getting me a new bonnet, but old women have no business with summer bonnets. And yet I can't see as that will help much, beings as I didn't know where the money was to come from."

"How brave they were!" Mary went on, her brown eyes glowing with enthusiasm. "Only five or six at first, they met at each other's houses; at last a church was built. It cost more than they expected——"

"La, child! it wouldn't of been a church if it hadn't done that," remarked her aunt.

"——And now, after employing their first minister, they find the roof about to vanish from over their heads! When mamma comes home from nursing Cousin Winthrop's wife, I will suggest that we give them Miss Goldie."

At that moment Timothy entered. "Who are you going to give Miss Goldie to?" he asked suspiciously.

Mary laughed. "I was speaking of her board-money," she explained.

"By the way, Mary," said her great-uncle gravely, "I am afraid your Cousin Winthrop's wife is worse." Mrs. Winthrop Thornberry had been thus referred to ever since her marriage to the richest man in the county. Winthrop Thornberry, in spite of his fortune of $500,000, was democratic and friendly to his poor connections. But the lady he had married grew, by virtue of that marriage, so elevated in feelings and demeanor, that she became known to the family as the engrafted Thornberry, who had never called a Thornberry "cousin." Therefore, not from retaliation, but simply to preserve one's self-respect, she was spoken of, not as "Cousin Janette Thornberry," but as "Cousin Winthrop's wife."

Will stepped upon the back porch, holding up both hands that all might see his bareness. His handsome face showed regret which, however, was partly illuminated by the light which Mary's presence shed.

"Where is the browned chicken?" demanded his grandmother sharply.

Will sat down, shaking his head. "Oscar has had bad luck," he said. "He got to reading and let everything burn up. He had to send nearly all of his customers to the other restaurant, but a few old tried friends are perched on his stools, waiting for him to do some more cooking."

"Will," said Timothy briefly, "light the fire."

CHAPTER VI

It was not alone absorption in the doings of the Peloponnesians that had caused Oscar Thornberry to let his restaurant-cooking crisp to unsavory coals. He was, indeed, still pursuing the dry and arduous path hewn into the past by the indefatigable labors of Mr. Grote; but as he thus pursued his way to the amorous gods and indiscreet goddesses, a vision not of Grecian, but of American beauty, flitted ever before his eyes. It was more than a year since Oscar had taken up his lonesome pursuit of knowledge; and it had been exactly the same length of time since he had fallen in love with Winthrop Thornberry's daughter. He had not desired to fall in love with Ethel; he had realized the difficulties of such a prospective condition. But there came a time when he said to himself: "Why disguise the truth? This thing in my heart is Love."

Since coming to this self-consciousness, a year had passed. Not one event had occurred to give him encouragement. Another must have looked upon his passion as hopeless. Ethel was rich; he, poor. Her father occupied a position of dignity and honor in the community, not alone because he was the richest inhabitant, but because he was a successful orchard-grower, an enterprising spirit, and a kind, friendly neighbor. Oscar, on the other hand, owned a small screened-in restaurant, whereof he was the chief cook. It is true that he had one brother "in the bank"; but his other *brother, as partner* in his grandfather's grocery, did little to shed luster upon the family. But all this was, after all, not the greatest obstacle. The most pronounced difficulty was Ethel herself. It was unanimously agreed in family council that "she took after her mother."

Ethel was not proud of her wealth, having been born to it, but of the position and advantages that wealth procured. Having attended the university, to say nothing of several sojourns in St. Louis, she had seen other men than those of Core City, and had gleaned ideas relative to restaurants other than those entertained by Oscar's acquaintances.

But why need we dwell upon these difficulties, since Oscar himself made little of them? Being a Thornberry, he was born to hope, and it was as probable to him that he would eventually win the hand of this cousin, five degrees removed, as it was that no rain would fall though the thunder was in his ears.

"Going my way?" inquired Col. Sylvester Mulkey as Oscar locked up his restaurant at three o'clock. The colonel paused upon the sidewalk, tall, narrow-faced, severe—a long exclamation-point of dignity, dressed in black.

"A piece," said Oscar, with inward regret. Oscar had made up his mind that this very afternoon he would declare his heart to Ethel, and he desired the preparation of solitude. He thrust his key into his pocket and waited a moment for Mulkey to go on; but Mulkey remained.

As they walked together, the colonel inquired, "Do you find the restaurant very remunerative in so small a place, Mr. Oscar?"

"How is that?" inquired Oscar, reining in his *thoughts and trying* to hitch the prancing steeds to the colonel's mind. The question was repeated with deepening solemnity. "Well, no," said Oscar, "it furnishes the boat, but I have to do my own rowing."

"It is not, I premise, an—er—occupation that one would assume from pleasure?" inquired Mulkey, with the air of one investigating a matter of curious, but remote interest.

"I learned how to cook when I was a boy," Oscar rejoined; "the fact is, all of us had to learn to scramble something for ourselves, as our housekeeping was irregular. As I knew how to cook, I rented that town lot, put up a light framework, tacked wire gauze all around it, shingled the thing, and opened my restaurant. There are no openings for a young man in small towns, bringing in a good income, that aren't gobbled up by people before you are born, and handed down to their families. I expect to go to the city in a year or so, where there are more opportunities."

"Ah," said Sylvester Mulkey, nodding, "I have no doubt a well-regulated restaurant in Little Rock, or Pine Bluff, or Hot Springs, would be a profitable investment."

"I suppose so," Oscar agreed indifferently, "but of course, I wouldn't run a restaurant away from home."

"And why not, pray?"

Oscar looked at Mulkey in surprise. "You know I wouldn't want to run a restaurant among strangers, where nobody knows my folks," he explained.

"But," said the other, with equal surprise, "but, my dear fellow,—*but*,—the vastly increased income——"

"What do I care about income?" interposed Oscar somewhat impatiently. "With us,—I speak of the Thornberrys,—money is as dust under our feet, if it is procured with a loss of self-respect."

"Sir," said Mulkey, with displeasure, "toil is honorable, whether among friends or strangers. And money, sir, money, honestly procured, is *not* as dust under—under anybody's feet."

"We do not agree," said Oscar quietly. "It is no matter."

"You are wrong," said Mulkey, raising his voice, as Hodgins Thornberry lounged toward them from across the street. "This is one reason why your people have not made the progress they should. You base everything upon family, as if that were a solid foundation. Look at your cousin, Mr. George Nicodemus! There's a man trying to develop the marvelous natural resources of northwest Arkansas, and what do your own people do? They scoff at the idea of his having found traces of oil, and copper, and silver, and diamonds. Is that the way to build up a community? It surprises me that one in your— it surprises me that *you* should uphold the aristocratic notions of Old England." Mulkey had no desire to wound Oscar, but if Oscar got in the way of truth, let him be run over!

"Look a-here," said Hodgins Thornberry, joining them, and speaking with unusual energy and distinctness. "Are you sayin' anything against our family, Mr. Mulkey? If so, you have me to answer to," the hackman continued, "and Sunday as it is, it will be my duty, and my pleasure, suh, to knock you down, suh!"

"No, no," Oscar hastily interposed, "we were merely discussing the money question, Cousin Hodgins."

It struck Mulkey as so grotesque that this restaurateur and this hackman should be upholding the nobility *of birth,* that he contented himself with a solemn wave of his hand; and having come to the street leading to his newly rented cottage, he left the cousins.

"I tell you now," said Hodgins, sinking his voice to a hoarse growl, "as soon as this comes to the fighting-point, I'm yore man. Just you go ahead and be as brash and spunky as you please; you've got yore Cousin Hodge to fall back on, an' you'll find me a feather-bed of softness as a place of resort."

Oscar was duly grateful for this backing, and having contrived to escape his ally, he reached home alone. His grandfather's family had not long since returned from their dinner at Mary Eden's, and when Oscar descended from his room, exhibiting a careful toilet which he hoped would escape the family eye, all were grouped about the front porch.

"Where're you goin', Osk?" queried Will, with a grin.

"Walkin'," said Oscar briefly.

"Give my regards to Cousin Winthrop," said old Timothy, nudging his wife. "Excuse me for nudgin' you, wife," he added hastily, "for if you have as little victuals aboard as I have, it's no time for nudging."

"Didn't you-all take dinner at Mary's?" inquired Oscar, seeking diversion from his own affairs.

"We made out," said his grandmother. "Oscar, if you should see Ethel——"

"I must hurry," said Oscar, closing the gate behind him in his agitation, "for I'll have to be back at my restaurant in a couple of hours." He hurried away.

"I never thought," said Peter, "that Oscar would bring so much honor on us as he has by falling in love with Ethel Thornberry. I expected him to pick out somebody unworthy of us. I'm always looking for that in our family," he added, with a stern glance at

Will. Then he closed his eyes to bring back the vision of Goldie Pickens.

"I'm afraid it'll rain on him, taking that walk to the country," said Mrs. Thornberry as a loud peal of thunder rolled heavily across the floor of dense clouds.

"Oh, I reckon not," said Timothy, lighting his pipe, "I just want this pleasant weather to continue."

Oscar left the torn-up sidewalk and followed the middle of the street, till it led him out of Core City. He was brought almost at once among the rounded hills which crown the uplift of the Ozarks. They were covered, almost to the summit, with blossoming apple trees. The air was delicious with pungent perfumes, and the eye reveled in billowy sweeps of pink and white. Here and there, an extensive strawberry patch showed acres of white balls, while beyond them stretched the waste lands so sugared with stones that the brown crust of the earth was completely hidden, as under a custard. The hard, red road wound among the hills, showing occasionally, as if lifted up for the gaze of the world, a hut with its surrounding sheds, litter of straw, and patches of innumerable stones. Sometimes a native Arkansawyer, in overalls and dilapidated hat, stood among his pigs, hearing in their every grunt a promise of growth and bacon. Such a one would send Oscar a hearty greeting down the hillside, and the young man would trudge on his way, the happier for the friendly hail.

When Winthrop Thornberry's farm was reached, it was not difficult to distinguish it from other plantations. Not only was his orchard of great extent, but every tree was as polished as a piece of furniture, and seemed to have sprung into the world with no instinct *telling it* that rough bark had once been in the family.

Nor did it incline according to individual whim, or send out superfluous branches, or exhibit a prodigality of sprouts. In brief, each tree was as thoroughly groomed as a most carefully curried horse.

The orchard sloped up to the side of Winthrop Thornberry's yard; and as Oscar trudged along the road, he came at last to a view of the large three-story brick, the most elaborate mansion in that county, as became the residence of its richest man. In the orchard, not far from the yard's side gate, where the trees stood unusually far apart, there was a quaint rounded building of lattice-work with a dome of curved colored shingles. Rose bushes pressed against its sides as if their green leaves and swelling buds were all trying to get a peep at the occupant of that summer-house. Oscar caught a glimpse of blue, and his heart leaped. Chance favored him. He climbed over the irregular stone wall, and approached the lattice door.

Ethel Thornberry rested upon the bench that circled round three sides of the room. She had just finished reading a letter which had already been perused several times. It was from an intimate friend in Hot Springs, telling her, in answer to direct inquiries, of the dissipation of Ethel's only brother. Ethel had long been persuaded not only that her brother drank too freely; but that he was in actual want, in spite of his large income, on account of heavy gaming at a resort where gambling, at that time, was legalized by the government and dignified by society. The question in Ethel's mind was, should she tell her father? Knowing his softness of heart, she hesitated to inflict a grievous wound with no certain prospect that its infliction could better the situation.

While meditating upon this problem, her heart grew

bitter against her brother, and throbbed with poignant sympathy for her mother now lying unconscious. Suddenly she caught sight of an angular young man, wearing spectacles upon his slightly hooked nose, who was advancing with awkward speed in spite of trousers much too tight.

In a word, Oscar had arrived. Seldom had he ever come to Ethel upon an auspicious occasion; but he could hardly have pitched upon one less so than the present. However, Oscar had the decided advantage of not knowing this; and, inwardly congratulating himself upon finding his distant cousin alone and thus, as it were, to all others "incommunicado," he entered the summer-house.

Ethel Thornberry,—who was sometimes spoken of, in family conclave, as being "a Thornberry in name only,"—presented, in her general aspect, the dignity one wears when it is merely a shining-forth of the natural character. It was the dignity of pride as well as of delicate sensibility. Clearly, she held herself high, and had Oscar not been so hopeful, he might have inferred that she held others correspondingly low. It had never entered her mind that Oscar aspired to her hand, but he had long shown a determination to become a familiar friend of the family; and, instinctively, she disliked intimacies. It counted absolutely nothing with her that Oscar's brother was "in a bank." Had he been President instead of simply cashier, it would have made no difference. To Goldie Pickens, who had nothing, money was an essential goal; but Ethel, having money, regarded appearances; and it can not be said that poor Oscar made a heroic appearance, either over the restaurant-oven, or upon Sunday *holiday, in tight* trousers and a sad-colored tie.

Ethel did not greet him until he was so near that it could not be avoided. Then she spoke without warmth. "Good-evening, Oscar. My father is at the house; if you are not afraid of typhoid, you will find him in the library."

"The fact is," said Oscar, "I did not come to see your father, but you, Ethel." He looked at her seriously, and his spectacles gave him an air even more solemn than his feelings. She sat before him, almost as tall as he, clad from shapely neck to slender feet in blue. Her eyes, too, were blue, and under the hair which gleamed too light for brown and almost too dark for yellow, those eyes, distant, reserved, critical, looked at him remotely. The erect form which ever suggested to Oscar's mind the term "queenly," and the beautiful face, too long to be perfect and too cold to be luminous, but beautiful in its type, was but the material form of the young man's longings. It was such an overwhelming happiness to be near Ethel and to gaze upon her, that Oscar was contented to the inmost fibers of his being. All that the world had to excite his ambition or to gratify his yearnings was within that small latticed chamber. Strange in how small a space the world can concentrate all its allurements!

"I'm afraid it is going to rain," said Ethel, by way of escape from the painful silence, "and you're so far from home; did you bring no umbrella?"

"Oh, I don't think it'll rain," said Oscar joyously. "Besides, what if it does? Let it rain!" Before him sat Ethel, the maiden of his thoughts and dreams.

The silence grew more intense.

"Oscar," inquired Ethel, desperately seeking a subject that might move the other to speech, "when do you open up your restaurant of evenings?"

"Just whenever it's handy," said Oscar, sitting down and rubbing his leg, seemingly in order to find if his trousers were intact after such a trying ordeal. "The boys come around when they're hungry, and if I'm there, it's all right; and if I ain't, they go to the other stand. But don't let's talk about the restaurant. I don't expect to be there much longer. I'm going to branch out. I've been preparing myself for real life. And I've come to tell you about it. I'd rather you'd know before anybody else,—except grandmother, of course. I've told her. You see, she took us three boys in when we were left helpless orphans, and she's been a mother to us; so, of course, *she* stands before everybody else in the world. But you come next, to *me*, for I love you, Ethel, I love you, *so!*"

Ethel stared at him, while a faint color came into her cheeks. She had never dreamed of this.

"I know I'm not much, now," said Oscar. "Well, whatever I may be above what you see, will be owing to you. I never would have thought of trying to—to branch out, if it hadn't come from loving you. And Ethel," he added, a modest triumph sounding in his earnest tone, "I can say all this in Latin. Yes, sir, while others have slept and taken recreation, I have studied. It would have been hard if I hadn't been doing it on your account; but loving you made even my Latin grammar interesting."

"Don't, Oscar," said Ethel hastily; "you mustn't talk to me in this way. I respect your—motives; but they are—it's no use, Oscar," she added. Her first impulse of displeasure had, somehow, been melted by his simplicity. She was touched.

Oscar said timidly: "It's in my mind to go to the *city*, Ethel, where there are so many openings for young men. I'll seek a position of honor. Don't you think I could make myself worthy of you, if I tried my whole lifetime?"

"Oscar," said Ethel, "it is not a question, after all, whether either of us is worthy of the other. I do not love you."

He said, somewhat faintly, "Don't you think you ever could?"

"I am quite sure I never could," she said, with gentle conviction.

"Well," said Oscar, drawing a long breath and turning his hat round and round in slightly tremulous hands, "and—how is your mother this evening?"

"She is not so well."

"Is Cousin Polly Eden still nursing her?" inquired Oscar. Of course, he knew already.

At that moment, a dash of breeze-wafted drops spattered upon the floor. Almost immediately after, Winthrop Thornberry hurried into the summer-house, carrying an umbrella.

"I brought this for you, Ethel," he said, panting. "Why, hallo, Osk, you here?" The richest man in the county clapped one of the poorest genially upon the shoulder, then darted a rather quizzical look at his daughter. "We'd better hurry to the house," he added. "Oscar, you're not afraid of typhoid fever?"

"No, sir."

"Then come along, boy."

Winthrop, a heavily-built, closely-cropped, and, but for an iron-gray mustache, clean-shaven man of some fifty-five years, started in advance, that Oscar might have Ethel's company. But Oscar hastened to his side.

"It wasn't any use, Cousin Winthrop," Oscar said dejectedly.

Ethel, overhearing these words, could not trust her ears. "What is it, father?" she demanded, holding displeasure in abeyance.

Oscar turned to her. "Of course," he said, with a homely sort of dignity that was not without its appeal, "I asked your father's permission to speak to you."

"And I gave it," said Winthrop Thornberry, passing his burly arm about the young man's thin form. "There are lots of worse fellows. I thought I knew what you'd say, Ethel, and I warned the lad; but he wouldn't believe me. And if you had agreed to him, *I* shouldn't have stood in the way."

Ethel felt an impulse to smile, but Oscar had won her respect, in spite of himself.

They reached the house. Oscar would have preferred to go on home; the rain would have helped to soothe his turbulent heart. But, alas! he did not know how to leave. Ethel ardently desired him far away; Winthrop felt the natural restraint of his presence; Oscar longed for solitude; but neither in his Latin grammar nor in Grote's *Greece* had he acquired the art of departure. He followed them softly into the hall, and thence into the library. It was a large and cheerful room, furnished, even crowded, with tiers of books. There were several tables with easy-chairs before each, and around them a semicircle of volumes, strewn upon the carpet.

"Ah, my son," said Winthrop, with hearty zest in his voice, "this is what I call life; my trees outdoors, and my books in the house. Eh, lad?"

"Yes, sir," said Oscar despondently.

"I will leave you here to enjoy each other's company," said Ethel, not without a malicious twinkle in her eye; she felt that she owed her father a retaliating blow; and Oscar's society for a couple of hours appealed to her forcibly, and it must be added, justly, as a means of condign punishment. She was about to leave, when the door opened softly and Mrs. Eden glided into the room, closing the door behind her with noiseless care. If Mrs. Eden's foot was large and her body heavy, her footstep never jarred upon the sick ear. Her form was bent out of plumb from years of toil, and her rugged face possessed a certain air of grimness and resolution, such as unflinching veterans acquire from engaging in life's most strenuous campaigns; but she ever grew to be something more than beautiful to those for whom she ministered. And thus, to the little company in the library, she was neither of low estate nor homely seeming. To their eyes, her hard lines and angularity appeared through a softening veil of tender service and patient waiting.

In life's most serious crises, there comes, at times, a shock that lifts us out of our little spheres of personal interest. We realize, then, that what we have considered of supreme importance, and for which we have planned and battled, counts, after all, for little in the great drama of human affairs. So it was when Mrs. Eden solemnly approached Winthrop Thornberry and laid her hand gently upon his arm. There was that in her face that made of Oscar's love and Ethel's pride mere passing breaths of a summer's day.

"Send for the doctor at once," said Mrs. Eden, in a low voice.

"She's worse?" said her cousin, starting toward the door.

"Yes,—and still unconscious. I think she has grown much weaker in the past hour."

A sob burst from Ethel's throat.

"I'll go," said Oscar briefly.

"Cousin Winthrop," said Mrs. Eden, "did you send for Atterton?" Atterton was his only son.

"No, Polly," faltered the other, "the doctor said it wasn't worth while, and Atterton wrote that he oughtn't to leave his business unless it were necessary."

"It is necessary, now," Mrs. Eden responded gravely.

Ethel recalled the letter from the friend of her schooldays, telling of Atterton's drinking and gambling at Hot Springs. She turned deathly pale and felt a horrible sickness of the heart. To hide her emotion, she hastened after Oscar, who had already reached the front door.

"Oh, how it is raining!" she exclaimed.

"Yes," said Oscar hurriedly, "but I'll have the doctor here mighty quick, I tell *you*."

"Take the horse!" called Ethel.

Oscar shouted from the distant gate: "Haven't time to catch it up. Good-by!"

Ethel ran after him, waving the umbrella, heedless of the rain that beat against her face. "Here!" she called. "Oscar! take the umbrella."

Oscar, never pausing an instant, hurled back from the highway, "You quit a-stoppin' me!"

That was his last farewell. Ethel ran back to the house, wondering not so much at Oscar's unchivalrous rebuffs as at her own impulsive conduct. But as she passed under the stone lintel, the memory of her brother's course of action smote upon her, chill as the breath of a prison-cell; and Oscar and his love were *alike forgotten.*

CHAPTER VII

"IT's a beautiful day for the funeral," said Mrs. Hodgins Thornberry, as she swept the dining-room after the noon-dinner. "Will you move your feet, Mr. Thornberry? She never would call any of us 'cousin,' but I am going to take my arms out of the washtub,"— this, of course, was spoken metaphorically,—"to attend her funeral. I don't think she would have come to mine, but I do as I'd be done by. Now put your feet on the other side of your chair, Mr. Thornberry, for you'd die, I reckon, of inhaling this dust, rather than get up."

"Poor Cousin Winthrop!" murmured her husband, by way of diversion. "Well," he added, "that'll be a mighty soft nest for the next woman he marries. He's awful rich; but nobody never see me knuckle to Cousin Winthrop, nor Cousin Winthrop's wife." (In youth, Hodgins had refused to take an education.) "She is dead, now, an' that's enough to say of anybody; but if she was a-livin' I'd have something to tell you of her high-heeled, down-looking superiority such as is broke out in her darter Ethel."

"Now hold your feet up. *You're* a fit subject to talk of others' faults, after deserting wife and infant for three years, then coming back like a parlor-boarder!"

Hodgins was discreetly mute.

"Anyway, Mr. Thornberry, you can't go to that church-funeral, for three o'clock is train-time."

"I'll be there," *said Hodgins, who thought it best to*

prepare his wife in advance. "The fact is, driving the hack and moving houses is too much business to put on any one man. Trains is too regular to suit me. I ain't regular, Marietta, and you know it; it ain't in the Thornberry blood; that's how I explain it."

"I'll tell you how *I* explain it!" cried the mistress.

Hodgins hastily rose and bestowed his most blandishing smile upon his younger child. "Tootsies," he said, "don't you want to go with pappy to the funeral? Pappy'll show you a big time, and he'll hold you up to look in the cawfin."

"Tootsies" pulled away and burrowed under his mother's apron.

"Huh!" cried Mrs. Thornberry scornfully, "you haven't been home long enough for your own flesh and blood to get acquainted with you."

As Hodgins afterwards said to his cousin George Nicodemus, "She had me there;" so he beat a retreat without making any reply. "Not but what I might have said something," Hodgins explained, "and then cut and run; but whatever I'd a-left there, I'd a-found when I come home again."

"There goes Groner to the funeral," said Mrs. Polly Thornberry, looking from the window. "Don't you think we'd better start, Timothy?"

"Nuck," said the old gentleman; "Groner always goes early to funerals, to get out of 'em all there is in 'em. We'll be on time. The card says three o'clock, and that means nearer four. I've shut up the grocery the whole afternoon out of respect to Cousin Winthrop; and if I've got to have a holiday, I might as well get some comfort from it. I wonder if George Nicodemus *will come* to that funeral. He may think it a good chance to sell some of his mining-sheers, while people's hearts is feeling meller."

"If he has any respect for us, to say nothing of himself," spoke up Peter severely, "he'll stay at home. Does he think it was a light thing to be sent to the penitentiary for years? Does he think he can lay aside his stripes, and mingle with the Thornberrys on equal footing?"

"He'll be there," said Will prophetically, "and on the front bench. Cousin George never did take his punishment as hard as his kinfolks. You see, it was the public funds, and he meant to replace every cent, so he doesn't feel that it was really stealing."

"Are you defending George Nicodemus?" exclaimed Peter, outraged. "Whatever he feels and whatever he did, he was clapped into state's prison by the laws of the land; besides, he admitted his guilt."

"Wherever he was 'clapped,'" observed Will serenely, "he will be found on the front bench when the choir begins to sing."

"Now, while we're on unpleasant subjects," remarked old Timothy, pulling hard at his pipe, "Waldo McCormack has moved back to Core City."

"Poor Elizabeth!" murmured Timothy's wife. Elizabeth was Mrs. Waldo McCormack. "It's dreadful to live near her and see her hectored over and badgered into her grave by a selfish husband. When they are at a distance, you can imagine he is treating her better. That's the only way to get any satisfaction out of Waldo McCormack; put him far away, somewhere, and you may imagine he's better'n he is."

"There's another burden for Cousin Polly Eden to carry," remarked Will. "Cousin Elizabeth is Cousin Polly's first *cousin, but they were raised together by*

Cousin Polly's mother, and I think that counts more."

"At any rate," spoke up Peter, with dignity, "Cousin Waldo McCormack has reflected credit upon the Thornberrys by marrying among them. I admit he's rather hard on Cousin Elizabeth, but he's an advantage to the rest of us. Cousin Waldo McCormack is an author. He has a book published. That lends dignity to all the connection. I don't see how we could spare him from the family circle."

"Of course," remarked his grandmother, "if Elizabeth was marrying a book, she got what she wanted. But I'm going to that funeral right now. I'm in a proper state of mind to attend anybody's."

As Timothy had foreseen, the funeral was greatly delayed. This gave the early comers time to dispose of much accumulated gossip. The ladies of Core City sat in the auditorium in their bright dresses and their newest hats, speaking in muffled voices as befitted the occasion, but with immense enjoyment. As the saying goes, "all the town was there," and all the town, untrammeled by any special liking for the dead, felt it to be a gala day. Sometimes the free and light spirit of such occasions is darkened by recollections of a loving tongue stilled and a generous heart cold forever. Not so in the case of Cousin Winthrop's wife. Perhaps none in the town, save her most intimate kinsmen, were debtors to her heart; and certain it is that her tongue had left more there than one with a large balance on the credit side of their account.

Groner Thornberry had come early, taking his stand in the unfenced yard that sloped down from the brick church to the torn-up sidewalk. He balanced himself stiffly upon his crutch, watching each arrival with hawk-eye, and engaging in conversation whom he might. Some of his acquaintances from the country, who rarely came to town save on court days or Saturday evenings, greeted him heartily, making him feel that it was "good to be there."

Presently he espied Hodgins Thornberry slowly ambling in his direction, smoking his inevitable cigarette. Groner's naturally discontented expression deepened on catching sight of George Nicodemus, following closely behind the hack-driver. Groner felt that there was one man too many.

George Nicodemus was low and slight,—a dried-up little man of about forty, who seemed even smaller than his clothes required. His brow was retreating; so was his chin. Thus his nose was left master of the field, and it peaked forth long and sharp, as if to cut the air. His step was soft, and his voice low; but he had a way of raising his tones in shrill unexpectedness, at the same time shaking his neck a little farther out of his collar, as if to show that there was plenty of him, if he chose to prove it. Hodgins was not much taller than his favorite cousin George, but he was so burly, so heavy, and his voice was so loud and rolling,—save always in the presence of his wife,—that he made less of his companion than the gentleman, without the contrast, might have made of himself.

Groner took a firmer hold in the hard red earth with his crutch, and greeted Hodgins with unusual heartiness, in order to make more marked his ignoring of the smaller man.

George Nicodemus inquired, "Have they set apart the front benches, and reserved 'em for the kinfolks?"

"Certainly," Groner answered acidly. "Do you

mean to tell me, George, that you are going to set yourself on one of those reserved front seats?"

"I made up my mind," said Nicodemus, shaking his neck out of his collar, "when I came out of retirement, that I wasn't going to give up. I'll take my place with the Thornberrys, and sink or swim with 'em."

"Right!" cried Hodgins, clapping him upon the shoulder so heartily that Nicodemus staggered.

The many lines upon Groner's round red face were increased by several of deep fixity about the lips. He said drily, "How old was Cousin Winthrop's wife?" Thus he disposed of George Nicodemus.

"Forty-nine," Hodgins answered, inhaling his smoke luxuriously. "I asked Ethel, when I taken the kerridge out there this mornin'."

"I always said she was about fifty!" Groner triumphantly exclaimed. "Ha! she can't keep it now. You can't take your money with you to heaven, and you can't carry your age into the grave."

"But we've all got to die," added Hodgins, with due solemnity.

"Yes," returned Groner, "and no doubt Cousin Winthrop's wife is better off."

"Yes," said Nicodemus softly, "she is out of the trials of life, which there are many of, as I ought to know, having tested 'em by a varied experience."

"Of which," snapped Groner Thornberry, "least said, soonest mended!"

"I have made up my mind," said Nicodemus, rising from his collar, and lifting his voice in assertiveness, "not to bury my past in silence. I'm not going to burden my future career by strapping the burden of other years upon its shoulders. Folks will have to take me for what I am. Perhaps I'm not a Daniel Webster;

but I judge there were several degrees between him and Nothing."

"That's right," said Hodgins admiringly.

Groner smote the earth angrily with his crutch, and relief appeared in Israel in the form of a tall, shaggy-haired man with a head much too large for his body, who came into sight, walking toward the church. His long white hands were folded before him. The broad forehead was bent in contemplative musings, and the long, thin legs sometimes grazed the edge of the sidewalk, dangerously near. Groner said in a hoarse undertone, "I heard Waldo McCormack had moved back, and there he is. Now Polly will have her hands full. She always had to support Waldo when he lived close enough,—and why? Just because he married my niece. Now all the best cooking will go over to his house and we'll have to wait meals, and with a boarder on our hands, too!"

"Of course, he's coming without his wife," said Hodgins, in a gusty whisper. "He never did take her nowheres, which I would always mine, if she would be took. I'm sorry they've moved back. I hate to see a Thornberry treated as Waldo treats his wife; and the worst of it is, he never knows he's done anything. He always thinks he's right."

"I'm of your mind," said Nicodemus. "I may have been in trouble; but never could my wife say that she was mistreated or spoken roughly to of me. Even in getting her divorce, she never claimed I'd been unkind, but that being as I was forced to spend a few years——"

"Look here, Nick," Groner exploded, "it was impossible to keep you out of the penitentiary ten years ago, and it looks like you're determined at any cost to go back to it. But what with Waldo McCormack coming and the hearse, too, I reckon both together can keep you off the subject."

The hearse drove up, and the driver looked disconcerted on finding that the front walk had been newly laid in concrete, and was guarded on both sides by several strands of barbed wire. The carriages containing the pall-bearers hovered in uncertainty on the outskirts. On one side of the yard there was a ditch, filled with cinders, preparatory for the finishing layers of concrete. The other side was flanked by a steep rise from the road. Suddenly everybody felt that provision should have been made for an expeditious entrance into the yard, and everybody was surprised that somebody else had not attended to the matter.

At this moment of suspense, it did not escape the general attention that Oscar was the only Thornberry among the pall-bearers; the others were of Cousin Winthrop's wife's family; also that Mrs. Mary Eden had come in the carriage with Cousin Winthrop, Ethel, and Atterton,—the son hastily summoned from Hot Springs. There was some speculating as to why Oscar had been made such a marked exception; of course, Mrs. Eden's presence was explained in virtue of the fact that she was the only one who would nurse the dying woman. But why Oscar? There was instantly conceived a shade of unfriendliness toward Oscar in the breast of every Thornberry waiting in the yard. As George Nicodemus whispered to Hodgins, "I believe in the Thornberrys all sticking together, sink or swim."

The word having been passed into the church, that there would be some difficulty in bearing the coffin over the defenses, the few men who had seated themselves in the auditorium came out to see the thing done. It was finally decided that it would be easier and more seemly to carry the casket up the steep incline than to cross the cindered ditch.

"It will be difficult," the undertaker said to the pall-bearers, addressing them as a captain might his men, "but if you take it on a run, there won't be no trouble, I don't *guess*. This ought to have been attended to before we came."

"I think," said Oscar, "that it would be much better for some of us to climb into the ditch and receive the remains, and then wait till the others climb across to wait for us, then all climb out and go on. I don't like to run with the coffin. It doesn't seem right."

"It's the best way," said the undertaker, with decision. "In changing at the ditch, there might be some accident. Just start on a run up the bank, and you'll be at the top in a moment; you'll have to make a short run; a solemn, proper kind of run; but you'd better be lively about it."

The church filled rapidly during the last moments. Ethel, heavily draped in a black veil, sat by her handsome father on the front bench. There was a marked resemblance between Winthrop, in spite of his large head and iron-gray mustache, and his son Atterton. That young man, whose face showed signs of recent suffering, was distinctly handsome, but of a more effeminate type than his cousin Will. Peter sat next to him, for Atterton and Peter had always been intimate friends. Mary had taken the seat next Uncle Groner, feeling that a funeral was not an occasion to enjoy the presence of any one; but Peter, because of his pleasure over Atterton's return to Core City, failed to miss her usual accompaniment. The pall-bearers walked slowly down the aisle, a little heated from their recent run, but duly grave.

Old Mrs. Polly Thornberry whispered her uneasiness to Will: "I'm afraid your grandfather won't get here on time."

"Don't be uneasy," Will whispered back; "I told brother Wells not to begin till he comes,—that he'd likely be late."

Tall and solemn Mr. Mulkey, with fleshy, short-winded Mrs. Mulkey, and their beautiful daughter Gladys Lucile, came down the aisle and sat as near front as any but a Thornberry might. Atterton whispered to Peter, "Say! isn't that girl a beauty!"

Then the coffin was rolled before the rostrum.

The Mulkeys had come to the funeral from a sense of Christian duty. "We will show these Thornberrys," Mr. Mulkey had told his wife, "by attending the obsequies, that we bear their family no malice for turning us out of Mrs. Eden's home in time of dire need."

Mrs. Mulkey, having seated herself and taken up her usual breathing, whispered cautiously: "That distinguished-looking young man must be Mr. Atterton Thornberry. Look at him, Gladys Lucile, I think he has noticed you. He is very rich, I hear."

Groner whispered to Waldo McCormack: "The choir'll be out pretty soon, we hope. I had it just now from Hodge; they're in the minister's study, arguing who's to sing the solo part in the quartette."

Timothy Thornberry now slipped into place beside his wife, with his usual surprise at finding himself late.

"Now," sighed Mrs. Hodgins Thornberry, "everything's ready but the choir."

The Rev. Mr. Wells turned the leaves of his Bible with a nervous hand.

Waldo McCormack, with the bewilderment of one but recently returned to his old home, and as yet unused to the ropes, whispered inquiry, "What's the matter with the choir?"

"Fuss," answered Groner succinctly.

"What fuss?"

Groner looked at him reproachfully. "Don't you remember?" he returned. "It was about whether the piano'd be tuned low or at concert pitch."

"But," whispered the author of a printed book, "that piano was sold two years ago, and yonder's the organ they've got in its place."

"They got shed of the piano," Groner acknowledged, "but they ain't shet of the fuss."

The choristers now slowly filed out of the little back room, and wound their way to the organ-loft.

"Hallo!" whispered George Nicodemus, "ain't the organist missing?"

"Yap," Hodgins answered, with great zest; "look a-there!" One of the choir, in fact the one who had gained the victory in the recent spirited contest, and was booked to sing the solo over Cousin Winthrop's wife's remains, solemnly tiptoed across the church to where Goldie Pickens was sitting.

There was a whispered conference. Then Goldie Pickens rose, saintly, spiritual, meek, as though she would say, "I offer myself as your victim; come and slay." She followed the soloist to the loft, and seated herself at the organ, thus, for the time, alienating from her all those who had demanded that the piano be tuned to concert pitch.

The services began. The solo was presented in a voice rather of triumph than mourning, and this was followed by a self-conscious quartette. The Rev. Mr.

Wells read the Scriptures, and in due time was launched upon his funeral oration. It was a great occasion, and he hoped to rise to it in an effective manner; and the only visible proofs he could bring of his effectiveness were tears. Therefore, for tears he sought. He began with general principles, proving by the kings of the past ("Where are they now?") that all must die. The audience, caring nothing for the kings of the past, and feeling little uneasiness about their own present condition, listened in dry enjoyment of the scene.

Even Mary, with her constitutional, if not inherited piety, found herself taking pride in the erect form of Peter, and in his uplifted face which promised so much for the Thornberry dignity. Here was a young man determined at any sacrifice to rise above his fellows, to make the name of Thornberry not only honored, but feared. He had even set himself the task of improving his immediate family. Mary was proud because he was her cousin, though but distantly related. She was prouder still that he had always shown preference for her society.

She woke with a start to the deepening voice of the minister. What would Peter think, could he know that her mind had wandered from the solemnity of the scene to playing in a garden of fragrant thoughts?

By this time, Atterton was shedding tears. He was the first of the family to succumb. Winthrop Thornberry followed his son to defeat. The Rev. Mr. Wells had his eye upon Ethel, but that young lady sat like a rigid statue, draped in black. The speaker had reached that part of his discourse beginning, "Nevermore will you gaze upon," etc. Ethel showed no sign. Atterton was deeply affected. He recalled a year of dissipation, and remembered how he had refused to come home to his sick mother, alleging business as an excuse when, in fact, he hesitated to leave a gay life for a home of shadows. He had, of course, believed that his mother would recover.

"I would have come," he told himself, "if I had known it was serious."

"Nevermore . . ." came the impressive voice from the pulpit. There were times when the Rev. Mr. Wells felt that the choir had the best of him; but now they were thrown into complete, if momentary, oblivion, piano, organ and all. Peter, seated beside Atterton, felt uneasily that his model—for he had long since accepted Atterton as his model—should not show grief so openly. He had always maintained, and usually with justice, that Atterton's behavior in public was irreproachable. These copious tears astonished and annoyed the Thornberry mentor. They seemed in a way common, even vulgar. They were giving people something to talk about, and Peter had a horror of gossip. He slyly slipped his foot over the carpet and trod upon Atterton's toes, at the same time giving the minister a look that ought to have dried his eloquence. But the orator saw only Ethel. If he could make that haughty head droop, the day was won! Atterton sought to compose himself. He realized that he was making an exhibition for the eyes of Core City, but for a time his repentant heart had burst the chains of conventionality. Winthrop was drying his eyes at this unusual exhibition of feeling upon his son's part.

Ethel slipped her hand into her father's and grasped it. "I am here," it seemed to say.

Outwardly, she remained cold stone to the last.

It was half-past four when the audience was invited

to pass up the right aisle, view the remains, and pass down the left aisle to the outer air. In the breaking of the ranks, people found themselves grouped in the front yard while waiting for the dead to be brought forth. A long line of empty carriages stood ready to carry relatives and friends to the cemetery.

"Cousin Winthrop," George Nicodemus remarked to Hodgins, "is doing things in style—hey, Hodge?"

"That's right, Nick. Cousin Timothy," he addressed the old captain, "what did you think of the sermon? It seemed to me the first part was over the heads of the audience."

"I think I clumb up and got 'most all there was," said the captain. Finding himself at Mrs. Hodgins Thornberry's side, the old gentleman pulled his white beard nervously and murmured, "There, there, Cousin Marietta, don't feel so bad! Let us hope that Cousin Winthrop's wife has gone to a place where she'll feel closer kin to us than she ever felt down here."

Mrs. Hodgins Thornberry dried her eyes hastily. "I'd never a-thought there was a tear in me for Cousin Winthrop's wife," she murmured hysterically. "I don't know *now* precisely what I'm crying for."

Groner Thornberry said, with an air of conviction, "Cousin Winthrop's wife is better off. We must all die."

Goldie Pickens, standing on the grassplot beneath the large stained window, looked up, and there was Peter. What a surprise for her! As in quick and unpremeditated impulse, she held out her hand to him, "I, too, have suffered," said Goldie, her eyes large and solemn. "I suffer now with you, my friend."

Peter took the slim hand eagerly. His fingers closed *upon it* tightly. He felt greatly comforted. Even when his grasp relaxed, she let her hand lie in his, like a cool pledge of ethereal affection. He was thrilled by her touch, by her calling him "my friend," by her steadfast, gentle, seraphic gazing.

Mary saw them standing thus, and her honest eyes showed a faint touch of surprise. Goldie caught a glimpse of Mary with the tail of her black eye, and for a moment her lids drooped while her expression suggested that the earth offered nothing proper enough for her to gaze upon, but when she looked up,—carefully keeping her blue eye next to Peter,—Mary had already passed on.

"Such a dear girl, your Cousin Mary," murmured Goldie.

CHAPTER VIII

GOLDIE PICKENS stood upon Mrs. Eden's front porch bidding a new music-pupil adieu. The girl had said rather ungraciously: "I haven't the least taste for music, Miss Pickens. I'm sure I shan't practise. But mother was so pleased at your filling the place of the regular organist, that she said I *had* to take; so here I am." In Mrs. Eden's front room where Goldie's piano was installed, the girl had "taken" with a cold, set face, as if the music were some contagious disease.

Goldie watched her depart; a plan was revolving in her mind. In vain, Groner in his lamblike voice,—he had a lamblike voice for favorites, and a lionlike voice for his immediate family,—petitioned the music-teacher to come and read aloud to him under the budding apple trees.

"Cousin Groner," said Goldie sweetly, "if you will go to the post office for me, I will never be able to repay you for your kindness; I hope to receive a letter from my venerable pastor." Groner Thornberry eagerly seized his crutch, ravished at being called "cousin" by the charming lady of the angelic voice. Thus having disposed of Groner to his delight, and her convenience, the young lady withdrew to her bedroom, which, thanks to a folding-bed, happily disguised its primary function. Goldie drew forth her writing-desk and began a note to Winthrop Thornberry. Occasionally she paused to stare blankly from the window. Being alone, it was unnecessary to pose; and it was as if the great loneliness of her life had rushed upon her in a mighty breath. Her face grew dark and hard.

Since her mother's death there had been no one to whom she cared to reveal herself. It was not that there was any crime in her past life, unless it were a crime to strive ceaselessly for daily bread; but she was ashamed of abject poverty. A drunken father had stranded her in St. Louis at a tender age, with a feeble mother to support. Goldie had served as maid, as messenger-girl, as nurse, as vendor. Yet in spite of these heavy odds against her, she had contrived through the generosity of chorus-girls and beer-hall musicians to pick up a superficial knowledge of music. Her lover, after his marriage to a rich girl, gave her a year abroad as a compensation for breaking her heart.

Goldie did not care much about people's hearts, after the deadening of her own. Life had not taught her the lesson of showing mercy. It was always a contest; her income was continually wrested, as by force, from unwilling hands. Sometimes it was the force of superior ability; often it was that of diplomacy. Goldie's feet, pretty and slender as they were, had not, perhaps, been shaped for straight paths.

Thus it came about, that she was never herself, her real self, unless alone. There was always something to hide,—her poverty, her past years of menial service, her disgraced and aged father who still lived to haunt her with vague terrors, her age, her determination to secure a competency through the legitimate channel of marriage,—in a word, everything in her past and every fiber of her purposes, that made her a distinct personality. In effacing all this, in carefully smoothing down any telltale prominence and individual trait, Goldie sought to generalize, to symbolize herself, to have herself accepted rather as a type than as a distinct characer.

The note was finished. Goldie read it aloud in a low, careful voice. She sought the expression she fancied Winthrop Thornberry would impart, when he should read it. She zealously avoided using the insinuating tone that would lend the best effect. Goldie might deceive others, never herself.

MY DEAR MR. THORNBERRY:
You will no doubt remember that I was induced to come to Core City as an instructor in music, principally, through your persuasion. You will remember your daughter engaged to take lessons twice a week. Naturally, Miss Ethel has felt, and still feels, a disinclination to take up the work. But I depend upon my teaching for my support, and it occurs to me that you might be willing to compensate me for my disappointment. Should such be the case, accept my lasting gratitude; but should you view the matter otherwise, be assured I shall acquiesce, knowing that you will do what is right.
Yours respectfully,
(MISS) GOLDIE PICKENS.

Goldie stared long at the note. It was neatly written. Would it offend? More than once, her craving for money had led her into false steps. Should anything be risked in the case of Winthrop Thornberry? He was worth $500,000, and,—reverently be it said, —he was a widower. . . . Goldie's mind floated with undeveloped fancies. Ethel could object . . . Ethel would be very hard to manage. . . . Still, there is no obstacle on earth so high that an elopement. . . . Young Atterton was handsome and dashing. . . . Peter was devoted. If Winthrop should send her some money for the lessons that had not been given, it would prove most acceptable. . . . Poor Mary!

After all, Goldie could not decide about sending the note. She thrust it into her bosom and went down-*stairs* trusting to inspiration. Mary was talking excitedly to her mother in the dining-room. Groner had just handed them a letter. They told Goldie the news all together. She gathered that Mary's sister, Ruth, was not coming home after all. The rich uncle with whom she had spent the past year was going to take her on a trip to Yellowstone Park and Niagara Falls. Mrs. Eden was joyously excited for Ruth's sake, but there were tears in her eyes over the prolonged separation.

Mary was just like her mother. Each laughed and cried in the same breath. Goldie could not understand such a conflict of emotions. As for her, she would either have been glad or sorry. Nor could she sympathize with this open show of feeling. No one could ever have read from *her* face whether she triumphed or felt anger. Even now, her rather contemptuous amusement at their simplicity was veiled under an expression of adorable meekness.

"I have never seen Niagara," said Goldie; "what an opportunity for Miss Ruth!"

"Opportunity, indeed!" snapped Groner. "I look on this as one more affront to me,—to *me!*" and he hobbled from the room, his round, creased face redder by far than its wont.

Mrs. Eden cast a tolerant look after Uncle Groner and explained: "Uncle Groner and his brother fell out over the organ question, when both lived in Kentucky, and for that reason Uncle Groner can never be reconciled to my allowing Ruth to stay in the East. But it's such an advantage for Ruth that I am quite firm. Her uncle is not only rich, but generous; and I made up my mind when young never to take up anybody's church quarrel. The church, I think, is not the arena for the contest *of personal* differences."

"Ah," sighed Goldie, "this religious firmness! I fear I could never have been a martyr."

"I do not think," said Mary, "that we are called on to die for an organ." She picked up the dusting-brush, which, since the reading of the letter, had been lying where it had fallen.

"This religious firmness!" Goldie repeated, shaking her head. "It reminds me, Miss Mary, of the fault Mr. Peter was finding with you."

Mary said nothing, but her body slightly straightened in surprise.

"Mr. Peter—Who?" asked Mrs. Eden, laying down the work she had just taken up.

"I should have said Mr. Thornberry," Goldie apologized, "only, there are so many of them. Yes, he was saying what a pity it is that Miss Mary is so *good* that it makes her—was *intolerant* his word?"

"I do not know what his word was," Mary replied quietly enough. "I do not think I was present when the conversation took place."

"He meant no harm in the world," said Goldie hastily. "You know Mr. Peter and I are such good friends that he speaks to me like one of the family. He only said that you are difficult to satisfy, because you are always so sure that you are right. He meant it for praise."

"Upon my word," said Mrs. Eden, "I think Peter had very little to do, to discuss Mary's qualities with—in that way."

"Now, Mrs. Eden," said Goldie hurriedly, "I don't want you to think that Mr. Peter meant the least harm, —he was complimenting Miss Mary."

"I can not suppose," said Mary, with quiet gravity, "that Peter meant any harm by his compliment; or, that you mean any by repeating it. But I have never liked compliments; and I hope you will not present me with any more."

Goldie looked hurt and sorrowful, but not angry. She withdrew as gracefully as she could. On gaining the yard, her impulse was to smile, but catching sight of Groner at the gate, she preserved her wounded look. He apologized for his abrupt exit.

"I am an embittered man, Miss Goldie," he said. "My own brother threw the organ in my teeth, and my only son married a woman who will not let me stay with them, though I pay my board. And when I think of Polly allowing Ruth to live with that brother who insulted me, and visit that son whose wife banishes me from my only child, do you wonder that I am bitter? I do not know which is worse; an organ or a daughter-in-law; both are of the devil, I think," he concluded, with exceeding fierceness.

When the music-teacher reached Main Street, she was still undecided about mailing the note to Winthrop Thornberry. She concluded to be guided in the matter by the result of a contemplated interview with George Nicodemus. The fame of the Nicodemus Mining Company had reached her ears before coming to Core City, and now, that she was so near the short cut to wealth, she was resolved to examine it before continuing her detour by the long road. She found Nicodemus in his office, explaining his various enterprises to prospective share-holders who were, as usual, from a distance.

Goldie had the advantage of detailed statements to shrewd business men, before Nicodemus came to deal with her personally. It appeared that the business was conducted by departments, one dealing with oil, another with minerals, a third with fruit-exporting, a fourth with the lands which had shown traces of diamonds. There were samples on the desk of copper, zinc, silver and even gold, all of which had been found near town, indicating that the Ozarks promised an inexhaustible supply of wealth which only needed development to make every large stock-owner a millionaire. Goldie handled the minerals, smelled the oil, and gazed upon an enormous quantity of prospectuses. Everything was in the future, but confident hope promised nine-tenths of the law. All of the shares were sold at a low figure, but the price of each was expected to be raised within a short time. Copper could be bought at two cents, but probably before the end of the month it would be hard to get it at three. No fewer than 100 shares could be purchased in any one department; but $30 invested in the oil-wells might bring a return of 100 per cent., within six months; and if the oil was not found in sufficient quantity to justify the expense of drilling, the $30 worth of stock would be transferred to another department,—say the diamond fields.

Goldie was pleasantly excited by so many prospects of success, and, so far from disguising her emotion, she exaggerated it. As she took leave of the master mind of so many enterprises, she was warm in her expressions of gratitude and interest.

"I have given you so much trouble," she said, "and you have been so patient! I appreciate your kindness, deeply. I am only a poor music-teacher, Mr. Nicodemus, and every penny I have was won by hard work. I believe you are to be the means of helping me to better things. As Mrs. Eden's cousin, I know *you* will advise me as a true friend."

George Nicodemus, hawk-nosed and hard-browed, looked at her with a speculating eye. Her little appealing graces came with the sweeter charm on account of his isolation from the society of all but business men.

"I feel quite sure, from what you have told me," said Goldie, lifting her mild face to give him a look of adorable confidence, "that I shall invest all that I have in your oil-wells. I must look over my poor little notes and meager bank-account, to find out just how much I can place in your hands. Good-by."

She hesitated a moment, looking down, as if in serious perplexity, then impulsively held out her hand.

"Miss Pickens," said George Nicodemus, a faint flush showing in his leathern cheeks, as he grasped the proffered hand, "don't you do a thing in this matter till I have advised with you."

As Goldie left, it was not without an effort that she prevented a triumphant smile from playing about her lips. If the Nicodemus Mining Company was unsafe, she would learn that from the head of the company; at the same time, if a fortune was to be made, she would get her nest-egg ready. Accordingly, she resolved to mail the note to Winthrop Thornberry.

From his window in the bank, Peter discovered her passing. He stepped out upon the sidewalk and greeted her with unmistakable pleasure.

His undisguised homage was grateful. She made a delightful bit of form and color against the grimy background of the advertisement-besplattered wall. It was a great relief to him, he told her, after hours of routine, to have this glimpse of a pure angel——

"No, you must not," said Goldie, gravely enough; "I do not like that."

Peter apolgized, but maintained his attitude of unbending dignity, letting her see clearly that he retracted his words because she wanted him to do so, and not because he was sorry he had called her an angel. "I was not speaking of you from personal feeling," said Peter, who really believed what he said. "I spoke of you merely as of a picture. That is how you appeal to me, Miss Pickens,—as some quaint, idealized form and face in which there is nothing wrong, nothing even human."

Goldie walked slowly toward the post office, and the young man kept at her side, enjoying the "picture" to the full.

"I do not think you should speak to me even in that way," said Goldie thoughtfully. "I know, however, what you mean, but after all, I am but human; and it can not be good for me to be told that I am beautiful. Do you not see?—in praising the angel, you make her a woman. I must judge of this matter from such light as I have, for I am in the world alone, with no one to direct me in wisdom."

"I shall obey you, Miss Pickens. To me you are, indeed, beautiful, but I shall not tell you so. It is not, however, your face that most pleases me, but the light of your inner soul which shines upon it." Peter felt he had done himself, as well as his companion, considerable credit by these balanced words, and he was ready to return to the bank.

"Before we part," said Goldie hastily, looking up at him with adorable wistfulness, "I ought to tell you that I repeated to Miss Mary what you said of her."

"What I said of her?" he echoed vacantly.

"Yes,—the Sunday all of us took dinner there; how she was always so, *so* dear and good, so pure and honest, that sometimes she did not have quite enough patience with those less perfect."

"I don't remember," said Peter, trying to think, "but it is true enough."

"She scolded me dreadfully, by her tone and look," said Goldie, with a shiver; "not that she said a word, Mr. Thornberry; I don't want you to think that she *said* a word. But her look was so unkind."

"I do not understand," said Peter largely, "how anybody in the world could ever look unkindly at you, Miss Goldie,—may I call you so?"

"Thank you,—Mr. Peter. But I must not keep you from your work. It is only we women who can sit with folded hands."

"I am glad," said Peter, "that such dainty hands have no work to do. Good-by, then."

"Good-by, Mr. Peter. Come to the choir-practice to-night."

"Oh, I can't sing," smiled the young man.

"I'm organist now," Goldie insinuated. "I need your support."

"I'll be there," said the young man, with sudden resolution. He returned to the bank, deeply thoughtful, but not of bonds and mortgages. The little meeting with Miss Goldie had been such a relief from dusty routine, and such a pleasure, nay, excitement, that he was resolved to make such more frequent. Why not belong to that choir? Why not escort Goldie home from it, after each practice? Why not develop this sweet, tender friendship? It seemed to the young man that life had suddenly pulled aside a curtain, revealing a long, beautiful vista of delight. The thought of Goldie beckoned. No ugly danger in monster form crouched by the wayside.

Peter had looked forward to a quiet life in Core City, admired by the Thornberry connection, honored in county affairs, a model of deportment and business dealings, revered by a wife in due time,—that is to say, by Mary Eden,—and justly lauded in his obituary as the man who had brought distinction and credit to the northwest of Arkansas. Little, indeed, of this life-program was yet altered, save the substitution, perhaps, of another's name for Mary Eden; but to this fancy-sketch were now added delicious prospects, not of increased respectability, but of happiness. He had thought he cared enough for Mary Eden to bestow his fortune and his name upon her; but in the splendid halo that surrounded Goldie Pickens, Mary faded and faded till she became a pale ghost.

As the days passed by, that ghost haunted Peter strangely. He grew impatient of it; he told it that he had never bound himself to its cold rule; that he had always been free; yet it would not leave him alone.

As in the past Peter's conduct and aims had been much influenced by Atterton Thornberry, so now this intimate cousin shaped his actions and his thoughts. For a few days following the death of Winthrop Thornberry's wife, Atterton had remained in seclusion on the farm. His remorse for the neglect of his dying mother kept him at home. Ethel, proud and cold, would have melted to warm tenderness at one word of repentance from her brother; but Atterton dreamed that his past course of debauchery was unknown to his family; resting in this fancied security, he still felt it necessary to speak of "pressing business," which could not sooner have been neglected. Thus in his repentance, he justified his course by vague statements which *served the more* to harden Ethel's heart against him.

Atterton's gay spirits could not long be subdued by the most pressing regrets, and soon the silent mansion, surrounded by its orchards, grew intolerable. He felt sincere sympathy for the bowed head of the father, not long since so jolly and full of hopes; but for him, there was an end to remorse. In the blackest hour of his humiliation, a face had flitted before his memory, to rob anguish of its sting. It was the face he had first seen at his mother's funeral.

"Yes," said Peter, as he and Atterton lounged like men of the world in the bank after closing-hours, "I'll take you around there, if you like."

"I do like," said Atterton emphatically, placing his heels upon the window ledge, and watching the smoke curl from his handsome, thin-lipped mouth.

They were alone in the building. Peter, according to his wont, had remained to balance his books, and Atterton as usual had dropped in by the back way. "Gladys Lucile is certainly the prettiest girl I ever laid my eyes on," Atterton continued. "I'll never leave Core City as long as I've a chance to look at her. I tell you, Pete, that girl has been right before my eyes ever since I first saw her. What do you know about her folks?"

"The family moved here not long ago," said Peter, who never allowed any one but Atterton to shorten his name. "Mr. Mulkey seems a very respectable man. He is inclined to look down on people who have to work for a living, but I suppose that is on account of his high family connections. He used to be in Congress, you know. You've heard of Senator Mulkey, haven't you?"

"I reckon so," said Atterton doubtfully, "I've heard of everybody. I don't like his looking down on working people. What can he expect of the South when the war wiped away about all it had?"

"He told Oscar," said Peter, drawing on his pipe thoughtfully, "that he ought to go to the city to run a high-priced restaurant."

"Good Heavens!" cried Atterton; "does he think a Thornberry would run a restaurant away from home amongst *strangers?* I reckon, then, he looks down on Cousin Hodge for driving a hack!"

"Yes," Peter nodded, "and on grandfather for keeping a grocery store."

"D—n him!" cried Atterton. "Still, Mulkey is not the pretty member of the firm. I am interested in little Gladys Lucile. It's a great mistake, Pete, to bother one's head about the parents of the girl you go to see. Now, I've been out in the world, and *I'm* experienced. Why, look here; suppose I hold a girl's hand on a moonlight night. Does that mean I must marry her? Well, I guess not! What do you think about it, Pete?"

"The same," said Peter, his horizon widening perceptibly.

"When you look at life from a man's viewpoint," added Atterton, "it gives you a man's wide freedom. What do you know about this Gladys Lucile except that she has a lovely face and a musical name?"

"The fact is," said Peter, "I don't particularly fancy her. She is as dumb as an oyster in company. And she can't play, or sing, or ride, or do anything to make her friends have a good time. She impresses me as a girl that expects other people to make her see the good time while it's her part just to look pretty. Her father and mother don't let her do any work; they seem to worship her. She reads a great deal, and if she does anything else, I don't know it." Peter's tone indicated marked disapprobation of the character he was portraying.

Atterton smoked a while in silence. Then he slowly smiled. "Well, Pete, the only way I can account for your apathy,—for when you admit her beauty, you admit as large a part in life as any woman need fill,— is to conclude that some other girl has captured your fancy. As to this negative attitude of Gladys Lucile, I do not object to it. I'm not looking for brains in a girl; I have plenty myself; what I want is beauty. Come, old man, you are too much of a fellow of the world not to have found some one who fills the bill with you as G. L. does with me, hey?"

Peter smiled consciously as he thought of Goldie.

"Ah, ha!" cried Atterton gleefully. "Ah, ha! Well, take me around to Senator Mulkey's to-night, and after that I'll try to swim alone. Do you know whether she dances or not? We must get up a—a——" It suddenly occurred to Atterton that a ball would be rather precipitate. "I think I'll stay over here all summer," he added hastily. "Of course, a—er—a hop is out of the question."

"I'll tell you what," said Peter suddenly. "Look here, At! You get Gladys Lucile in the choir, and we'll go down to the ice cream parlors after the practice, then stroll a bit before going home. That, perhaps, would be the best thing under the—the circumstances. A splendidly furnished resort has been opened up in town."

"Splendid resort, nothing!" cried Atterton, with decision. "We will go around to Oscar's wire-gauze joint, there's where *we'll* go. You don't think I'm going back on the family, do you? Not much! Well, it's a good idea, Pete, and I'm for the choir. Say! were you for tuning that old piano low or at concert pitch?"

"Low," said Peter, with emphasis.

"All right,—I'm for the same. I'll coach Gladys L. This is great. Man! there's a lot of rot talked about religion being no good, but I tell you, it tides a man over many a rough spot."

Peter had usually reached home before the other men of the family, who were delayed at their places of business by tardy customers. It began now, however, to be an ordinary thing for him to come in late at night, as a result of lending his companionship to Atterton.

"I want to cheer him up," Peter once explained, for, on general principles, he considered late hours reprehensible.

One evening, on coming home from the choir, his ears filled with the mellow voice of Goldie Pickens, and his eyes bright from gazing upon her timid face, he found the family assembled upon the porch steps. It was a balmy moonlight night, and old Timothy was adding the fragrance of his pipe to the less assertive perfume of bursting buds.

"We were just saying," remarked Mrs. Polly Thornberry, who sat in the hall-entrance, for protection from the dew, "that we ought to invite Waldo McCormack and Lizzie here to supper. They have moved back to Core City, and Waldo will expect it."

"Honey," said Timothy, "better call her Elizabeth, even here in private, for you know Waldo makes a point of it."

"There's another thing," said Peter. "If we have them here, grandma will be almost certain to say something about step-mothers, and that always hurts Cousin Waldo's feelings."

"I'm going to watch myself," declared the old lady, nodding her black lace cap with decision.

"And there mustn't anybody," spoke up Will, who was lolling on the lower steps with the luxurious air of seeming to spread out all over them and to fill every crevice in blissful repose, "talk about literature, or art, or science, for Cousin Waldo doesn't believe anybody else knows anything about 'em."

"Well," said Timothy, "I am pretty safe to leave *them* topics alone. And Oscar is no talker at best. We ought to have Mary Eden and Polly over. They would like to meet Elizabeth, and I reckon they can stomach Waldo if we can. We might make it a family getherin', and invite Winthrop——"

"No," said Mrs. Thornberry, "*they'd* feel too bad to come to a supper."

"I don't know about that, Polly," said Timothy argumentatively, "you know it ain't a-going to be no festive occasion where Waldo McCormack is. It would be 'most like another funeral. And I like Winthrop powerful; I don't feel like having it without him."

"Honey," said his wife, "you know Elizabeth would never get to be with her folks if she wasn't invited to their houses, for Waldo won't let her have us in his; it disturbs him in his writin' and musin' and meditatin'. So the supper would be for *her* sake. I don't know as Winthrop would want to come to a family supper so soon after his wife's death; but he oughtn't to, if he does, and I'm not goin' to tempt him. If Polly and Mary come, that Pickens girl will have to be invited, for you can't get shet of her,—that comes from takin' in a boarder; they're like a nightmare a-ridin' on the backs of the fambly."

"Miss Goldie," said Peter, taking offense, "will be a distinct gain. She can sing and play for Cousin Waldo and make him pass an agreeable evening. *There's* a young lady who makes herself useful wherever you put her. By all means we must have Miss Goldie."

"Peter is right, as usual," drawled Will. "As Cousin Waldo doesn't pretend to sing and play himself, he will let Miss Pickens detail him off to one side, and that will give Cousin Elizabeth a chance to talk to her kinfolks."

"What about Cousin Hodgins and Cousin Marietta?" inquired Oscar, rousing from his abstraction, and feeling that they might think it his time to say something.

"That would never do!" Mrs. Thornberry exclaimed. "Marietta is too plain a talker. She would be sure to say something worse than 'step-mothers.'"

Oscar did not defend his suggestion. He had spoken, thus showing that he regarded himself as belonging to the family conclave. His mind, at once, fell back to struggle with a Latin paradigm. Ethel's refusal had not deflected the young restaurateur from the paths of knowledge, any more than it had lessened his love. Ethel had told him she could never be his wife; she, no doubt, believed this; but Oscar didn't. It is true, he had no reason to doubt her sincerity, or to trust in his persuasive powers. Still, he hoped. It was a fearful thing, at times, to contemplate the mounts of knowledge which his feet had not climbed. There were days when he seemed to lose all that he had, by arduous toil, acquired; new ideas crowded old facts out of his mind, and old and new suddenly rolled away like a thundering avalanche, leaving his brain bare and dizzy. *He had not* yet determined what he would do with all this information. In answer to Will's inquiry, he merely said:

"I'll find a place to bring it in, somewheres."

A few days after the family conference over the supper, Oscar was alone in his cheap restaurant, and being alone, he was, of course, studying. It was too late for dinner, but not late enough for an evening lunch, and the young man was gleefully contemplating a prospect of uninterrupted mental toil, when three young people came up the sidewalk and stopped at the screen door. They were Atterton, his sister Ethel, and Gladys Lucile Mulkey.

"Not in there," Ethel objected; "it is so public,—it is like eating out on the street."

Atterton stared through the gauze-wall. "Oh, come on," he said. "Nobody's in there but Osk; I'm not going back on Osk. You don't mind, do you, Miss Mulkey?"

"Certainly not," said Gladys Lucile.

They entered. "Hallo, Osk," said Atterton heartily, "we want some ice-cream. Sit here, Miss Mulkey. Ethel, are you comfortable?"

Ethel did not look comfortable as she bowed distantly to her rejected suitor. Gladys Lucile was strikingly beautiful, but correspondingly dumb.

Atterton was bubbling over with satisfaction at having accidentally met his sister in the other lady's society. He had thus taken advantage of the situation. "What have you got, Osk?" he inquired, with zest.

"Anything," said Oscar cheerfully, his bosom thrilling with happiness at the nearness of Ethel. To his fancy, his rude structure had become a bower of bliss.

"Give me pineapple," said Atterton. "That will show that my heart is longing."

"Well," said Oscar, "I don't believe I have *that* flavor."

"Try your luck, Miss Mulkey," said Atterton gallantly.

Gladys Lucile suggested chocolate.

"I will look and see," returned Oscar heartily, "but I believe the chocolate is all out. I talked about ordering some more, but somehow I haven't got to it yet. Yes; it is all out, just as I thought. Cousin Ethel," his eyes brightened at this chance to address her, "what will you take?"

It wounded Ethel's pride for Oscar thus to stand behind the counter, and she answered quietly that she did not want anything.

"Oh, nonsense!" cried Atterton. "Bring on your ice cream sodas. Flavors are not the important part, the groundwork is the main thing. Put in your frozen stuff, and let 'er fizz!"

Ethel acquiesced. It was seldom that her brother paid her such attention. Atterton, charmed with the looks of Gladys Lucile, chattered incessantly. He was very happy, and Gladys Lucile herself appeared pretty well satisfied, though of this it was always difficult to make sure. But Oscar was the happiest soul present. His eye had already marked the tin spoon with which Ethel took her soda. That spoon would henceforth be laid aside, a sacred thing. It was so cheap that one could spare it from the general stock without inconvenience. Oscar breathed into the deepest extent of his lungs the faint individualized perfume that emanated from Ethel's handkerchief, as it lay upon the *counter.* Oh, if she should go away and forget to take that handkerchief! Oscar eyed it covetously. He saw it pressed daintily to the proud lips. His heart stood still.

While refreshments were being discussed, Oscar suddenly espied an old customer approaching, evidently with some idea in his brain of ordering "a chile." He was practically unclothed down to the waist line, and his ragged trousers and shapeless boots seemed fit complements to the uncombed hair. He was a section-hand who had left his digging, but not his dirt. Oscar slipped from the room and engaged him upon the corner.

"See here, Mr. Wullens," said Oscar, "I've got some high-toned folks in my stand taking ice cream."

"Oh, that's all right," said Mr. Wullens cheerfully, "I don't never let nothin' tek my appetite,—I never did."

"It's their appetite I'm thinking of," said Oscar frankly. "It's just like a party in there, and you're not fixed up properly to sit with 'em. You go on over to the other restaurant, and order whatever you want, and I'll foot the bill."

"Not much," said Wullens, now catching sight of the three through the gauze. "I'll jest sit around at your back do' till they come out. If the railroad company gets tired waitin' for me, let 'em go hire another worker, if they can find another willin' to work. I'll stand by your joint, Osk, you bet. Nothin' like tried friends."

Ethel, silently taking her soda, witnessed the encounter and smiled rather bitterly as Wullens, with a courtly bow, passed the wired front. What disreputable friends Oscar had! Strange that with such surroundings he *should* dream of winning the hand of

Winthrop Thornberry's daughter. Her cheeks burned red. When they departed, she was unusually distant in her bearing.

But she left Oscar inwardly singing. Life was brighter and sweeter for the little incident. Ethel had carried away her handkerchief; but she had left the spoon. Oscar pounced upon it.

Wullens poked in his head cautiously from the back door. "Gone?" he inquired, in a stage whisper. Then he entered and perched upon his favorite stool. Oscar brought the smoking chile and said gravely, "As owner and proprietor of this establishment, I will sit with you, Mr. Wullens; but being also the waiter and cook, don't hesitate to call upon me for anything you want." Oscar seated himself upon the inner side of the counter and furtively polished the tin spoon.

"You're a great reader, Osk," remarked Wullens, blinking as he took down his liquefied pepper, "I often see you at it. I ain't never learned yit to read or write. Men has been my books, and I've saw considerable of human nature. And I may say as I have turned out some creditable works of my own. You have saw my kids, hain't you, Osk? Well, suh, thar's four little volyumes which I am considerable proud of being the author."

"You're a lucky man, Mr. Wullens," said Oscar emphatically. "How can a man fret over troubles of the outside world when he has a faithful family? When I see a man or woman naturally sour and fault-picking, they just seem to be advertising that their home is unhappy. Why, Mr. Wullens, if I had a wife —Oh, Lord!" cried Oscar, rubbing hard at the cherished spoon.

There was a pause filled by gurgling sounds from

Wullens. Then he asked abruptly, "Mrs. Eden,—Mrs. Polly Eden,—She's the best woman that ever lived,—Whar do you s'pose she is now? At my shack. Yes, suh, thar she sits, readin' aloud to my wife. Look a-here, Osk. I'm forty year old. D' reckon I could learn to read, my time o' life?"

Oscar regarded him doubtfully. "Are your wife's eyes still failing?"

Wullens made no answer for a few moments, then he answered abruptly: "She has went blind, Osk. Now, look a-here; if I could read——"

"I'll teach you to read," cried Oscar, his face glowing.

"Will you, Osk? Retch your paw over here! She gets so lonely, you know. And at nights, when we set thar together, and not a mortal word to say that hain't been said time out o' mind,—would it take long to learn, Osk?"

"It ain't a quick proposition," Oscar responded.

"Well, I look at it this way," said Wullens hopefully; "my oldest kid is six. I'm going to crowd him mighty fast, but I 'low he can't git a-holt of it for a considerable spell. D' reckon I kin master the first principles before he comes on? I don't want all this proddin' for nothing."

"I am sure you can beat the boy to the goal," said Oscar. "I'll try you the first evening I can get off."

Thanks to this mission of kindness for the blind woman, Mrs. Polly Eden reached home that evening at a late hour. Hungry Uncle Groner was fretting in the front yard, with Goldie Pickens as a sympathetic listener. There had been many loaves of bread to bake for their regular customers, and Mary, upon whom all this work had fallen, was flushed and tired. But it was not physical toil only that caused her face to look worried and pale as her mother entered the kitchen; for several days she had been battling with unpleasant thoughts. The source of them was Peter Thornberry.

It was quite apparent that he was changed, but the girl failed to understand that this change arose rather from accentuation of his real nature than from alteration to another. She had shared the family belief that Peter would arise to lead the Thornberrys out of the wilderness. His unswerving adherence to ideals had won her childish admiration, and she failed to perceive that his ideals dealt with the forms and externals of society, and had no moral significance save as the world regards morality as proper. He had been her hero, the strong young man who did not hesitate to point out the errors of others, and who, sure of his own propriety, was rather dubious of the conduct of those he loved best. He had not hesitated to show Mary her faults and she had taken pride in his surveillance. But this yielding of a spirit, naturally free and independent, was based upon two assumptions; first, that Peter was practically infallible; and second, that his reproofs and corrections were dictated by affection as well as by justice.

Somehow, Peter appeared to have lost his keys recently. Mary thought it was his association with wild young Atterton Thornberry. She was not so sure, now, that all he did was right. His attitude toward her had plainly cooled to indifference; the cause was Goldie Pickens; but there had never been a word of love between the cousins, and Mary solemnly interrogated herself, to learn if it ever had really existed.

She was not sure, but she was too honest with herself to deny that love had been possible. The Thornberry connection had rather taken for granted that she would marry Peter, and to Mary herself it had seemed more than likely. So it had to Peter, till he met Goldie; but he was not bound by promise or implication. In a word, there was nobody to blame for the present situation, though Mary was hurt that Peter should have discussed her peculiarities with Goldie.

She thought she must speak of that to Peter. But why? Alas! was it true that she cared for him too tenderly to see him led away blindly by the siren of the organ? Mary mistrusted Goldie Pickens in a vague, mystified way; she was so utterly beyond her experience that, to Mary, she scarcely seemed human. Yet to admit to herself that she shrank from Goldie, seemed to hint of jealousy, and that brought the hot blush of shame to her cheek.

Mrs. Eden bustled into the kitchen, almost hoping supper would be ready, and yet knowing, in a dull sort of subconscious manner, that it could not be.

"Oh, Mary!" she exclaimed, "you do look so worn out! I couldn't leave Mrs. Wullens any sooner, the poor soul was just thirsting to be read to, and they are *so* poor, yet have to hire a nurse, since her sight has failed. And poor, dear Mrs. Wullens, she doesn't want to hear anything read but her church doctrine!" Mrs. Eden sank upon a chair and looked at the kitchen stove with a disinterested eye. "How piping hot it is in here!" she continued. "I think we will have to stop selling homemade bread till next winter."

"But we must sell the bread," Mary objected. "Our regular income won't do more than keep us; it would be like living in a prison."

"That's so," said Mrs. Eden thoughtfully. "I was wishing, as I came home, that we could raise a little fund to get one of Mrs. Wullens' own church members to read to her. Her nurse won't look at the religious papers, because they teach that everybody out of Mrs. Wullens' church is going to be lost, and they seem rather glad of it."

Mary laughed. "Well, mother, isn't it just as hard on you?"

Mrs. Eden laughed. "Poor Mrs. Wullens!" she said plaintively. "If they made her the gate-keeper, I'd never get inside! Well, what will we do about supper? Something has to be got, I suppose. I'm not hungry, though."

"Neither am I," said Mary hopefully; "perhaps nobody will want anything."

"*I'm* hungry," said Uncle Groner, stretching his neck around the door. "And so is Miss Goldie, *too*," he added, with marked significance.

"We're all just tired to death," said Mrs. Eden. "There's a fine bed of coals in the stove; let's get that beefsteak, and warm it over on the coals."

"Like a little picnic," said Mary cheerily,—"eating from our hands."

"Yes," chimed in Mrs. Eden, "as few dishes as possible."

Groner Thornberry, with a gloomy brow, went out to hatch conspiracies with the boarder.

When he hobbled back to the kitchen, the steak was on the coals and a most delicious smoke was tickling the lungs. Groner was moved to his inmost soul, that is to say, his stomach; but he hid his lust and looked on *gloomily*.

Arkinsaw Cousins 127

"Turn it over!" cried Mrs. Eden gaily. "You've already burnt it, child."

"I fear I have," said Mary, trying to dig a burning coal out of the hissing meat.

Groner announced: "Miss Goldie doesn't want any supper like this."

Mrs. Eden stepped to his side and, putting her mouth close to his ear, said with slow distinctness, "And—I—don't—care—whether—she—does—or—not!"

Will Thornberry entered the back door without the ceremony of knocking. "Land alive!" he cried, "what a smell! Hallo, everybody! What's the fun? Got a bite for me?"

"There's always a bite here for you, Will," cried Mrs. Eden; "at least, if there *is* a bite. Sit down at that kitchen-table and push those knives and forks out of the way."

"Oh, I'm not going to soil any dishes," Will protested. "Just give me a slice of bread with some of that steak on it. That's it; yes, thank'y, Mary, let the butter drip on the bread. Why, this is great! Come on, Uncle Groner!"

Uncle Groner gave a sour smile and said nothing. They stood about the floor, eating from their hands and going back and forth as they talked.

"I'm mighty sorry," said Will, "to pay for my lunch with a piece of bad news, but I guess I'll have to prove ungrateful."

"Anything happened?" asked Uncle Groner hopefully.

"Nope; but something is goin' to happen," said Will. "In a word, you are all invited to take supper with us Friday night to meet Cousin Waldo McCormack and *Cousin Elizabeth.*"

Mrs. Eden sank upon a chair. "I reckon you-all 'll *have* to do it," she said, "but I 'most know Aunt Polly will say something about step-mothers."

Will nibbled at his meat and shook his head in sorrowful anticipation. "Mary, could you come over Friday afternoon and help get up a cake, or something? Grandmother's afraid her doings won't exactly suit Cousin Waldo. And you know if he isn't suited, he'll turn to snubbing his wife. If we can possibly keep him jollied up, we hope Cousin Elizabeth will enjoy the evening with us kinfolks."

"Of course, I'll come," cried Mary. "Will, here's a little more steak than I want. If you don't mind eating after me——"

"Just hand her over!" cried Will promptly. "Say! this is fine. We didn't have anything to-night but bread and molasses at our house. But I must run back to the store now, so grandpa can go and get *his* bread and molasses. My! won't I crow over him, though!"

Mrs. Eden looked after Will and murmured, "Just like a ray of sunshine!"

Mary went to Timothy's house obediently on Friday afternoon. She was attired in her plain work-dress. It was her intention to go home after cake-baking to make herself suitable for the august gathering. Once installed in her Aunt Polly Thornberry's kitchen, she took possession and drove her aunt, without much coercion, to the room to rest up for Cousin Waldo McCormack. Being alone, there were too many things to watch at the same time, and too many burnings in her past experience, to admit of connected thought. The clock ticked on to four, and then to half-past. *The bank* was closed, but Mary did not think of that till the door suddenly opened; and there stood Peter.

He was more surprised than she; for, with a mind inherently above all petty details of commonplace life, he accepted his cakes and pies, not questioning whence they came. Being thus shocked out of the routine of his thought-grooves, it was as if he saw Mary with new eyes. He suddenly woke to a conviction that she was pretty. Perhaps it was the pink apron; perhaps it was the disordered hair; the flushed cheeks; the shy gladness in the dark orbs.

For Mary was glad.

In an instant, every cloud had vanished, and her old hero had made his appearance, the keys of infallibility once more in his grasp. There was, without doubt, an air of distinction and dignity about the young man, imparted by an assured bearing and a devotion to what he regarded as the correct. In an odd way, although his soul was far above the commonplaces of a kitchen, it seemed to him that Mary's form had never appeared so graceful or her face so winning as in these homely surroundings.

"*You* here!" he cried, advancing with a pleased bow. "This isn't fair, to make you labor that we may enjoy the result."

"Oh, I like it," said Mary happily. "It is like working behind the scenes, and you know I am invited to the show, also. I am getting ready the ropes, so there may be no hitch in the performance." She laughed out.

Peter, standing behind her, laid his hand upon her head. She stopped suddenly in her work, amazed. There came the wild thought that perhaps he was about to express remorse *for* something—she knew not what

—for his passing subjection, perhaps, to the charms of the music-teacher.

"Mary," said Peter, in a low, thrilling voice, "I never realized before how beautiful you are. Mary! you are so beautiful!" His arm had gone swiftly about her. He kissed her abruptly.

Mary tore herself from his embrace. She wheeled about and looked him in the eyes. Her face was scarlet. Her bosom rose and fell with quick irregularity. Peter stood bewildered, partly overawed by her long, solemn look; but, principally, because he realized that he had acted on a blind, fierce impulse,—an impulse common to the vulgar herd. It was not so much that he had offended Mary, as that he had offended himself. He was even displeased with her in an illogical, but natural way, because she had been the cause of his acting in a manner unworthy of Peter Thornberry.

There was a deathlike stillness in the kitchen, broken only by the sharp ticking of the clock.

Then Mary spoke in a low, tremulous voice which seemed not so much accusing, as humbled: "What have I ever done," she asked, "that you should insult me?"

"Mary!" he faltered. "I beg your pardon. I am so sorry. I——"

A low cry came from her pale lips,—the lips he might easily have won the right to press. She put her hands over her face, and fled from the room.

CHAPTER IX

"You must be sure to be at home on time," Mrs. Polly Thornberry warned her husband as he started to the grocery after dinner on the eventful Friday. "Remember it is to be at six o'clock, and if Cousin Waldo is kept waiting three minutes, he'll be in an ill temper all evening; not that it matters so much about him, if he didn't take it out on poor Elizabeth. And you mustn't let the cat into the dining-room while we are at the table; Cousin Waldo wouldn't know what to think of us, if Thomas Jefferson was allowed to eat at the side of your chair."

The old gentleman paused at the gate, knowing from long experience that there was more coming. Mrs. Thornberry raised her voice,—she stood on the screened-in porch at the rear: "And if Cousin Waldo undertakes to read us any of his compositions, Timothy,—now listen at me, Timothy,—don't you yawn and fidget as you did that time you mortally offended him. And I'll put the pearl-handle knife at your plate,—one at Cousin Waldo's and one at yours; and every time you take up yours, it'll remind you not to put it in your mouth, as Peter is always advising about. Cousin Waldo can't eat with any one who puts their knives in their mouths, Timothy."

"Honey," Timothy called back cheerfully, "just take all this burden off of your mind, for I'm going right downtown to deed the place to Cousin Waldo; see to it, that you don't mention step-mothers when he comes to take possession."

The old lady laughed and so did the captain; but they saw the hour of six approach with a gradually increased weight of solemnity. Timothy was at home betimes. The house was spick and span, and poor Mrs. Polly was in the last degree of exhaustion.

"He'll have a clean house to look at," gasped the hostess, picking up one more pin, "but I don't promise him any old woman at the head of the table. Timothy, I'm most dead."

"You couldn't be in a better state, to receive Cousin Waldo," remarked Timothy. "Ain't it a pity people have to get on a strain to receive their nearest kin? There's my half-brother,—I never get with Groner that I don't feel as I was drying up and getting ready to catch afire. I'll go sit out on the porch and wait for 'im. It's just six now, and they won't nobody be here for half an hour, I reckon. Where's Will's new hat?"

The article referred to was a new straw hat with perforated crown, which Will and his grandfather used in partnership on great occasions. Thus, Timothy wore it to church while Will carried his last year's "straw"; but Will had full possession at picnics and other occasions devoted primarily to youth, while at such times the grandfather hovered on the outskirts in his slouch-hat, already faded and brown.

"I guess Will has it on," said his wife, who had cast herself upon the couch in an ecstasy of delayed repose.

"Nope, honey, he told me expressly that he'd left it here, so I could do the honors to Waldo. But, good fathers alive! Polly, there comes the man down the *street at this* minute! He was invited for six, and he's *come* at six!" Timothy groaned as his wife bounded to her feet with considerable agility. "What on earth will we do with him? The others won't be here for half an hour. Waldo McCormack was always that way. Polly, don't you leave me alone with that man. I won't stand it."

"Where are Will and Peter?" asked Mrs. Thornberry wildly. "Timothy, you slip out the back way and hurry them home—and Oscar will have to shut up his restaurant. And drop by Polly Eden's and stir them up. And see that you get back here *yourself*," she added, with marked emphasis.

As Waldo McCormack knocked on the front door, Timothy fled from the rear.

Waldo McCormack was a tall, thin man whose unusually large head gave him a distinctly intellectual appearance. The brow was broad and white and smooth, the nose was straight and delicate, the hair, which grew in masses of irregular waving locks, was brown and silken, sweeping his collar; the face was clean-shaven, the eyes dark and somber. He was not unlike a portrait of Hawthorne at middle life, and the whiteness and slimness of his hands accented the predominance of spirit over matter. He was simply but elegantly dressed, in a suit of fresh black, against which a little gleam of gold here and there, by way of pin or chain, bespoke the fastidious gentleman. In appearance and appointment, he had ever been a credit to the Thornberry connection.

"And where is Cousin Elizabeth?" the old lady inquired timidly, her heart sinking.

Waldo McCormack waved his aristocratic hand. "She sends her regrets," he answered, in a musical, low voice, "but at the last moment she dropped a lighted match upon her dress and burned a hole in it, so she begs to be excused."

"Oh, Cousin Waldo!" cried Mrs. Polly, the tears coming to her eyes, "this is such a disappointment! Won't you let me run over and beg her to come dressed in just anything? Cousin Elizabeth always looks lovely to us."

"It would not be seemly," said Waldo. His voice was quite low and soft, but there was a line at the corner of his mouth which crossed out any possibility of his wife's coming.

In the meantime, Timothy had sped as fast as his veteran legs could carry him, to the grocery; and, having dispatched Will after Oscar and Peter, he himself posted off to Polly Eden's. Here he routed out Mrs. Eden and Groner and Miss Goldie Pickens, who, already attired, were waiting for time to put them in fashion.

"He actually came at six o'clock!" cried Mrs. Eden, in dismay. "Well, well, these geniuses are so eccentric—I'd lots rather read after 'em than live with 'em!"

"I understand," murmured Goldie, as she drew on her long lace gloves that almost reached the angelic elbows, "that Mr. McCormack has written a book that is published."

"Yes," said Timothy, "and a heap sight more that ain't been published. Where's Mary?"

Mary looked in from the adjoining front room. "You must excuse me, Uncle Tim," she said faintly, "I—indeed I would just be a burden to the company—my head aches dreadfully."

"Why, bless your heart, honey," cried Timothy *cheerily*, "that's all right. I'd have a headache, too, if

I didn't live in the house where the thing's to come off. You get you a good book and go to bed,—Polly'll understand."

"Mrs. Eden," said Goldie, "may I stay and minister to your daughter? Ought we to leave her here alone in the house?"

"Come along, all of you, and leave Mary to her novel," cried Timothy. "She just has the McCormacks; she'll get over 'em when Waldo has gone home."

In due time, Timothy rounded up all his guests, and none too soon, for Waldo and Mrs. Thornberry were growing weary of looking at each other in solemn waiting for rescue. Supper, of course, had not been commenced, but, as the hostess whispered to Mrs. Eden at the first opportunity, there were some important dishes already prepared which "would do cold."

Goldie found Waldo delightful. She learned him as she learned everybody, experimentally; that is, she broached various subjects as leaders in order to find those cherished principles or prejudices which make one man different from another. As all principles and prejudices were as one to Goldie, it was easy for her to enter into sympathy with all men. She soon found that Waldo McCormack had his own views upon a great number of diverse subjects which ranged, indeed, from the best authenticated dates, regarding the Pyramids, to the best way of regulating the speed of automobiles. Although his fund of general information was truly extensive, and the number of his personal convictions astonishing, all these were given coherence and unity by the underlying feeling that others need have no knowledge or convictions when he was present. He was made of the same stern stuff as the old Mohammedan; if people's views coincided with his own, they were superfluous, and if they differed, they were an affront. His manner said, "I am here to tell you what I think; you are here to listen. This is life."

Occasionally, some one ventured a remark in carefully generalized terms, but Waldo usually took it up and exposed it. To the astonishment of the entire family, poor Mrs. Polly Thornberry, in her effort to make herself pleasant to this literary connection, and at the same time keep off the subject of step-mothers, brought up Dickens and Thackeray and exploited their charms, even going into details regarding her younger years, when the world used to thrill at the announcement of a "Dombey and Son" or a "Pendennis."

Waldo McCormack, frozen with cold amazement that this old woman should venture upon the critical arena, and especially to take up arms for antiquated favorites, sat perfectly still.

The hostess, deceived into the gratified belief that she was contributing to the enjoyment of her niece's husband, elaborated: "Why is it," she asked, "that now-a-days we can't have stories such as were given us in the old days? Everybody is trying to write, it looks like, and yet the books that sell best are the ones we forget the quickest. People say folks want trash. Ain't the American public as smart as it was when we used to read 'Great Expectations,' and 'The Virginians,' and 'Middlemarch'?"

"Honey," interposed Timothy, "hadn't you better start that supper?" He read danger signals in the darting eye of Waldo.

"Go on, Aunt Polly!" cried Mrs. Polly Eden, who

d been listening with her bright eyes beaming ap-
oval.

"These authors of whom you speak," said Waldo,
iving his hand and thereby putting them far from
m, "did not portray life, but the vague shadows of
eir own imaginings. I have no sympathy with any
t the rigid realists."

"Oh, Mr. McCormack!" cried Goldie, "have you any
 your own writings with you? Do read us some-
ing—oh, do!"

Goldie had made a hit. Everybody was grateful
her, and inwardly applauded. The sternness melted
om Waldo's face. His hand went to his breast-
cket.

When supper was announced, the manuscript was
ll under way. Waldo, displeased with the inter-
ition, felt that eating ought not to intervene. "To
 the force of this little story," he said, "it should be
 n at one sitting."

ut it was no use. Not even for Waldo the Great,
 d a meal in the Thornberry mansion go begging,
 it had been made ready. The author sat at table
 r sulkily. The fire which had burned in his breast
 nd of his polished sentences, left him feeling cold
 rear. He looked up after awhile and said plain-
  "Do you not think it a terrible thing to have
  ies?"

 , I don't know," responded Timothy drily, "it
  s the mind."

   does not understand," said Goldie softly. "I
  hat great loneliness, that isolation from all
  y."

   pose," sighed Waldo, "it is the punishment of
   ritualized emotionalism. Ah, Miss Pickens,

we, who seek to reach the peaks of divine experience, must pay the penalty in groping for some understanding hand to clasp."

"William," said Timothy, "drive that cat away from the door, will you? Waldo," he added as Thomas Jefferson, taking advantage of the open door, rushed in, "you must excuse his eager cries. We had only bread and molasses for supper yesterday, and the smell of all these things has temporarily unbalanced the poor beast."

"*Timothy!*" said his wife reprovingly, rolling her eyes at this levity. Waldo stiffened as the hungry feline crouched at his feet.

"What a delightful cat," said Goldie. "He has evidently taken a fancy to you, Mr. McCormack. What is the old saying about a cat looking at the king?"

"Let us give the creature a morsel," said Waldo, suddenly in the sunniest of humors. "What do you feed him on, Aunt Polly? Has he a separate dish? I will give him something with my own hands. Why, look at him; he has taken quite a fancy to me."

"He'll get his hairs on you if you aren't careful," Will cautioned.

"I have seen cats before," was all Will received for his pains. Waldo, who had little appetite, fed the cat from time to time, looking down upon him with a benign smile; then at Goldie, to make sure that she enjoyed his condescension.

Timothy, finding himself freed from Waldo's surveillance, ate rapidly with small regard for the pearl-handle knife. Groner, who felt Waldo's usurpation of Goldie's company peculiarly irksome, proved himself *unusually* disputative, giving little comfort to any one who appealed to him for confirmation of the most obvious facts. Mrs. Eden, finding Waldo wholly occupied with Goldie and the cat, chatted merrily with Will and Oscar, and treated Peter to the grave respect better suited to his tastes. Suddenly Mrs. Polly Thornberry, now in fine spirits over the progress of the supper, launched forth in reminiscent strain until she realized, as a gleam of horror showed in the eyes bent upon her, that she was "on step-mothers."

It was a subject of which Waldo McCormack was peculiarly sensitive. Elizabeth Thornberry, on becoming his second wife, had learned of the existence of three children (the result of a former marriage), concerning whom she had, before the wedding ceremony, been ignorant. The high-spirited girl, with the true Thornberry hatred of concealment and sham, had expressed her mind in no uncertain terms, to such effect, indeed, that Waldo was mortally offended. She was never permitted to see her step-children, and when, in after years, with spirit quite subdued and heart dulled, she begged that they be brought home, it was not granted. They were kept in another state. Waldo visited them frequently, and sometimes spoke feelingly of the necessity of living apart from them. Thus it was he punished his wife. He felt he was in the right.

"My conscience tells me," he had been heard to say, "that I am absolutely right in this course." He knew the Thornberrys thought otherwise; that they regarded his conduct as the revenge of an unforgiving spirit. But what else could you expect of Thornberrys? It was enough for him to know that he was right. Whenever he heard a Thornberry speak of step-mothers, he instinctively felt that they were thinking of Elizabeth. On the present occasion, the guests sat staring at Mrs. Polly Thornberry with bated breath, her last words still ringing upon their ears,—"And I said to Matilda, 'The man who gives his children a stepmother without knowing well how she will regard the situation, deserves—he—I—ah——' " Mrs. Thornberry's voice trailed off into miserable confusion and then silence as she realized that all was lost.

It was an awful moment. Waldo, who had lifted a bit of chicken from his plate for the delight of Thomas Jefferson, poised the dainty morsel in air as he stared at the speaker. The cat reared upon his hind legs and cried for the meat; but Waldo did not hear him. To such a sensitive and self-conscious soul as his, those deadly words could mean nothing but an intentional insult. Why else should Aunt Polly speak of stepmothers? Why else drag such extraneous subject-matter in by the head and shoulders? Why else invite him here to supper save for this purpose? Aha! gladly would the thrust have been made in Elizabeth's presence! but, thanks to his firmness, she had been spared this shock.

Waldo rose from the table, and, in the heat of the moment, glared at the bit of chicken in his fingers, not knowing how it had come there. Then he looked at "Aunt Polly" as if he suspected her of having thrust it into his hand.

Mrs. Thornberry was dumb. Would it be best to pretend not to know that Waldo had taken her words to himself, or better to apologize openly, and thus point her words directly at him? She did not know what to do. Thomas Jefferson, seeing his coveted morsel dropped back into the plate, gave a loud wail and backed upon Timothy's feet.

"*You* get out of here!" exclaimed Timothy, giving

his favorite a light, but lifting kick, that sent the astonished Jefferson flying. "I might known something would happen. It always does when we get on a strain."

He rose. "Well, Polly," he said, "the meal's over, I reckon."

Waldo, with brow as dark as a thunder-cloud, marched toward the door.

Goldie was at a loss. It was, of course, not in the way of nature that Waldo could be a step-mother, yet plainly that relationship of law and compliment had offended him in its discussion. Before he could reach the door, it was thrown open from without, and the author retreated at the new affront. It was one of their old neighbors.

"Hallo, Timothy," said the newcomer, dispensing with all ceremony, "they's a crowd down to your grocery store, wanting to git in, and they live five mile in the country. They're out of flour and they say they must have it, and they won't go to no other grocery store."

"I'm a-comin'," said Timothy.

"Grandpa, let me go," Oscar cried.

"No, me," said Will. "It's my place to go. I've got a half-interest in that grocery store."

"I aim to go, myself," said old Timothy sternly.

While the men were discussing, not to say wrangling, as to who should leave, Goldie Pickens stepped up to the furious McCormack.

"Will you not let me sing for you?" she begged, plaintively.

"Thank you," said Waldo shortly, "but I don't understand music."

Goldie said to herself, "What a blessing!" She

murmured, "I have the dearest little song I would like to sing for you. I should like to be able to say, some day, when people are discussing your works,—'I have sung for him.'"

"Miss Pickens," said Waldo, hesitating, "I do not know one note from another."

As Timothy walked rapidly down the front path to the gate, he heard Goldie Pickens singing to Waldo McCormack. "Wonderful girl!" Timothy exclaimed, below his breath; "wonderful, indeed!"

Old Mrs. Thornberry retired to the dining-room after seeing Waldo to the parlor, with that casual air one sometimes assumes, as if going to see how the servants are getting along, while being, in fact, the servant of all.

Mrs. Eden, finding Waldo absorbed in Goldie's melancholy little ballad, slipped out to the dining-room and found her aunt slyly stacking up the plates. "Aunt Polly," Mrs. Eden whispered, "if you will do up something, I will slip over to Cousin Elizabeth with it, while Cousin Waldo is engaged. Is there any drinking-water in the kitchen? I am perishing for a drink."

"Merciful fathers!" ejaculated Mrs. Thornberry, holding her wrinkled hands above her lace cap, "I forgot to put it on the table, and bought ice expressly for it." She lowered her voice as Will crept out of the parlor. "Go back, son!" cried Mrs. Thornberry, in agitation, "all of you mustn't sneak out that way; and I'm disgraced anyhow. Cousin Waldo must be as dry as a bone."

Will answered, as he rumpled his hair in some embarrassment: "Say, grandma, what do you think of sending Mary something for supper? She helped get *it, and it's no* more than fair."

"Now, don't you think of such a thing!" exclaimed Mrs. Eden, immediately adding, "That's just like Will to remember Mary."

"Of course, I'll fix up something," said Mrs. Thornberry heartily. "Hold on, Will, where're you going?"

"I'm going after some water, my own self," said Will. "Want a drink, Cousin Polly?" They went to the kitchen together, giggling like school-children. When they returned it was agreed that Mrs. Eden should take a basket of lunch to Elizabeth McCormack, while Will should bear a similar burden to Mary. During the making-up of the lunches, Goldie's voice came to them soft and sad. "Poor Osk," murmured Will, "he's sitting up in there as stiff as a monolith. Cousin Waldo can't be very thirsty while he's drinking in all that soul."

Goldie sang:

> "' His love was dead,—he wished to die.
> He could not. Ah, he murmured, Why?
> No hope his broken heart can give;
> His weary lot it is to live.' "

The flute-like voice ceased, and they could hear Waldo McCormack's deep mellow voice in tremulous earnestness.

"I'm glad I can't catch his words," murmured Mrs. Eden. "Give me the basket, Aunt Polly."

She departed with a fierce protest in her heart against Goldie's song. Out in the balmy night, she repeated mockingly, " 'His love was dead,—he wished to die.' " And Waldo had spoken forth in feeling approbation of such a sentiment. "*My* love was dead," she thought as she trudged along the deserted street, swinging the basket a little too violently for the good of the chicken-gravy, but perhaps thus assisting the evolution of a new poem for her religious weekly. "My love was dead. So was Christ. But both have passed through death to life. That ought to make a stanza. Perhaps it may cheer some lonely heart. It would have cheered mine, had some one written it for me years ago. Oh, you lonely, lonely girl!" she whispered, looking back at the picture of her young widowhood with Mary, an infant, in her girlish arms. "If my older self could have been sitting there, telling you how blessed the years would be, when you grew to understand! Poor thing! you, too, wished you could die, and asked why you could not. And now, just see what you have gained by living," she continued argumentatively. "There is Mary, raised to be the best girl in the world. And there are the lives you have brightened,—you, Polly, who thought your own heart broken! God doesn't need us in heaven. He can brush away all tears up there,—Dear me! if I haven't gone right by Elizabeth's yard!"

Mrs. Eden retraced her steps and knocked at the door. It was presently opened by a pale, timid woman, whose unnaturally large eyes showed startled surprise. Elizabeth McCormack had evidently been weeping, and, just as evidently, had sought to disguise her tears. She was of Mrs. Eden's age, forty, and these two had been inseparable in girlhood. Their love for each other had not flagged through the tiresomeness of years. They looked alike, too, though Mrs. McCormack was thin and her cousin stout; but this thinness was the result of suffering and unhappiness.

The footstep on the porch had startled Mrs. McCormack with the fear that her husband had returned. *His coming* home was never a gladsome event, but at this hour his appearance could mean only that he had been offended, and if he became offended at the Thornberrys, of course, she would be forbidden to associate with them. The great hollow eyes suddenly made out the hard, sunburned, line-marked face of Mrs. Eden.

"Polly!" she cried out, flinging her arms about the other, basket and all. "Oh, you darling!" She squeezed the other to her breast and tried to keep back a sob.

"Why, Lizzie!" cried Mrs. Eden heartily, "what's the matter? Let's shut the door. Here's a bite from Aunt Polly. You wouldn't come to the supper, so the supper had to come to you. I'm not used to being made over this way." So saying, she gently disengaged herself, and leading the way to the dining-room, drew back the tablecloth.

"I know you see I have been crying," said Mrs. McCormack, following. "It was such a disappointment not to get to be with you-all—that, when Mr. McCormack left, I closed up the house and just sat down to have a good cry, all by myself. I didn't dream any one would come; no one hardly ever does, you know; it disturbs Mr. McCormack to have people here."

"But why didn't you come, Lizzie? It spoilt everything. Try that chicken salad. Elizabeth, do you remember that old red and yellow rooster Uncle Tim had before you moved away the last time? 'Boss,' we called him—he could catch grains of corn when you threw them in the air. This is he. Old Boss. Try it."

Mrs. McCormack laughed out, and Mrs. Eden said, "La, Liz! that sounded just like a recess-laugh at the old college."

"Oh, Polly!" exclaimed the other, "it takes *so* little to make a person happy!" She ate, almost choking on old Boss, but not on account of his age. Presently she made explanation: "I was lighting a lamp to look in the closet for my pink ribbon—I was all ready except that, and remembered how Uncle Tim likes me in pink—and Mr. McCormack said in his nervous way,—you know,—'Now be careful!' so I dropped the match on my new dress; my only really decent dress, Polly."

"And did it burn badly?"

"Oh, no, the place doesn't hardly show, but you know how particular Mr. McCormack is; he is *so* particular. I think he was displeased because I was startled at his voice. You know I have never pleased Mr. McCormack, because I was never careful enough. He always says I'm a perfect Thornberry, and I believe I am."

"Well," said Mrs. Eden, with a little warmth, "didn't God make the Thornberrys, too?" However, she brought herself up short, reflecting that she was not answering Waldo. "Honey," she said, "I'm sorry all that gravy is in Mary's new cake. I got to making poetry, and swung the basket to keep the meter."

"Oh, that doesn't matter, Polly, you can scrape chicken gravy off of cake. I've done that several times, and even Mr. McCormack wouldn't suspect it. What was the poetry?"

"It isn't in rhyme, yet, but substance," responded the other, pushing one dish after another upon Elizabeth, as the latter forgot to eat. "I'll put it in rhyme as soon as I can get to it. It's based on the idea that when some great blow falls upon the heart and seems that it won't ever feel any more,—it's sort of paralyzed, *you know*——"

"Yes," said Elizabeth, "I know."

"And," Mrs. Eden went on slowly, "you see the sunshine so beautiful, and feel hard at God for letting it shine,—and you hear children's happy voices and wonder, dully, how the world can laugh——" Mrs. Eden stopped abruptly.

Elizabeth laid down her fork and, rising abruptly, went to her cousin, sat down on her lap, and put both of her thin arms about the stout neck. Mrs. Eden, with tears streaming down her face, looked steadily upward as if seeing a vision. She went on, clasping the sobbing form tightly: "And then you think of Jesus, who, although He saw just ahead of Him the fearful agony and shame of the cross, could weep with Mary because Lazarus was dead. . . ."

"Oh, write it," sobbed Elizabeth, "write it for your poor weak cousin!"

"Then who am I, to give up?" cried Mrs. Eden, with enthusiasm. "What grief of mine can compare with His? Be brave, poor heart, be brave. There is work —No,—Life has its work, to cheer you now, and there's rest beyond the grave."

While Elizabeth McCormack was thus intimately dwelling beside the workshop where poetry was being evolved, Will Thornberry was carrying his basket of food to Mrs. Eden's home. Mary was, of course, in the house, and the young man made nothing of the deathlike silence that followed his repeated knockings at the door. Finally, he went around to the side door, the key of which, to his knowledge, was lost. It was hardly ever bolted within, except just after a rumor of gypsies in the vicinity, for the bolt had grown old and clung tenaciously to its groove. Will found the door unfastened. He marched into the front room.

"I'm in here, Mary," he called, "so you might just as well come downstairs."

Mary appeared, but her countenance was not encouraging. "Oh, is it you, Will?" she said coldly. Then perceiving the basket,—"It was kind of you to think of me; but I feel so badly I can't take a bite." Then her natural kindness asserted itself. "Perhaps I can eat a little. Just leave it on the table. Thank you, Will. I am sorry I let you knock so long; I didn't know who it was, and wouldn't look for fear I'd feel that I ought to come down."

Will found some newspapers, and having spread them upon the table, took out the dishes one by one. Mary stood at the foot of the stairs, which were boxed up and came down into the middle of the room. One step projected beyond the stair door, suggesting that there had been so many, one had run over. Mary stood with one foot upon this step, looking disconsolately at Will. She ardently wished he would go back. Indeed, she faintly suggested that Cousin Waldo might be displeased at his absence.

"Your own mother has sneaked off," said Will. "I reckon I'll hide behind her example. Here's ham. Chicken. Sweet potatoes. Come on, Mary,—butterbeans. Gravy. Salad,—remember old Boss? Hot biscuits wrapped up in a clean rag,—grandma said you needn't send it home. Sweet peach pickles. Cake,—*you* made that, Mary."

A hot blush of mortification swept over Mary's cheeks and brow. She still clung to the stair door as if with half a mind to dart away. Will tried not to look at her, but occasionally he couldn't help it. She made, he thought, a most bewitching picture;—the slender *foot upon* the stair, the hand, little, but it must be admitted, not very soft, clinging to the knob; the dark hair and eloquent face seen against the dove-colored woodwork of the stair-walls; and the large dark eyes looking at him with deep thoughts he would have liked to fathom.

Ever since her parting from Peter, Mary's emotions had been well-nigh intolerable. She felt that her fresh maidenhood had received a wound which would ever scar her consciousness. She did not feel herself the same free, honest spirit since that hateful moment in her aunt's kitchen. The very thought of Peter roused her soul to hot rebellion. Never before had she shrunk from the kind, handsome face of Will, but now she shrank from him, too. Will's slow announcement of each dainty was like listening to a catalogue of horrors. Had Peter told Will? and was that why Will no longer met her eye?

"Very well," said Mary, with an effort at self-command. "Thank you. Maybe, after awhile, I can taste something. I think you had better go back, now." Then with a sudden fierce resolution to know the truth, she said sharply, "Will, why don't you look at me?"

Will, with a start of surprise, and only too glad to be invited, lifted his rumpled head and said, "Kisses; very pleasant no doubt to contemplate; but really, Mary, there is no heart in them."

The foot vanished from the stair and Mary went toward Will, her face red with righteous anger. Will had never before seen her in an ill-humor. "How dare you say that to me?" she cried, bringing her eyes close to his. "How dare you?"

"Why, good gracious, Mary!" exclaimed Will, retreating a step. "How did I know you'd take it that way?"

His words gave her fresh offense. "And how did you think I *would* take it?" she exclaimed, her voice quivering between tears and passion.

"Look here, Mary," said Will, still bewildered, "if you think *I* wanted to kiss you, you are mightily mistaken. Why, it never entered my head. I was talking about these here muffy-looking candy-kisses that Oscar sent over from his restaurant. Did you think *I* wanted to kiss you? All I meant was that you could poke your finger through 'em; they're just like round chunks of air surrounded by sugar. Look,—I'll show you." In his eagerness to demonstrate his innocence, Will seized one of the kisses and thrust his finger through it in triumph.

At first, Mary stared at him dazed. Then she began to laugh hysterically. She sank into a chair, still laughing, but the laughter soon changed to sobs. He was rooted to the spot.

"Oh, Will," sobbed Mary, "don't mind me,—I am not well,—I don't understand myself, either. Forgive me," she went on, "you are so honest, and true, and matter-of-fact, and I am such a wretch,—there isn't any use of—of—anything."

Will was in despair at sight of her mysterious grief. He went over to her chair. "Don't, Mary," he said anxiously, "don't talk that way." He laid his hand upon her head.

Mary remembered how Peter had done the same thing. She shuddered violently, but somehow, it seemed different for Will to touch her.

"I've made an awful mess of it, and I wasn't even thinking of getting off a joke. I was not thinking about anything. Get cheerful, Mary; it isn't right to *give in, this* way. You mixed me up so that I said '*these here*' after promising you never to make that mistake again."

Will's homely comfort was like balm to the wounded heart. "He doesn't know," she reflected. "After all, Peter has told no one." The sobs ceased.

"That's it," said Will, patting her head, then withdrawing his hand. "You're better now. If I was a girl, I reckon I'd understand."

"Poor Will! how I cried out at you."

"Oh, I'm all right, if you are," said Will genially. "Suppose you try one of these sweet peach pickles. They are simply lost in the haze beyond the limit. Where's your spoons?"

"Spoons?" Mary repeated, still half-bewildered. "Why, I don't know. I needn't have a spoon. Hand me one of them, Will; that's an honest hand."

"It's honest," said Will, "but some of the gravy has got splattered on it."

"And I don't care if it has!" cried Mary, rubbing her weary face with her handkerchief; "I want that peach out of your hand. My! isn't it large! Isn't there a smaller one? I want just a bare taste."

"I'll bite off half of it," Will suggested. He held it up by the sugared stem. "Or, maybe you'd druther, —*rather*—bite first."

"No indeed, I want what you leave."

"Well, it's immaterial to me," smiled Will, and he took off half the peach with his strong white teeth.

"Dear fellow!" thought Mary when he had departed, "how simple-minded, how perfectly simple-minded! so trustful and innocent and honest, and—and—simple-minded."

Will also had his reflections as he slowly trudged back to help entertain the difficult McCormack; and being alone and without restraint of any kind, his reflections showed a disdain of grammatical forms. They ran thus: "It must of been Peter; yap, it was shorely Pete!"

The family broke up some two hours later. Groner Thornberry had stifled his almost intolerable sense of grievance over the blandishments bestowed by Goldie upon Waldo McCormack; but, as they walked back home, his emotions burst their bounds. Pretending to be forced to a slower gait than his lameness really required, he presently placed himself and Goldie out of the reach of Mrs. Eden's ears.

"Look here, Cousin Goldie," he said fiercely, "I consider this a lost evening. You have neither spoken to me, nor looked at me, and I consider this a—a—lost evening."

"I'm so sorry," murmured the other. "But I felt that I owed my attention to the guest of honor; and I can speak to you, and see you, every day."

"Yes, that's the trouble with me," snapped the other. "Everybody thinks that I don't crave attention, just because I'm always so patient and good-natured when I'm snubbed. Look here, Cousin Goldie," he continued, his tones seeking their most dovelike accent, "you know what I think of you. You know I love you. I'm not a man to mince matters. I love you, I say. And you have led me to think that I'm not disagreeable to you. Goldie, tell me this night how you feel toward me, and if I'm to be the happiest man on earth."

For a few moments Goldie looked down, while her hat shut out the moonlight from her face. Groner made his crutches resound, as they smote the loose planks of the sidewalk with unusual violence. At last, *the music*-teacher spoke with the utmost gentleness.

"Cousin Groner, it is sweet to be loved, and you can not know how it pleases me to find that I have won your affection. *You* disagreeable to me? You know you are anything but that! Indeed, I do love you sincerely; I feel almost as if you were my own father. Do you not feel that way?"

Groner choked in amazed wrath at the turn she had given his declaration, and coughed so loudly, and so long, that Mrs. Eden, far up the street, stopped in some uneasiness.

As he paused, purple for want of breath, Goldie murmured with tender distress: "Oh, that cruel cough! I wish there were some way to stop it."

Groner strangled and cleared his throat with such violence that he could have been heard a block away. "No," he gasped, when able to control his vocal organs, "no, I do *not* feel like your father!"

Mrs. Eden waited for them to come up, then said, "Uncle Groner, that cough gets worse and worse."

"I think," murmured Goldie, "that a cooler climate would do him good. There's nothing like a change of air for it."

CHAPTER X

AT Core City, two daily events assumed the importance of social functions; the coming in of the afternoon train, and the opening up of the night mail. If shops were found closed, or offices deserted, it was sufficient excuse to offer subsequently, "I went down to the depot." It was at the "depot" that Atterton Thornberry now waited in his new buggy; and it was to the "depot" that Peter Thornberry came for diversion. Atterton was there to meet his father, who had been several days from home; Peter had come to escape certain unpleasant reflections caused by the brief scene with Mary. He was still offended with himself because, in a sudden impulse, he had kissed the charming girl in the pink apron. A kiss was, he reflected, a very little thing; and Mary was his cousin; and besides, such salutations are more frequent than people would have you believe. It is true that, in novels, they usually come at the close of the story; not so in life. But Peter had always taken himself most seriously, and he felt that he had not acted up to his part as a proper person.

Moreover, there was Goldie Pickens to consider. What would she think of such a transgression? Pure, simple, virgin-souled little Goldie, how her eyes would open at the hint of such an act! She could never again trustingly slip her fluttering hand under his arm, if she knew herself in danger of being kissed. Peter in- *wardly* groaned. It was when the memory of Goldie

Arkinsaw Cousins 155

Pickens almost overwhelmed him with its sea of sweetened thrills, that his act seemed most reprehensible. He could hardly hope that Goldie might one day learn to care for him, because she seemed so far above the vulgar emotions that form, for most of us, our customary atmosphere. Still, Peter could hope it, because his opinion of himself was exalted. His mind was not definitely made up to win the hand of the music-teacher, but he had begun to consider it very likely.

"If I keep on like I feel now," thus the Thornberry who was "in a bank" compromised with himself, "I guess it will come." Deeply as Peter was infatuated by the subtle, not to say subtile, charms of Goldie, he wanted to be perfectly sure of himself. Had he not more than once almost spoken the fateful word to Mary Eden? and now see how he and Mary stood!

Atterton hailed Peter and invited him to share his seat in the buggy. The hack was drawn up beside the platform, and so was the dray. Various buggies stood near, and upon the shady side of the walk lounged some of Core City's leading citizens. It was not that disreputable, shoving, guffawing mob that one often sees hanging about small stations. The men were orderly, with kindly feelings toward everything on earth except the opposition political party, and a new railroad that some "upstart concern" threatened to bring to Core City. The very poor and the prosperous were there on a footing of equality, and Atterton, from his buggy, joked one and all in his bright, winning way, utterly regardless of the fact that his father was the richest man in the county. The young man who drove up a delivery wagon, to lift out some squawking hens by their legs, and the station-master who received them, regarded each other as brothers. Some of the loafers, descendants of illustrious families, had been prevented in the terrible days following the war from obtaining an education; but they held themselves as untutored princes; and no occupation could lessen their self-respect, or their holding in the community. It mattered not to Core City how certain occupations were regarded by society at large; here, man made the position, not position the man.

Peter admired Atterton to such an extent that he could enjoy, in a heavy way, the badinage that brought loud laughter from the platform, though badinage was not in his own line. After awhile Atterton turned to him; and in a low voice explained a scheme he had on foot, to the end that life might not stagnate. There were references to "some strolling musicians," and "the hall," and "making out a list," which to the initiated could signify nothing save a projected "hop." Peter approved.

The train whistled. "There she comes!" some one cried, and the figures on the platform were thrown into violent agitation. As the engine came abreast, the crowd shouted, "Hi, there, Jake!" and Jake, the engineer, one of life's faithful soldiers, and the son of a colonel in the late war, gave a military salute as he glided past. The train stopped and the conductor cleared a path for his passengers, by good-humoredly pushing his old friends to right and left, getting several hearty back-handers in exchange.

Two or three more intimate comrades crowded up to the officer with "Say, Dick, how's your wife?" and "Dick, is the little woman any better, to-day?"

The conductor shook his head as he gripped sympathetic hands. "She stays mighty porely, boys," he said. Somehow, his heart was a little lighter as he bustled about his duties.

Winthrop Thornberry descended from the car, burly and perspiring. His sunbrowned face was graver than had been its wont before his wife's death, and the iron-gray mustache suggested that the lips seldom smiled. This impression, however, was deceptive; it was only when quite alone that the orchardman was wholly depressed. A playful disposition was too much a part of him to be laid aside when old faces greeted him.

Although he was, on this afternoon, peculiarly disturbed, the sight of the section-hand, Wullens, awakened his boyish spirit. Wullens, standing with his back to the track as became an old section-hand who could see a train any day, was leisurely scraping the yellow mud off his boot with a huge, horn-handled claspknife. Winthrop tiptoed across the platform and, bending over the edge, suddenly grasped Wullens by the ear. The section-hand felt that momentary sense of hot irritation which usually goes with the grasping of one's ear, but wiggling round, and seeing Winthrop, he grinned, and his captor laughed.

"Well, Harvey, old man," said Winthrop Thornberry, "I couldn't help thinking of you as you stood that day with a knife just like that at school—you remember, I know; the day I licked you. Oh, come, don't tell me you've forgot. That was your first and last day at school, eh, Harve? No school for Harve Wullens. How old was you when you ran off to the war, anyhow? fourteen? Twelve? Oh, say! it wasn't *twelve!*"

"That was my first day at school, Winthrop," said Wullens, rubbing his grimy hand over his outstanding black hair, and then giving his trousers a much-needed hitch, "but it hain't my last, no suh. I taken it up agin. Oscar is comin' this very night to indoctrinate me in the alphybet."

This was news to Winthrop, but he understood everything in a flash. "Doc said there wasn't any chance, didn't he, Harve?"

Wullens swallowed and answered, "She won't never see again,—Mandy won't."

Winthrop said, "Well, you've got her with you, old man, that's a comfort." He turned away suddenly and went to his buggy.

Winthrop was unusually silent as Atterton drove him toward their country home. When he spoke, it was to condemn some of the orchards along which they were passing. "I don't know why folks will let their trees just come up of themselves," Winthrop declared. "There's some money in it, but not much. You can't have perfect apples off of imperfect trees. That's mighty true, Atterton."

Atterton, not interested in trees, said, "Yes, sir."

They drove on. "See how they lean every way," said Winthrop, pointing. "Look at that undergrowth. And the rough bark left on the trunks. And no spraying done. And yet these fellows will grumble because my apples bring a higher price than theirs."

No response. Suddenly Winthrop said: "Son, I'm going to be frank with you. That's the only way I know. You think I've been to Fort Smith on business. Well, so I have. But my main business was at Hot Springs." Atterton started. "Yes, I went down there. Atterton, I know how you've been living. It wasn't treating me right, but I don't mind that so much. *It was not treating your mother right.*"

Atterton flushed. "I didn't know how sick mother was."

"Of course, you didn't, boy. But suppose she hadn't been sick. It was a discredit to her. Son, you have been *wicked!*"

"Now, father," Atterton expostulated, "that isn't the way to look at it."

Winthrop interrupted with exceeding gravity. "I'm not speaking of your debts, enormous as they were. I have plenty, as you know only too well. Every cent is paid off. But that is little. It is concerning the things that those debts stand for, that my heart is heavy, —very heavy, Atterton. In fact, son, I didn't suppose so soon after your mother's death that anything could make me feel sorrow as keenly as I do this day."

"Now, father," said Atterton gently, "I am awfully sorry I've hurt you, just awfully sorry. I hoped I could tide over without your knowing anything about it. So those rascals couldn't wait, couldn't they? They wrote to you, did they? Villains!"

"But, son, suppose I had never heard of it; that would not affect your guilt."

"Father," said Atterton kindly, "you and I regard life from a different point of view. You are a country man; I am a city man. I don't mean to offend you, indeed, I do not, father; but really, you understand trees just as I understand men. Being a man of the world merely means enjoying a larger liberty than a little place like Core City could understand. In fact, I have *lived*. Down here, where you are all simple in your tastes and provincial in your prejudices—I do not say this as a reproach, but as an explanation,—the glare of the city blinds and its noises deafen you. It is, father, just as if you-all were stranded off on the edge of some little pool that has been formed among the cat-tails and cresses at the margin of a rushing stream."

"Atterton," said Winthrop patiently, "you led me to think you were in business in Hot Springs. You deceived me. If deception is the prerogative of a man of the world, you had better leave the rushing stream you speak of, and come take up your post with us frogs among the cat-tails and cresses. For I fear, son, you'll get drowned out in that current. You tell me *you* have lived. Of course, *I* have not; I've just grown up and matured like a tree. Did you ever reflect that everything God plants gets closer to the sky, the more it grows?"

"I never was religious, father."

"I judge not," said Winthrop drily. "Now, Atterton, we must bring this to the issue. As regards the past, I am willing to blot it out. But I must know definitely if it is still your purpose to spend your time with wild people. I'll set you up in any business you fancy; I'll deed you a splendid orchard, if you will agree to stay with it. I'll do anything for your good and happiness, son, anything. But I will do nothing,—mark me, Atterton,—nothing for your hurt and unhappiness."

"Why, of course, I understand that, father," said Atterton affectionately. "I know you'd do anything on earth for me, and I'd do anything on earth for you——"

"Then give up that sort of life," said Winthrop quickly.

"——Except how I shall live," said his son. "A man must choose his own way of living. To stay on an orchard farm would kill me. As to some business in a large city, I think well of it, and perhaps will take it up with you at a future time. As to my spending my time with what you call wild people. I can't govern myself according to old-fashioned ideas of the world. A man must be a man, his *own* man, and not somebody else's. I must always say, 'Does this seem right to *me?* Can a gentleman perform such and such an act, in his perfect freedom, in his large liberty?'—and then, if so, go and do it."

"As you have acted in the past?"

"Perhaps I overdid it occasionally," Atterton confessed, "but the principle is the same. A man has the right to do anything that is honorable,—that is, that doesn't interfere with other people's rights. Now, to tell me that I am not to sip a glass of wine or hard cider——"

"This is not a question of hard cider," his father interrupted.

"Ah!" cried Atterton triumphantly, "but where are you to draw the line? When you say 'Must not,' you have to draw a line. If hard cider, why not beer? Why! you will have to quit eating grapes. You like to play chess. Well; couldn't you gamble over chess? You will have to fold your hands and do nothing. Let us take up the subject of dancing and dispose of it at this point. If we can't dance, can we skip jauntily? and if not skip, why run? why walk? Indeed, father, all this,—now you must understand that I mean no disrespect and no offense—all this seems just silly to a man of the world. But I don't blame you for looking at such trivial matters as if they were important. You are a part of your environment. Core City, a hundred years behind the day, thinks thus and thus, and you naturally fall into line. That brings me back to my original point; when you begin to forbid some things, and to allow others, how are you going to draw the line?"

For several minutes, Winthrop was silent. At last, he spoke in a tone of quiet conviction, "Well, I'm going to draw the line; and if you watch me, you'll see how."

When the house was reached, they found Ethel waiting at the door. During the lifetime of her mother, the daughter had never been demonstrative toward her father, partly because demonstrativeness was not a characteristic of her nature; but primarily, because the late Mrs. Thornberry had been of an exceeding jealous temperament. It would hardly be just to say that Winthrop had bestowed marks of his affection upon Ethel in sly secrecy, or that there had been absolute premeditation in his swift meetings with her in the hall or on the stair; but he knew that his wife could brook no woman's approach to his loved presence, even though that woman were his own daughter; and Ethel knew this even better than he, since she did not depend upon her intellect to find it out. Neither had rebelled under this tyranny of love; a husband like Winthrop is seldom disposed to complain of a fond woman's monopoly, and a daughter like Ethel is inclined to take one's mother as a matter of course.

Mrs. Thornberry had been known as one of those women who seldom leave home, and who, when they do break this sedentary rule, make it extremely uncomfortable for other people. It is impossible for a man to thread his way through life without being thrown more or less in the society of women; some pretty, some designing, some magnetic; Mrs. Thornberry recognized this necessity, and preferred to stay on the farm where she might hold all women at bay. The old myth of a "woman-hater" was, doubtless, based upon the prejudices, not of a surly bachelor, but of a woman who looked with a cold eye upon her kind.

On the present occasion, Winthrop took his daughter in his arms heartily, and kissed her several times with not a particle of disloyalty toward his late wife, in his sense of larger freedom. Atterton regarded his sister with an approving eye as all three went into the library. Winthrop opened the letters awaiting him, which for the most part related to spraying, dry-rot, bitter-rot, bugs, and other topics dear to his heart. There was one, however, which breathed a perfume not such as ordinarily clings to the garments of your true orchard-man. Winthrop read it with a pursing of his lips, and tugging occasionally at his iron-gray mustache, like a drowning man catching at a straw.

Ethel sat at the window, her long supple form clad in a black gown, which set off her yellow hair and reserved face to peculiar advantage. She was wondering if her father could be prevented from hearing about Atterton's gay life at Hot Springs. Atterton, moving restlessly here and there, picking up one book after another, but considering none, was recalling his late conversation with his father.

"Ethel," said her father abruptly, "if you had begun to take music-lessons the day she came to Core City, and had taken twice a week, at fifty cents a lesson, how much money would you have paid Miss Pickens? Get a pencil and paper, and figure it out, will you? Don't let's delay this matter. This is important. This is vital. Let me get my check-book."

"Why, father, what do you mean? I took no lessons of Miss Pickens."

"We are not to consider what you did," said Winthrop severely, "but what you might have done." Then he laughed. He handed her Goldie's letter. "After all," he said, "she is poor, and needs it; and I'm well-off, and used to being imposed on."

"I wouldn't pay it," said Ethel. "Such impudence shouldn't be encouraged."

"If I don't pay it, there will be trouble. This lady looks like a perfect saint, and, no doubt, thinks she is one; and, when it comes to having trouble with saints, I'd rather offend the very—er—the *hum!*" Winthrop cleared his throat.

"Go on, father," smiled Ethel, "doesn't it begin with a 'D'?"

"That's where you find it in the dictionary," said Winthrop, laughing. He turned easily to his son, as if there were no differences between them. "What do you think of Pickens, Atterton?"

"Peter is head over ears in love with her," said Atterton, glad to be brought into conversation. "He thinks, as you say, that she is a perfect saint. Why, father! Cousin Groner sits and listens to her play, and although he fell out with his own brother, to say nothing of the Lord, over having an organ in the church, he goes to hear *Pickens* play at meeting. And you know how unsatisfactory Waldo McCormack is; well, Pickens has *got him*. I believe he actually thinks she could write a book. And the choir swears by her—even a few of those who wanted the old piano tuned at concert pitch have come back to the church."

"Figure up that bill, Ethel," said Winthrop. "I'm not going to butt out my brains aginst a rock of per-*fection.*"

"As for me," said Atterton, "I don't fancy her, somehow or other; she doesn't seem human enough. I have my faults; I'm not perfect, and never claimed to be; but I'm human."

"I think myself," said his father drily, "that you are inclined that way."

The next morning, Atterton drove to town behind his favorite mare, and drew up the swift, high-stepping animal at Hodgins Thornberry's gate. With the elastic rapidity that characterized his movements, he threw out the iron weight, leaped to the ground, tethered the horse, jumped over the fence in preference to opening the gate, and rushed around to the back door, in the neighborhood of which Mrs. Hodgins Thornberry passed the greater part of her life.

The stout, energetic lady was making soap, and looked up from the stirring of a huge iron kettle to peer at Atterton through its steam.

"Howd'y, Cousin Marietta!" cried the young man with great heartiness, "where's Cousin Hodge? I have a note for him to take. He always says when I have one to send, to call on him so he can make the dime."

"He's not at home," replied his cousin, "but I'll take the note, for we certainly need every dime on this place we can get."

"All right, Cousin Marietta, and if you take it I'll give you a quarter. Why, hallo there, kidchen!" he added, pouncing upon the younger offspring and lifting the delighted boy to his shoulder. "Is the other kid at school? Of course! How's he getting along? Here, man, see how you like this chocolate-drop."

"A dime is all I'll take," said Mrs. Thornberry; "anybody'd take it for that, and this is a business deal,

Atterton, a business deal. But I can't go now, and leave the soap. Can you wait an hour or so?"

"No, Cousin Marietta, I want an answer right away. Say! I'll sit on the wheelbarrow and stir the stuff, if it gets to boiling over. Isn't that the main stunt in soap-making? Never made any, but I've smelled it a-making. You'll stay with me, won't you, kidchen?"

"You know he will," said Mrs. Thornberry, smiling in great admiration as the child's grimy hands dived after more chocolate-drops. "Where's the note to go?"

"You know pa's house down by Lee's—the last one he bought. That's the place. Mulkey has rented it. The note's for his daughter."

"Oh!" Mrs. Hodgins Thornberry exclaimed. "Of course, I know. Hodgins is down there now, moving the house farther back; Cousin Winthrop agreed to it, as Mr. Mulkey doesn't like it being so near the road,—he's one of these aristocratic, retiring kind of beetles,—shuts up from the world,—was a congressman once, or senator, I forget which—and they *say* he was a colonel."

Atterton, perceiving a slight disposition to criticise, said gravely: "A very nice man, I understand; fine family and high political position. He's come here to practise law, and, as he's rich, he can well afford for some time not to get any cases. All right, Cousin Marietta, good for you. I'll mind the soap and the kid; both are warm propositions, but I wasn't born yesterday."

The hackman's wife hurried into the house to smooth her hair,—an indispensable ceremony with every right-minded woman, though the guillotine await her—then trudged down the street, warmed by Atterton's sunny kindness. Atterton was one of the very few of all the Thornberrys to whom Marietta, at one time or another, had not "spoken her mind"; and to herself, she was obliged to admit, that he was one who needed it most.

"But somehow I just can't," she would reflect with a slow smile.

She came to Winthrop's last purchased house. The yard was in the utmost confusion. The foundation had been taken from under the building, and rocks were strewn across the front path. The cottage stood airily upon slender needle-like supports known to the initiated as "jacks."

Huge timbers were cast crosswise here and there, like straws dashed in a gale. A large section of the fence lay out in the road. In spite of this aspect of activity the silence of absolute repose brooded over the place. It was as if a storm had passed, leaving demolition in its train. Hodgins Thornberry's wife picked her way carefully to the front porch. The steps were gone and the low, heavily-built woman struggled violently to the airy platform. Having paused to regain her breath and her natural color, she knocked.

"Come in," answered a polite though quavering voice. It sounded like some one in distress, and she made haste to open the door.

The front room was deserted, save for Mr. Mulkey's father, who sat stiffly in his particular chair,—a chair with a carpeted foot-rest and a back on hinges. He looked at Mrs. Hodgins Thornberry with startled eyes; for, remembering how he had been routed out of her cousin's house, he considered her, with justice, an energetic and determined character.

"Good-morning," he said faintly.

"Good-morning," said the other; "is this Mr. Mulkey?"

"We have met before," said the old gentleman. "I explained on that occasion why I can not arise to greet visitors."

"Yes, but I was not presented to you. Are you Mr. Mulkey?"

"I am Mr. Mulkey's father."

Marietta fixed him with relentless eyes, and coming closer added: "Are you, I say, Mr. Mulkey? I am Mrs. Thornberry; *are* you Mr. Mulkey?"

A slow color came to the other's pallid face. "No, I am not!" he exclaimed forcibly. "My name is Munkey, it was always Munkey, and will always so be. And I will not deny my name when I am driven. I was born Munkey. My son had his name changed by law and statute. He did not like it. He changed it as little as he could, but change it he would. But I have not changed my name, nor will I change it."

"I am pleased to meet you, Mr. Munkey," said the other heartily. "A Thornberry married a Munkey up in Iowa. I thought your daughter-in-law might be the one; but I was told that her name is Mulkey, and that Mulkeytown, Indiana, is named after your son."

"I don't know who Mulkeytown is named after," said the other, still in extreme agitation. "*My* name is Munkey. I don't proclaim it; I don't force it on anybody; but when I am driven, deny it I won't. Did you want to see Mrs. Mulkey? She knows nothing of the Arkinsaw Thornberrys. When my son decided to alter his name, they cut loose from both sides of the house. You have no idea, madam, how very strongly the Munkeys feel about this matter. They are proud *of their* name. I have no feeling in the matter, but when you insist upon my name, I tell you it is *not* Mulkey."

"I respect your position, sir," said Mrs. Thornberry, in a mollifying voice. "Is your granddaughter at home?—I bring a note for her."

"I am sorry, madam, but all the family have gone out to hunt your husband. He said he would bring the horses very early this morning to move the house back, but he has not made his appearance. Ah, yonder comes Gladys Lucile."

Gladys Lucile scaled the outer fortifications and entered, unusually handsome, thanks to such unwonted exertions. The note was presented, and as soon as the young lady had written her answer, Mrs. Thornberry bore it away.

Gladys Lucile, finding herself alone with her grandfather, reached for the novel she had begun an hour or so before. The old gentleman hastened to forestall her before she should be hopelessly lost to the world.

"What was the note, child?"

"Mr. Atterton Thornberry wants to take me to a hop, to-night," said the girl, smiling kindly at her grandfather, and hunting for her "place" in the fat volume. "I wrote I'd go, of course."

"Don't you think, dear, it was strange for him to send his note by his lady-cousin, instead of by some lad?"

"Yes, grandfather, but all these people are so queer, you know. Mr. Atterton calls everybody by their first names, and hails every person he meets, black or white. It's the funniest thing to walk down the street with him; he doesn't overlook a soul. You know papa was always so utterly different from that. Well, do you know,—I like it." Gladys Lucile now had her finger on the "place."

"Don't begin to read yet, dear," said the old gentleman wistfully. "Oh, I did have such a time with that fierce woman! She *made* me tell that my name is Munkey. I wouldn't deny it. That's the only thing of my own that I've got left, and I'll *not* part with that. But it worries your father so."

"Oh, I wouldn't mind," said Gladys Lucile absently, as her eyes caught these words at the bottom of the page: *"Then he put his arm . . ."*

"Dear, did you find a trace of that house-mover?"

"No; but a man said he wouldn't be likely to come till to-morrow, he is always so slow. But all these people are slow. Nothing ever seems done in a hurry. Grandfather, are you cold? It seems too warm for me."

"It's my legs, child. The excitement with the fierce woman drove all the blood to my head. If I could just get to my room,—I've a fire in there. But if I walk, I won't be able to get down again."

Gladys Lucile laid aside her book. "Maybe I can drag you in your chair. But do you think you can possibly sit by a fire? It is like an oven to me in this room, with everything open. I couldn't live where there is a stove."

"Your legs are young, dear," said the old gentleman simply, "that makes all the difference. There is very little caloric in *me*. If I can just get to the fire, I can straddle my legs on each side of the screen, and keep the heat off of the rest of my body and members."

Gladys Lucile was tugging at the chair when her mother entered.

"Why, Gladys Lucile!" cried her mother, who never

allowed her daughter to do anything, if she could help it, "you are exerting yourself! you have made your face quite red. Father, I wonder you permitted it. Let me here, Gladys Lucile. You were never strong."

Gladys Lucile gladly enough relinquished her task, and resumed her novel. The old gentleman sought to justify himself by explaining how Mrs. Hodgins Thornberry had affected his "caloric."

"Now, that's just too bad," exclaimed the fleshy matron, who was seldom flurried unless Gladys Lucile's comfort was in jeopardy. "I'll put you by that fire, and rub your limbs, too." She bustled to the washstand drawer for the flannel cloth, then exclaimed: "What is all this, father? Your drawer is filled with little sticks of wood."

"Gladys Lucile brought them for me," he said. "I was afraid I might get out. The rag is in the wardrobe."

Mrs. Mulkey went to the wardrobe. "Why, father, this is filled with wood, too." She squatted down and peered under the bed. "Wood, wood! Do I not always keep you warm enough, father?"

"You are the best daughter to me man ever had," said Mr. Munkey (not Mulkey), with a miserly glance toward the stock of fuel, "but I just love to know the wood's there. It gives me a peace of mind nothing else can. This is June. As soon as July and August are passed, the mornings are quite chilly."

Mrs. Mulkey stepped to the door and said firmly: "Gladys Lucile, I do not want you smuggling any more wood in to your grandfather. It isn't suitable work for you. I will bring it, or your father, when it must be brought. It isn't that I begrudge the wood; I would put a whole forest in here if there was room for it; but your hands, child, are not made for work. You are not strong enough. And besides, it's not respectable. Do you hear me, Gladys Lucile?"

"Yes, ma'am. All right, mother," said Gladys Lucile. She softly rose and carried her book upstairs. There was too much conversation and contention below. Of course, her mother was right. It must look strange to the neighbors; and until they could find a servant,—servants were so scarce!—it would appear better for the older ones to do the work. But whether right or wrong, Gladys Lucile was eager to escape human voices, that she might read her novel in peace.

CHAPTER XI

LIFE presents so many problems for consideration, and so many duties to perform, that it is sometimes next to impossible to remember to feed one's chickens. It was nearly four o'clock when Mrs. Eden, thanks to much superfluous crowing from the back lot, cackling without eggs, and singing without music, awoke to this truism. Remorsefully she hastened to the barn, for the old battered tin pan, in which feed had been mixed with water for as long a time as a tin pan may, without too copious a leakage, be used in that tri-daily service.

Mrs. Eden had passed an unusually busy day, which means that she had done a prodigious amount of work; and when the chickens were pacified,—we say not "satisfied," for what fowl is ever altogether at peace with the world, save one scratching in a neighbor's yard?—Mrs. Eden returned rather stiffly to her cottage. She sank with a deep sigh into her chair, and reached wearily for her sewing. Mrs. Eden reflected that no matter how much she might do, there was always something "next." She did not often give way to this rather discouraging train of thought, but to-day she was troubled. She knew that Mary was unhappy. Peter's devotion to Goldie Pickens was discussed by "everybody." Mrs. Eden had never been partial to Peter, but she had sympathized with Mary's pride in the one Thornberry who sought to drag his rather reluctant family up the mount of popular admiration. She was not sure that Mary had been in love with the Thornberry mentor, but there had, at least, been sentiment on the part of both. And now for the "whole town" to become aware of Goldie's ascendency was bitter to the mother-heart.

To speak of the "whole town" knowing that Peter had ceased his frequent visits at Mrs. Eden's, to become a very shadow to the "new music-teacher," was scarcely an exaggeration; for what one inhabitant of Core City knew, was usually the property of all who wanted it; and this want, namely, to discuss personal affairs, particularly those which did not concern themselves, was well-nigh universal. It mattered not so much to Mrs. Eden that Peter's heart should be deflected, as that anybody should pity Mary. This was, no doubt, the unconscious reason that Mrs. Eden was particularly kind and agreeble to Goldie Pickens, and the reason, conscious or unconscious, that she began to entertain a decided disapproval, not to say suspicion, of her boarder.

In order to think well upon the situation, and to indulge a little selfishly in despondent thoughts, Mrs. Eden had sent Mary out for a wlk, maintaining that it would do her good. She said to herself, "I just want to be as unhappy and miserable as I please." Poor Mrs. Eden had little opportunity to be miserable, on account of work that must be done; nor was she allowed to enjoy this melancholy luxury very long on the afternoon in question, for Mary had not been gone long before she returned.

"I thought," said Mrs. Eden weakly, "that you were going to take a nice, long walk, Mary."

Now Mary knew what Mrs. Eden had thought as well as did that lady. "Oh, no," she answered lightly. "I've brought you a treat. Let's hurry to the kitchen."

She held up an oblong paper box which cried "ice cream" as distinctly as if it had vocal organs.

"Oh, what have you done!" cried Mrs. Eden, reproach and delight queerly blending in the exclamation. "We can't afford ice cream, darling. But it's the first we've had for so long—that—how much did it cost?"

"It cost fifteen cents, but I'm sure it's a quarter's worth. Oscar didn't want anything; but when I said I would never get any more if he didn't take the money, of course it was all right."

They reached the kitchen in tingling excitement. The afternoon was as warm a one as Arkansas ever prepares for her children in June, and the coolness of the box was delicious.

"You ought *not*, Mary!" said Mrs. Eden. "I'll get the saucers. This is living like rich people. You mustn't spoil me this way. But just one time won't hurt. We will have to call down Miss Goldie."

"She's not at home," said Mary comfortably. "Just before I went to town, I knocked and knocked on her door, but there was no answer."

Mrs. Eden poised some ice cream on her spoon, and said darkly, "I'm glad."

Mary said nothing to that. Her gaze was riveted upon the other's head. "Oh, mother!" she exclaimed, laying down her spoon.

"What is it?" cried Mrs. Eden, clapping her hand to her head. "Oh," she said with relief, "I was afraid I had left it on the dresser."

"Mother!" repeated Mary, rising abruptly. "Hold your head this way, to the light. Oh, mother! it's a gray hair."

"No!" exclaimed Mrs. Eden, startled and awed, "not a gray hair, Mary!"

"Yes, it is," said her daughter, with a quiver in her voice. They were both standing, looking at each other with solemn eyes, as if they had just felt the breath of Time's cold wings sweeping above their heads. It took a very little thing, after all, to break down their reserve. A full heart overflows from one drop of a passing shower.

"Gray hairs are nothing," said Mrs. Eden bravely. Mary's arms were about her.

"I never thought that you might leave me," said Mary, wiping away her tears; "this is like a hint. It's a real blow. You are sure you didn't know it was there? You haven't been keeping it a secret?"

"I never dreamed of it, darling. But what does anything on this earth matter, except getting ready for the long journey?"

For she knew it was not the gray hair, nor even what the gray hair typified, that caused Mary's sobs. They were seated now, beside the window. Mary was in her mother's arms. Perhaps she did not know why she was crying, but the mother knew; and, for a time, made no effort to check the tears. Finally, she spoke in a softened tone: "The thought has come to me, when looking at some dear old lady, that by and by angel wings are going to be fashioned out of the beautiful feathery white locks."

Mary's tears ceased, but in her mother's embrace she could not be ashamed of them. She kissed the other and rose. "Well," she said, "if this gray hair is a first feather, I'm going to rob your wings, mother, for it must come out."

"What is the use? Others will come. Do you think we can fool wise old Father Time?"

"I'm going to put him to guessing, anyway," said

the daughter, in a determined voice. "Bend over this way. There! Oh, you traitorous, stealthy, heartbreaking, first gray hair! But, mother," she said suddenly, "our ice cream is all melting. Hurry-hurry! it's too bad."

"Never mind, honey," returned the other, coming back to the table; "I like the juice, and there is a little solid left." Just then came a knock at the front door.

"That's too bad!" exclaimed Mary, with something like indignation. "Our first ice cream, and company has come! But maybe they won't want to see you. Eat as fast as you can, while I am gone."

"I'll link in," Mrs. Eden declared heartily. However, she had taken but a spoonful or so, when Mary opened the door. "Mother, Cousin Winthrop wants to see you on business."

Mrs. Eden hastened into the front room and found the widower standing near the door.

"Cousin Polly, how do you do!" cried the rich orchardman warmly. "Now, I might as well say at the start, that I've come on private business, and I want no one else to hear what I have to say. Mary, Ethel is sitting in the carriage at the gate. Run along and chat with her."

Mary obeyed the spirit rather than the letter of this command, for Ethel was not one with whom she could "chat" naturally. The cousins were as wide apart as two dispositions may well be; they looked at life from dissimilar points of view, and thus saw a different life with different aims. That which interested the one could not appeal forcibly to the other. Their intercourse, therefore, was usually upon that uniform, icy plain of social convention whereon, if one slipped not, one might glide expeditiously out from his little cove into the open skating.

Ethel brought up the matter which had recently threatened to check the wheels of state,—how one cabinet member's wife had stepped before another cabinet's member's wife at a reception in Washington. It was impossible for Mary to pretend deep sympathy for the lady who had been preceded. She, for her part, touched on a poor family in the outskirts of Core City, which was in distressing circumstances. Ethel inquired if the head of the family was the man who had refused to work for her father at twenty-five dollars a month. Mary was obliged to admit that the man was the same, and the destitute family was banished with the cabinet members' wives.

It was always thus. As Ethel told her father later: "It is not that I find Mary dull, for she is bright and cheerful, and filled with all sorts of queer interests; but she always makes *me* feel myself dull. It is so uncomfortable to be made conscious of one's own dullness!"

As soon as Mary left the house, Mrs. Eden said to her rich cousin: "I must go upstairs and make absolutely sure that Miss Goldie is not up there. As for Uncle Groner, he's gone away on a visit. You know there are times when he can't bear us another moment; he comes back reconciled." She went upstairs, and gave vigorous knocking at Goldie's door. Not the faintest whisper came in response.

Mrs. Eden descended. "Mary said she had gone out, but we can't be too sure of that, if there is a secret to be discussed."

Winthrop looked at the other with a bright, appreciative eye. "You're right, Cousin Polly. That young woman is a sly character, in my opinion. Then shall we sit down here? Are we quite safe here?"

"Perfectly safe," said the lady abstractedly. Suddenly she added: "Cousin Winthrop, I have a little ice cream in the kitchen; would you like some? Mary had just brought it in—at least, it is a little melted, but I think it will do."

"None, thank you," said Winthrop promptly. "I don't care for anything." Suddenly it occurred to him that ice cream must be a rare event in his cousin's life. "Ice cream, you say? Well, that does sound rather festive. Now if I may come right out in the kitchen——"

"Of course, you may!" cried Mrs. Eden gleefully. "Sit right there at Mary's place. She had hardly begun; and here's another spoon. It's pretty mushy, but——"

"Mushy?" exclaimed Winthrop, "it's just right for me. This hard ice cream you get nowadays is bad for my teeth. Poor Mary! I'll have to pay her back another day." Winthrop gravely sipped the melted milk, glad that his protesting stomach had no voice. "Cousin Polly, you'd better keep an eye on that Pickens girl. I'm afraid of her. I don't know exactly why, but I believe she's a designer. However, let's get to business. I want to talk about Atterton. I'm just going to open up my heart to you, Cousin Polly, as I couldn't to any other living soul."

He paused, and looking at his ice cream with a frown went on slowly: "Atterton is dreadfully wild, Cousin Polly, and he has been doing all sorts of things down at Hot Springs, except the right thing. He has wasted money like water spilled on the ground; well, you know he was that way in the university days. His dear mother wouldn't hear a word said about it; but I've come to you for advice—just as I used to come, with this difference: I've decided on one thing. Now, don't try to dissuade me. I have decided to stop Atterton's allowance and throw him entirely upon himself. But that isn't all. I've decided to deprive him of his half of my property."

"Oh, Cousin Winthrop!" exclaimed Mrs. Eden, in agitation. "Poor Atterton! Do you know when you came in here you reminded me so of him? You two are so much alike. You wouldn't do that, I know," she added earnestly.

Winthrop took a nibble at his spoon to encourage the other, then answered positively, but sadly as well: "Yes, that's what I've come to see you about; to ask your advice as to how this money should be disposed of to best advantage. In other words, I mean to take what should have been his, and spend it, that it may prove a blessing to many instead of a curse to one weak soul. I want you to understand that this is not to punish Atterton. Yet I fear he'll look at it that way. No, it's the last effort to try to make a man of him. When he finds he has nobody to fall back on, I hope he may prove his own master."

"But don't you think when he is older——"

"He's twenty-four, Cousin Polly; old enough. These habits are already formed. They can never be broken except by privations and hard work."

"I think, Cousin Winthrop, it is right to stop his allowance and make him support himself; in that way, he will find that money is easier spent than earned—oh, much more, much more!" she added, with something like eloquence in her impassioned tone. Then *she remembered* herself. "Wouldn't that be enough?

Suppose he turns over a new leaf,—I am sure he will. Wait till he has proved himself a strong man. Then his fortune ought to be ready for him."

"I have thought it over carefully; I have thought it over in agony of soul," said the other mournfully. "This way seems best. As long as he knows I have that money held back for him, he will go ahead making ruinous debts and living a useless life. You know how hopeful the Thornberrys are. He will always be expecting to get his property. Why! he has already squandered ten thousand, at the very least. He's taken just that much from Ethel, and for nothing,—for worse than nothing. It will be that way till the end of the chapter, if things go on as they are. No, I shall make Ethel's share over to her this week; I'll deed her the farm. I will reserve what I consider sufficient for my own support; and the rest—poor Atterton's share—two hundred thousand dollars—Lord! it's a hard thing —when I think how it was made and increased and watched over—but I can't help it. I'm going to give it away, absolutely. And what I want you to do, is to tell me how to spend it. I want it to do good, and that's why I've come to you."

There was for a time perfect silence in the kitchen, save for the ticking of the clock. Winthrop, obvious of his homely surroundings, stirred his ice cream without tasting it. Mrs. Eden looked through the open door at the sunlight sleeping upon the grape-arbor.

Winthrop began abruptly: "Now, Cousin Polly, if you had two hundred thousand dollars all of your very own——"

Mrs. Eden interrupted him with a smile. "I couldn't though," she said. "It wouldn't be my very own, if it were placed in these hands. For I do not look upon

she said. "I never was taken ver
there's one blessed thing about me,
self; I think what I think without t
cram it into anybody else's brains.
at my grape-arbor. Isn't that a fine
But they are not *my* grapes. Thei
the church and to the sick and aged.
say, 'What a lot of grapes you have

"But what do *you* get out of it?
throp, with a queer glance at his cous

Her face grew brighter. "You se
the clusters? Well, that belongs to
a deeper silence, and then Mrs. Eden
Winthrop, I want you to reconsider
want you to give Atterton another ch
to the worst, I will advise about spe
I know where every dollar you ha
blessing to the world. But it wouldi
this from Atterton, unless we knov
himself with it. We don't know

himself. But God knows I would do all I could to make something like a man out of what he has left of himself. And if you say there is still a hope, there must be. *Let* you try to persuade him? Why, bless your heart, if you can do anything with him, I'll be ready to go down on my knees in gratitude! It is just because I believe this money will prove his curse that I mean to give it out of his reach."

"Then I will undertake this charge, and do what I can," said Mrs. Eden, her eyes shining.

"Now, bless your dear soul!" cried Winthrop, grasping her hand. "I'm mighty glad to add one more guardian angel to Atterton's coterie, for looks like the balance of 'em has had more on their hands than they could manage."

Footsteps were heard in the front room, and Mary opened the door. "Mother," she announced, "here are Cousin Hodgins and Mr. Mulkey,—and Miss Goldie, who tells me she has *not* been away."

Winthrop rolled his eyes at Mrs. Eden like a schoolboy caught in a prank. "Well, I must go," he said hastily; "my business was ended, anyhow."

Mrs. Eden followed him from the kitchen and greeted her guests.

Goldie Pickens, serene and gentle as was her wont, explained to the hostess: "Miss Mary tells me she was knocking on my door some time ago. I was asleep. Oftentimes my slumber is quite profound. I came downstairs for this book; and as you have company——"

"Pray don't go," said Mr. Mulkey gravely. "My visit partly concerns yourself."

Goldie looked surprised, but seated her slender form in a distant corner. Winthrop and Ethel rolled away.

Hodgins Thornberry, clad in his fishing-clothes, with a folded rod in his hand, and a box slung from his shoulder, waited near the door.

"You are no doubt surprised to see me here, Mrs. Eden," said Mr. Mulkey, with most portentous gravity, "but I have determined to bury all feeling and forget the past in view of the interests of Christianity."

"Mr. Mulkey," replied Mrs. Eden gravely, "I do not know what you have buried, but I'm always glad to see any one who has the interests of Christianity at heart."

Mr. Mulkey, tall, thin, stiff, waved his long arm, and his huge black mustache seemed to gather additional heaviness as he continued. "I'm here on a painful mission, Mrs. Eden, very painful."

"As for me," interposed Hodgins Thornberry, "not seeing as I can do any good here, and being elsewhere expected, and me being a man of my appointment——"

Mr. Mulkey rose hastily. "Stay, Mr. Thornberry!" he cried, in agitation. "You have agreed to move my house; we are extraordinarily inconvenienced, with the house propped upon pins, as it is, and the night wind sweeping under the floor. You must *not* go fishing till the house is moved." Mr. Mulkey turned to Mary and explained, "I just found him by accident, starting off on a week's camping-out, and I am taking him about with me till I can get home." He then turned again to Mary's mother. "Several parties have told me, Mrs. Eden, that you, an important factor in the church, have ruthlessly insulted Mrs. Lee and her friends."

"You have been greatly misled," said Mrs. Eden calmly. "Human beings, Mr. Mulkey, can not be *important* factors in the church, in the sense that the cause of Christ depends upon them; and that is what I understand by the church."

Mr. Mulkey drew himself up, evidently with the feeling that he was an exception to the "human beings" in the other's mind. "You say nothing as regards Mrs. Lee," he observed. "She was, I am informed, a great worker in the church before you insulted her; therefore, it was a blow to the church and, regarding it thus, I feel bold to come to you. This is unpleasant to me, but I must act as conscience dictates."

Hodgins Thornberry, though ardently longing for a shady nook at the margin of some stream, began to take interest in the world around him. "See here, Mr. Mulkey," he observed, "do you think you've got a monopoly on that there commodity? I'll have you to know that Cousin Polly has got as much conscience as you ever dared to have; I've got plenty of it, myself."

Mrs. Eden, knowing Hodgins' proneness to partisanship, and that though he would endure almost any slight himself, he could not see a Thornberry abused, hastened to answer Mr. Mulkey in a concilatory strain. "Mr. Mulkey—I believe I should say Colonel Mulkey? —I never consciously insulted Mrs. Lee. You labor under a mistake. My offense is as follows, sir: I said, some years ago, when we used a piano in the choir-loft, and the tuner came to tune the piano, and the question was raised whether or not it should be tuned to concert pitch,—I said, on that occasion, that in my opinion it should be tuned at concert pitch."

"Exactly so," cried Mr. Mulkey, "and yet you knew that Mrs. Lee, sweet and delightful as her voice is, could not reach the highest written notes without a straining, a manifest effort, perchance a cracking, so to speak, a—a——"

"Cracking is a good word," spoke up Hodgins, "as I have heard her leave one half of her voice on top of high 'f' and drop the other half to 'e-flat.' " Hodgins, rather proud of this proof of his own technique, chuckled.

"Now," pursued Mr. Mulkey, with awful dignity, "although you knew that it would accommodate Mrs. Lee's voice to tune the piano low, you said you thought it should be tuned high. And the organist,—she was even then on a bed of sickness; yet you added this burden to *her* heart, by saying that the piano ought to be at concert pitch. I feel this so deeply, that I have come to you, Mrs. Eden, although I was once put, as I may say, out of your house."

"Say the word, Cousin Polly," said Hodgins, "and he'll be put out a second time. This here talk is mighty sickenin' to me."

"No, no, Cousin Hodgins. Colonel Mulkey, when asked if I thought the piano should be tuned at concert pitch, I said I thought it should. I'm no musician, but the tuner advised it, and I thought he ought to know."

"Was that tuner a member of the church?" inquired Mr. Mulkey austerely.

"No," spoke Mary, "and neither was the piano."

"Miss Mary!" said Goldie Pickens, in the softest and gentlest accent of reproof for this trifling with holy things.

"Then is my mission to fail?" cried Mr. Mulkey, in a grieved voice. "May I not go to poor Mrs. Lee and tell her you are sorry you advocated concert pitch?"

I still think," remarked Mrs. Eden, with a smile, "that that piano ought to have been tuned at concert pitch."

Mr. Mulkey dropped his long arm with a groan.

"It is useless," he said. "I bid you good-afternoon. Come, Mr. Thornberry."

"Were you a musician," murmured Goldie Pickens, rising, "you would view the matter differently. I agree with Mrs. Lee. I *know* the piano should have been tuned low. I *know* it. Had I been here at that time, it would have been a matter of conscience with me. I could never have gone back to church again had it been tuned high against my conscience. But you did not understand. I could never feel offended at you, dear Mrs. Eden, because I know you do not understand the artistic temperament. I am sorry Mrs. Lee is not more magnanimous."

"How fortunate *you* are, Miss Goldie!" Mary remarked.

"Thank you," said Goldie sweetly.

"Honey," said Mrs. Eden to her daughter, "come over here, and see if you can't find another gray hair!"

CHAPTER XII

GOLDIE PICKENS, having contrived to make Mrs. Eden feel that she was in the wrong about something, tripped out of the cottage, and went forth, as it were, to seek her fortune. She had an appointment with George Nicodemus for the discussion of his mining operations; moreover, there was the probability of a *tête-à-tête* with Peter, and the possibility of a meeting with Atterton. True, she had disposed of Groner, having found him impecunious and inclined to monopolize her, and hamper her movements; while from the tenor of a note received from Winthrop, inclosing a much-needed check, she concluded that she had removed the wealthy widower from the sphere of her attraction. But Peter always remained, and his position in the bank assured him a living. He was such a certain quantity, that Goldie could well afford to speculate on the x's and y's in life's equations.

As she skirted the barbed wire that protected freshly laid cement, she first took up Atterton. Here was a young man, the son of an immensely rich orchardman, unmarried, and, according to the neighbors, who felt sure in the premises, impartial in his attentions to Core City girls. Were he in love with any one living at a distance, of course, everybody would know her name and degree. There was, therefore, no such complication. Now, Goldie possessed a vital secret concerning *this young* man, a secret she had gained by listening at the kitchen door with as meek and conscientious a face as is consistent with the act of eavesdropping. She had overheard most of the conversation between Mrs. Eden and Winthrop Thornberry. How could this secret be used to bring Atterton under her influence? It was a matter that required delicate handling; perhaps it would be best to allow natural events to shape her course.

Catching sight of Sylvester Mulkey, the young lady quickened her steps. Here was a man resolved to assume importance in the community, even if he must use a church-quarrel as a stepping-stone. Goldie could not but respect such a desperate straining after respectability, and it was more from sympathy than from any calculating motive, that she made haste to overtake the opponent of concert pitch.

That grave and conscientious gentleman had been delayed, owing to the strong reluctance Hodgins Thornberry felt toward proceeding with the house-moving. Hodgins had finally agreed to go for the rollers and ropes, and take up his work where he had dropped it some days before, owing to constitutional inertia.

"Colonel Mulkey," said Goldie, in gentle sympathy, "I grieved to be present at your interview with Mrs. Eden, for it wounded me to witness her unforgiving spirit. You were acting as you thought best, and when conscience directs, what do we care if all the rest of the world opposes us?"

"You're right, Miss Pickens. I thank you. You understand me. If that piano had been tuned low——"

"There would never have been any trouble," sighed Goldie.

"To the church," Mr. Mulkey concluded. "I have done my duty. I feel at peace with all the world, perfectly satisfied,—or at least I should be, could I but get my house moved."

"There is another thing I desire to speak to you about, senator," said Goldie sadly. "You will remember when you were driven out of Mrs. Eden's home with your family, in time of need, the excuse given was, that Miss Mary's sister would soon come home, and must have your room. Well; I have just learned that that sister is not coming home for a whole year. Mrs. Eden herself told me that Ruth—that's her name—is traveling in the far West."

"You amaze me!" exclaimed Mr. Mulkey, stopping abruptly upon the sidewalk. "I knew that Mrs. Eden advocated concert pitch in the teeth of the best church-workers, but I never dreamed that she could be guilty of dissimulation."

"Perhaps," sighed Goldie, "dissimulation and concert pitch go together."

Having sown this good seed, the music-teacher parted from the "senator" and went to the central office of the Nicodemus Mining Company. She was expected, and George Nicodemus waited alone in the stuffy little room over the printing office where so many golden hopes were anchored.

"No, I must not sit down," said Goldie, modestly realizing that she was alone with a marriageable man. She gave him a deprecating glance from under her drooping lids, as if excusing herself for having come without a lady companion. A slight flush showed in her pale cheek.

George's desire to win her approbation made him appear drier and stiffer than ever. He rattled the prospectuses, and jarred the can of crude oil. To hide his embarrassment he began talking as to a man:

"There can be no doubt that we have a deep vein of copper, and almost—well, practically, an inexhaustible vein, Miss Pickens. It is right here——" He smote a rude pen-and-ink map with his clawlike finger. "I will read you the geologist's report."

He did so. It was a very long report. Goldie thought that if dryness was an indication of copper, there must be a vein running through the report. When he had finished, she asked, as she wearily rested her hand upon the desk:

"Then would you advise me to buy copper shares, or oil shares?" George Nicodemus looked at her intently. Goldie waited, her meek face drooping, in a confiding attitude.

The master mind said abruptly, "It's a great cross to me, Miss Pickens, that I am thrown with people like you only in a business way!"

"But," said Goldie shyly, "you are more than a man of business to me, because you are dear Mrs. Eden's cousin. Do not feel like a stranger, please. Call me 'Miss Goldie.' All my friends call me so. I like that."

"And I like it!" George declared. He laid his finger upon another part of the map, and said, "I wish there were as much gold in this section as there is in your name!"

"Then—but—— Then you think the oil-wells——"

"Miss Goldie," said the other abruptly, "look here! I own the canning factory, and the evaporator, and the produce house, and the shipping houses where apples are sorted and barreled. All these things bring in a handsome income. But what are apples to diamonds? What is a canning factory to an oil-well? Now, look here! I haven't sold out my business, and put my money in these wells and mines, have I?"

thought possible. It is strange wl
weight of hope may hang by the s
when that thread is attached to a min

"But there's other advice I shou
George evaded. "Miss Goldie, I feel
you. I should like to have something
your affairs to advantage."

"Come to see me," said Goldie impu
Having brought George thus far al
had previously mapped out for him
office. She had made Mulkey her fr
ing him against Mrs. Eden,—for the
to her of winning friendship was to
against somebody else,—and she ha
Nicodemus to peep at her from behind
day was, thus far, well spent; and it v
ful heart that she turned in the di:
Street.

She passed the bank with drooping

and don't think me a heathen, but we—I——" he paused in fear. Goldie looked shyly down. He resumed desperately. "There's to be a hop, to-night, and I want you to go with me. It's awfully select. Just a few there—Atterton and Gladys Lucile and the Lee boys and three or four more—and some strolling Italian players—it's all arranged—and if you don't go, it will spoil everything!" In his eagerness, Peter was not Peter. He might have been any other ordinary young man, wildly in love.

Goldie looked up swiftly. "Mr. Peter, you ask me to go with you to this—er—ah—hop. This is the night for choir-practice; *my* place is at that organ."

"Of course," said Peter, as they walked on; "but after the practice, you know. Of course, we'll practice the hymns and things—anthems, I mean. But when it's all over—say about half-past nine——" He paused.

"Mr. Peter," said Goldie quietly, "would it be right? That's all I ask. I will trust you; would it be right?"

"Now, it's this way," said Peter earnestly, as he saw hope ahead. "No one will know about it. The fellow that rents the hall always keeps mum about our hops, on account of people's prejudices. For the same reason, the town papers never mention them. We'll just slip off there after practice, and nobody will ever know you were there."

"But, Mr. Peter," said Goldie firmly, "the question still remains, whether people hear about it or not,—is the hop itself wrong?"

"It will be a very quiet hop," said Peter.

"Yes, I understand; but, still——"

"It will be an absolutely *quiet* hop; just a *quiet* hop."

"You mean, then, that there will be no dancing?"

"Oh, there will be *dancing*," Peter allowed. "But it will be a *quiet* little hop, and it will be perfectly right and proper for you to attend it."

"Then I will go," said Goldie. "I am so glad, because I really want to go. Thank you, Mr. Peter."

Atterton Thornberry came down the street seeking Peter; but, finding him thus agreeably engaged, slowed his footsteps that he might not spoil a romantic parting. In this loitering attitude he was discovered by Sylvester Mulkey, who swooped down upon him, and made him the prey to a senatorial anecdote.

Mulkey was still chafing from the insult he felt he had received from Mrs. Polly Eden. He kept the point of his anecdote buried from sight as long as possible, dug it up with maddening caution, lest it get out too soon, and presented it after Atterton had seen it coming a mile away; but Atterton's loud, forced laugh could not cheer the colonel's heart.

"Mr. Thornberry," he said abruptly, "I am not in my usual spirits. I have just learned that one whom I regarded as the soul of honor is a maker of devices. All the world seems distorted to me, just now. It is a terrible thing, sir, to have your faith in a friend shattered."

Atterton espied his father driving Ethel along Main Street, and grew restive. True, this dignified statesman was the father of Gladys Lucile, but one does not waltz with fathers, and Atterton's mind was full of the projected hop. He saw Goldie Pickens drift away, every movement of the lithe form seemingly set to dreamy music; Peter was left rooted to the pavement, as if unable to find his way back to the bank.

Sylvester Mulkey continued: "This is a lady,—a lady, as I believed, a Christian. I am not speaking of her advocacy of concert pitch. She is frank enough about *that*. It is her deep-laid plot that I mean,—her secret planning, her watching, her *plotting*. But I say no more," he added, as he suddenly remembered that Mrs. Eden was Atterton's cousin.

Atterton sought escape, not so much from Mulkey, as from the approaching carriage. He shrank from wounding his father by a refusal to go out to the farm, and, of course, he must stay in town for the hop.

Winthrop noted his flight, but, pretending ignorance, called Ethel's attention to the young cashier. "Eth, that young Peter's making a fool of himself, eh?"

"Yes, father," said Ethel, a note of tenderness unconsciously slipping into her tone. She was in the back seat, tall, reserved, pale. Atterton's avoidance of them had been pronounced.

The orchardman turned sidewise to look back at his daughter. "Honey, I'm lonesome this evening,—lonesome for a man's company. You're mighty sweet and good, but you can't sit and smoke a pipe with me till one in the morning, and that's what I need."

Ethel's flexible mouth tightened. She understood; he pined for his son's society.

Winthrop sighed profoundly. "I'm as blue as Waldo McCormack!" he declared, with a rueful smile.

"I wish I were a man," cried Ethel. "I'd sit in the library, and smoke, and talk old times and politics, till morning!"

"I wish to the Lord you were, just for to-night," exclaimed Winthrop, "and that Atterton was a young lady in skirts and tight shoes. I'd have her then, fixed in her own room with key turned in the lock. Whoa!"—this to the horses. "Honey"—this to Ethel, "here's Oscar's stand. Let's take him home

..., ..., he'll pay more attenti...
me."

"I fancy he will," said Ethel drily.
might think——"

"No, he won't. You can give hi...
seen you do that often, when you w...
beau down a peg. He's in there all
can see the top of his head."

Ethel felt that her father was aski...
her; but knowing of his recent disco...
wildness, she was disposed to do n...
temporary comfort. She descended...
and walked to the screened-in res...
dignity and grace of a princess visitin...
humble retainer. She hoped Oscar w...
afar, and come to meet her, but the s...
if he saw people from afar, usually f...
them. She was forced to enter the
the young man held his nose to the pa...

"Oscar!" said Ethel. The young

He stammered something, no matter what. Ethel did not feel the humiliation she had once experienced when passing this Thornberry makeshift of a restaurant, with its common wire gauze, its common high stools, its common hot kitchen in plain view, its common though neat counter. It did not even shame her that the proprietor was a distant cousin. Since her mother's death she had felt for him a respect she could not extend to his surroundings.

"Oscar," she said, with a friendly smile, "father wants you to go out home with us, to spend the night."

"Oh, does he?" ejaculated Oscar, dazed. He stared at Ethel as if he still regarded her as a fairy sprung from the ground, and then looked away at the carriage, as if half-expecting to find bits of pumpkin rind adhering to the spokes. Ethel waited for him to lay down the book, but he was as if petrified.

"Father is lonely to-night," Ethel went on. "You know he is nearly always full of high spirits, and even under his worst troubles he is brave. But he doesn't feel brave now, and he wants you to cheer him up."

"I'm so sorry," Oscar groaned, "but I can't go."

Ethel stared at him as if she couldn't understand his words. Then she said: "But we are waiting for you. Father wants you,—needs you. Brother won't be at home to-night, and when happy people are blue, they are *so* blue."

"Yes, that's a fact!" cried Oscar fervently. "But I can't go. I'll explain."

"But you *must* go. *I* want you, Oscar. You are not offended with me, are you?"

"Offended with you? O Lord!" cried Oscar, almost wringing his hands.

Ethel looked at him blankly. She had not thought that he could repulse her personal petition.

"Ethel," said Oscar, "do you know Mr. Wullens?"

"Mr. Wullens? Certainly not."

"Well, your father does. His wife has gone blind, and Mr. Wullens wants to learn to read, so he can cheer her up at night. And I've agreed to teach him,—he's poor and can't afford to hire a reader. And to-night is to be his first lesson. I have to go there at eight. He is a section-hand, and won't be done work till six. And after he has rested and had supper, it will be late. So I just can't go. I'm *awfully* sorry."

"But can't you teach him some other night?"

"He has to go up the road to-morrow, and he won't be back home till Saturday. It would discourage him like anything to put him off now. And I couldn't get the word to him till suppertime; and after his looking forward to it all this time!—No, I must go there, Ethel."

"Oh, very well," said Ethel blankly. She left the shop with head erect and, having gained the walk, mechanically shook out her skirts as if to rid them of the restaurant atmosphere.

"I'm mighty sorry," Oscar called mournfully after her.

"What!" exclaimed Winthrop, "he ain't comin'?"

"No," said Ethel incisively, "he is going to spend the evening with Mr. Wullens."

"Why, sure enough!" cried her father, slapping his leg, "Wullens told me Osk was comin' there to teach him the alphabet. If I'd thought of that, I wouldn't have asked him. Well, Osk is true blue, bless his heart!"

"What do you mean by true blue?" asked Ethel curiously.

Winthrop whipped up the horses. "Why, see here, honey," he answered, throwing one arm over the back of the front seat and sitting sideways to look at his daughter, "you know it must 'most have broke him all up not to come. He likes me, and worships you, and nothing could have kept him in Core City but the bindingest sort of duty. And look what the duty is; a promise to poor old Wullens, and he being unwilling to disappoint the hard-working fellow, him bent and determined on being a comfort to his afflicted pardner. Now, I hain't no idee," Winthrop went on—in intimate conversation, the language of "the older Thornberrys" suffered, at times, severe lapses—"I hain't no idee old Harve Wullens can learn 'A' from a step-ladder; but it's his undermining intention to try that has won Osk."

"I hadn't thought of it that way," said Ethel reflectively. And thinking of it in that way increased her bitterness toward Atterton. Oscar, for the sake of a promise to Wullens, could forego the pleasure of being with the woman he loved, whereas Atterton, in order to gratify artificial pleasures, did not hesitate to crush his father's heart.

Those who saw the carriage rolling away toward its country home, noted the set face of the queenly daughter. "She will be like her mother," they thought.

Atterton, unconscious of the unhappiness he was causing, spent the afternoon in the manner congenial to his tastes. In his wider view of life, those things which, in Core City, were typical of outer darkness, appealed to him as the playthings of a self-respecting Thornberry. When it was dark he repaired to Peter's room, in the liberty of intimacy, and made himself look as handsome as possible. He was always a handsome fellow, and the additional touches at hair and tie and shoes increased his winsome appearance.

Old Mrs. Polly Thornberry smiled at him in open admiration as he came down the stairs. "How fine you look!" she exclaimed. "It makes my old eyes feel young."

"And how good you always look, Cousin Polly!" cried the open-hearted Atterton. "Whenever I look at you, it reconciles me to growing old." He kissed her and went away humming gaily.

In the meantime, there was trouble in the house toward which his feet were directed. Mr. Mulkey had just been handed a soiled slip of paper with pale blue lines running across it, and some straggling words, very black and apparently laborious, which made nothing of the parallel helps to grace. It was a note and ran thus:

> i bein not a expert at rytin i have got this ear wrote by fren off mine to say which ole Jim Coalwin he have moved houses as mabe heel do you see him immeadyate before e leeve Core City which e is off a mine too doo tonit noaboddieealse cante doot but him-minme, an for mee, i am of too the hapie feeshingroundes Hodge Thornberry esq.

Mr. Mulkey set forth expeditiously to find this Jim Coalwin, and Mrs. Mulkey was called upon to join in the search, as there were two trails developed, and the "senator" could follow but one. It was almost traintime, and Jim Coalwin must be stopped at all costs.

"Gladys Lucile," said Mrs. Mulkey before she departed, "I am as sorry as I can be, and so is your father, that both of us must be gone when Mr. Atterton Thornberry comes for you. But we've got your grandfather installed in his own room by a rousing fire, and we think he will stay there. You know, Gladys Lucile, that your grandfather is—er—curious. And Mr. Atterton's family is so rich and particular, they wouldn't know what to make of such a—a—a—character as your father's father. So don't let Mr. Atterton wait here but a moment. Take him right off to the hop. And if you hear your grandfather moving in his room, just slyly sidle up to the door and turn the key."

Gladys Lucile did not reply. It was not her custom to speak, unless she wanted something; and at present she wanted nothing.

"How perfectly beautiful you look," her mother went on breathlessly. "But I must hurry. You have dropped your gloves, dear."

Gladys Lucile looked with languid interest at the gloves, knowing her mother would pick them up for her. "Here," said fleshy Mrs. Mulkey, handing them over, "don't exert yourself, dear; don't get your face flushed." The mother sped away in quest of the house-mover,—and, soon after, Atterton arrived.

The sight of Gladys Lucile made his heart leap in warm admiration, while the appearance of Atterton gave Gladys Lucile an interest in life distinct from suspense engendered by works of fiction. To himself he declared that this was the loveliest creature his eyes had ever beheld, nor was this declaration entirely unexpressed, for his eyes spoke the conviction. She read his heartfelt approval, but she was not flurried; for, all her life, it had been her part to receive admiration and pay nothing for it. He took his seat in the parlor while she went upstairs to put on her hat and cloak, that the ball-dress might not be flouted in the eyes of Core City.

The movements of Gladys Lucile were never hurried, and her absence now was unusually delayed because she was accustomed to her mother's assisting hands in the toilet. She was always hard to please, as to the set of her hat and the hang of her garments, and she passed some time before the glass, thinking, with a pleased little lift of the corner of the mouth, of Atterton's shining eyes. It was a fact of transcendent importance to her father that Atterton's father was rich, and Mrs. Mulkey but reflected the sentiments of her husband. But Gladys Lucile did not care for riches. Was she not herself rich? There had always been plenty of servants in the house till they came to this town where people would not work unless they felt like it. If she desired anything, that thing became hers.

Atterton, carried beyond himself by the enchanting picture of Gladys Lucile, as she flashed past the hall door on her way upstairs, closed his eyes. He desired to preserve that image; but he was interrupted in his musings by the opening of a door. Old Mr. Munkey, leaning heavily upon his cane, slowly dragged his unwilling feet into the room. Atterton sprang up with a sunny smile. "This is Mr. Mulkey, I believe?" he said, holding out his hand. "I am Atterton Thornberry."

The old gentleman shook hands, and waited to find if he were to be pressed about his name; but as Atterton seemed satisfied with his assumption, the other sighed with relief. He explained to his daughter-in-law afterward, "I didn't say I was Mulkey, and I didn't say I wasn't."

Atterton seized one of the easiest chairs, and pushed it toward the feeble old man.

"It isn't any use, sir," said Mr. Munkey, shaking his

head. "It is kind of you, but I can't sit down. I heard you in here, and knew you must be all alone, and I got up to extend the hospitality of the house, sir."

"That's kind of you," said Atterton heartily; "do sit down. I'd like to get acquainted with you, Mr. Mulkey."

"I can't sit down. When I get up, I can't ever get down, till my son comes. He understands my leg-joints. There's a trick about pushing the connections. Ah, Mr. Thornberry, it's splendid to be young and have all your connections intact. But my son's wife is just like an own daughter. There's nothing either wouldn't do to make me comfortable."

"Now, see here, Mr. Mulkey," said Atterton decidedly, "if you want to sit down, you just show me where those joints are, and I'll make the connection."

"Nobody can do that but my son; I thank you kindly. You see, that isn't all there is wrong about me. I have lost some of my caloric."

"Your caloric, sir? What——" Atterton checked himself, as it suddenly occurred to him that the old gentleman might mean something not fitted for polite conversation.

Mr. Munkey hastened to set him right. "My vital heat, I mean. I am never warm enough. I don't care how hot you get a room. You might pile on the wood *ad libitum*, but that wouldn't do any good. You couldn't *get* me warm; not all *over*, you understand. Part of me would be perspiring, and some member or other still cold to the hand. Calves are what give most trouble; calves and arms. Now," he went on with zest, "there's this fresh-air cure idea. I've read considerable after it. In fact, I never see a piece in the newspaper concerning ailments—no matter what ailments—for if I haven't 'em, I may get 'em—you never know what's coming—that I don't read it. Now, Mr. Thornberry, there's a great deal in that fresh-air theory. It's good. I've taken up the determination to breathe all the fresh air I can. But how am I to keep my calves warm while doing so?"

"That's certainly a problem," said Atterton sympathetically, "and I'll tell you what I'll do; I'll think it over and see if I can't hit on something to solve the difficulty. But I don't like to see you standing there, Mr. Mulkey; you don't look strong."

"Strong?" echoed the other, in vehement repudiation of the word.

"Then you let me set you down," said Atterton decidedly. "Now, what do you do? Which leg?" Atterton pushed the chair up behind the old gentleman, then knelt before him and hovered over his members, his bright eyes tilted inquiringly.

"Both. Take 'em just under the kneecap," said Mr. Munkey, dropping his cane and grasping the arms of the chair in the expectation of being seated, "and give a quick push up, and a long pull down, and a turn to the right—Why! bless my soul, here I am, doubled up as nice as you please! Give me your hand, sir!"

They were shaking hands warmly when Gladys Lucile came downstairs. She was a good deal surprised, but smiled good-humoredly. She was not a girl to excite herself over other people's peculiarities, or to lose her temper over her own. She and Atterton went away, carrying the blessings of the old gentleman with them. There was some pleasurable delay in climbing off the front porch and skirting the scattered rocks and timbers. They reached "the hall" in unusually high spirits.

"The hall" was a narrow room over a grocery, reached by outside stairs that ran along the wall. The opera chairs had been taken up, and heaped at one end. The wandering Italians occupied the stage, ordinarily devoted to the minor drama and public school entertainments. The chairs were so arranged that they formed a retreat from the main room, presenting between it and the dancers, a wall of chair legs and arms that had the effect of latticework.

"Let's go in here awhile," said Atterton; "it reminds me of Oscar's restaurant,—eh, Pete?"

Peter was already in this nook, seated beside Goldie Pickens. They were so absorbed in each other's society, that Atterton laughingly told Gladys Lucile he didn't believe they wanted a crowd. There seemed nothing about this evening's hop to distinguish it from the ordinary social function debarred from the town papers. No one would have thought, unless it were Goldie Pickens, that the dark-browed fiddlers were playing an overture to broken hopes, and that the beautiful forms flashing back and forth under the insufficient electric-lights were dancing, as it were, at the death of noble thoughts.

There was one thing that was impressed more and more deeply upon Peter's consciousness as the evening sped on; namely, that Goldie Pickens was not so much an angel, as a woman; or, rather, that the fact of her being an angel did not deprive her of a woman's charm. At their first waltz, he had put his arm about her with a cold feeling, half expecting her to recoil from his embrace. She had not done so, and, while he wondered vaguely at the unconsciousness of the saint, he exulted in the awakening of the mortal. When she yielded her form to his rapturous embrace, not as if compelled by social convention, but as if her curve fitted naturally and gladly to his arc, he was intoxicated with surprise and joy. When he took her hand, he felt a warm, confiding pressure, a naïve clinging of the flexible fingers. This ethereal, nebulous creature had been humanized by love. Could Peter doubt it? Her shy eyes, her clinging tenderness, bespoke a heart vanquished.

After the waltz they retired to the barricade of opera chairs, where, being alone, he poured forth his passion in broken words.

"You know I do," Goldie whispered. Then like a fluttering bird seeking escape,—"Mr. Peter, you're a tyrant!"

"You *shall* tell me," the young man whispered. "I have a right to know. Tell me, Goldie, in so many words: Do you love me?"

"Oh, Mr. Peter—you are cruel——" But in spite of her distress he was as adamant. "Yes," she whispered, with drooping lids, "Yes,—I love you."

"Oh!" was all Peter could say.

"Go, now," said Goldie hurriedly. "The Lee boys are watching. I mustn't dance the next set with you. Send Mr. Atterton to me, and you take Gladys Lucile for the next number."

Peter stumbled over the barricade, half-blind. His brain was whirling, his eyes aflame. Goldie was his; the world was at his feet! He delivered Goldie's message, and Atterton looked ruefully at Gladys Lucile.

"Say, old man," he remonstrated, "why don't you go ahead? I'm satisfied; aren't you?" Resistance was useless. He went to the music-teacher, but his face was downcast. He had not admired Goldie's ethereal charms since reading the note she had written his father.

"You must excuse me for claiming you," said Goldie softly, "but I have been seeking an opportunity to tell you something."

"Oh, it's all right," said Atterton, endeavoring to speak with his accustomed heartiness. "Certainly; no explanations are necessary. A fellow oughtn't to try to monopolize a girl at these hops,—it's right to give all a chance to change off. Are you ready?"

"Not yet, Mr. Atterton. Let us be seated in this quiet nook. There is something of grave importance that you should hear."

"Yes," said Atterton drily. Hearing anything of grave importance had always proved to Atterton a weariness of the heart and mind. "Grave importance" was but an epithet for fault-finding. He seated himself stiffly, and, through an opening in the wall of chairs, watched the beautiful face of Gladys Lucile as it was lifted toward the duty-serving Peter Thornberry.

Goldie did not take offense at this abstraction on her companion's part, for she felt that it would not be long before she had his entire attention.

"I hardly know if I should tell you," she murmured. "We are not very well acquainted. But you are Mr. Peter's most intimate friend, and I feel that for his sake, as well as for your own, I should do all I can to help you."

"This sounds serious," remarked Atterton. "Don't you want to dance?"

"Not just yet, thank you. I believe, after all, that I must tell you. Yes, I will tell you now. It is something that Mrs. Eden said this afternoon."

"You mean Cousin Polly sent me a message by you?" asked Atterton, frowning slightly.

"Oh, dear, *no!* She had no idea I would ever repeat her words."

"Then please don't repeat them," said Atterton promptly. "Whatever Cousin Polly wants me to know, she will tell me, herself."

"Wants you to know! But that's it,—she doesn't want you to know." Goldie went on hastily, fearing she might be checked before she could accomplish her purpose of making this rich young man her friend for life. "It most vitally concerns you. Mr. Atterton, your father has decided to give away all the money he meant to leave you,—two hundred thousand dollars. You are not to have a penny. Wait! let me tell you as your friend. He—your father—came to Mrs. Eden this afternoon, and said he was going to cut you off without another cent. Poor Mrs. Eden! She begged him to reconsider. He wouldn't. At least, he wouldn't, at first. Finally Mrs. Eden effected a compromise. They are going to *watch* how you act, and Mrs. Eden is going to try to persuade you to do as they think you *ought* to do. And if you change, and get to be like *they* think you ought to be, and live according to *their* idea, your father will change his mind, and *excuse* you, and *let* you have the money when he dies. He is going to deed the farm to Miss Ethel this week, and he'll *watch* you and see how you *act*. And if Mrs. Eden can't *do anything* with you, or get you to do as *they* see fit that you *shall* do, you are to be *sent out* into the world with your *bare* hands, like an *outcast*. That is what Mrs. Eden said this very afternoon. I had been asleep in my room, and when I woke up I saw your father's carriage standing at the gate; your sister was holding the horses and Miss Mary sat with her in the vehicle. When your father departed, I descended from my—from my—er—my bedroom," said Goldie hastily, speaking the word in a hushed voice.

Atterton's brain reeled under this sudden blow, but he exerted all the forces at his command to hide his surprise and humiliation. As the other spoke, there came back to him the bitter words of Sylvester Mulkey. Mrs. Eden had advocated concert pitch. It must be Mrs. Eden whom Mulkey accused of secretly "planning and plotting." Mulkey would have warned him, but had not known how to do it! Atterton's face grew white, but his voice was steady as he said, "Really, it is too bad for us to miss all the dancing."

"I would not have told you," murmured Goldie, rising slowly in order to detain him; "but, since Mrs. Eden is going to *watch* you to *prove* you, be careful,— I should grieve for you to lose your property. Bear in mind all the time that Mrs. Eden is watching, watching, watching!"

"Miss Goldie," said Atterton quietly, "have you any further suggestions?"

It did not occur to him to doubt Goldie's story. His father's significant threat to "draw the line," and his visit to town that afternoon, would have been enough to bear out her statements. But the internal evidence was convincing. Mrs. Eden's peace-loving disposition, his father's provincial prejudices, the words quoted,— words his cousin would use under the circumstances,— left no room for doubt nor would the music-teacher have invented such a tale. She had risked much in making this bid for his favor.

Goldie did not understand the other. She had anticipated an outburst from which she felt sure of reaping a decided advantage. But, except for the white face and clenched hand, Atterton remained outwardly unmoved. This strange reception of so important a secret, caused her to look at him in some uneasiness.

In reality, Atterton was furious. Strangely enough, his resentment was not awakened by what Goldie considered of the utmost importance, that is, the loss of his property, but by what she had implied rather than affirmed. Atterton blamed Mrs. Eden with exceeding bitterness for confiding in this stranger. He was forced to the conclusion that his cousin had regaled both Goldie Pickens and Sylvester Mulkey with his most private affairs. The result of his erroneous conclusion was reckless defiance. So Mrs. Eden was not only watching over him, but made a merit of her espionage, and discussed it with her visitors!

"Well!" thought Atterton, his face settling into rigid lines, "she'll not watch in vain. I'll give her something else to talk about!"

"Mr. Atterton," said Goldie, watching him covertly, "I'm afraid I have not acted wisely. But I want you to know I am your friend."

Atterton flung back his handsome face and laughed. "Let's dance!" he said.

At twelve o'clock, Core City is usually deserted, save for the night watchman dozing on some doorstep. The streets are white from the electric arcs, and the deserted shops, with curtains rolled up and the interiors revealed to any passing gaze, seem to dare the thief. The livery barn stands open, and, occasionally, a sudden thud of hoofs startles the drowsy servant lying dressed upon the dingy carpet-covered couch in the office. There are no business houses, save those surrounding the city park,—a square of rough grass, scattered trees, and an old well. The country presses so closely upon the heart of the town, that the air is thrilled with the crowing of those cocks that do their crowing at twelve, and the barking of dogs sounds startlingly near.

It was not unusual for Oscar to linger to a late hour at his restaurant, studying. On this night, twelve found him seated behind the counter, bending over some difficult volume. His visit to Wullens had consumed much time, for Wullens had been painfully anxious to learn, and had learned little, with exceeding difficulty. Oscar was making up for lost time, when he heard a quick footstep just outside the wire gauze. He looked up, supposing it the night watchman; but Goldie Pickens entered.

"I'm so glad to find you here," she said breathlessly. "Oh, Mr. Thornberry, something dreadful has happened! I must ask you to take me home. I'm frightened almost to death."

Oscar, bewildered, stared at her as at a ghost, his finger still warming the last word he had conned. The light gleamed in little sparks of red fire upon his bright spectacles. He had known nothing of the hop.

"There was a little wine-supper," Goldie confessed, "after Gladys Lucile and that younger crowd had been taken home. Mr. Atterton would have it, after the hop. I was used to that in Germany,—I never thought anything of it. And I had no idea Mr. Peter would be overcome. We started home, and he said the shortest way was through the park; so we cut across, and when we reached the old well, he could not stand any longer; so we sat upon the curbing and were there a good while. I waited for him to recover himself. But he was quite overcome and, at last, lay down there and went to sleep, while I was still talking to him. Oh, I was so alarmed! He's there now. Oh, oh, Mr. Oscar, what shall I do?"

Oscar descended from his high stool. His face was stern and pale. "Do you mean," he said harshly, "that Peter is drunk?"

"He is quite overcome," said Goldie appealingly.

"A wine-supper!" Oscar exclaimed. "I never dreamed that Peter could so forget himself. You say it was Atterton who got it up?"

"Yes, sir, it was Mr. Atterton's idea. He seemed so—so excited and—and gay. Mr. Peter hesitated about it, but I thought it would be rather nice. Do you condemn me entirely?" Goldie spoke with genuine emotion, knowing that she had caused the storm which afterwards she had been unable to subdue.

"You stay here," said Oscar abruptly; "I'll be back in a moment." He ran over to the city park, found Peter supine and insensible, and returned. "Come," he said shortly.

She walked at his side, timidly sending up sideglances from her blue eye. Seldom in her life had she been placed so manifestly in the wrong.

"You blame me," she presently observed, appealingly.

"None of us boys ever got drunk till this night," said Oscar almost roughly. "We were left orphans very young; but we've managed to behave ourselves. Peter was the strictest of the family. No matter how hard you tried, you could never exactly please him. And now he's disgraced the family!"

"Don't say that, sir," pleaded Goldie. "He will be all right in the morning, and nobody will ever know about it."

"Of course he won't do it again, once he's begun!" Oscar sneered. "And what do you suppose is to be done with him? Lug him home to grandfather and grandmother? or leave him all night, to be chilled by the dampness, and made ill?"

"Who would ever have thought it?" moaned Goldie wretchedly. "Who would ever have thought it?"

"I should think," said Oscar frankly, "that any good, sensible girl would have thought it. You say Gladys Lucile wasn't there?"

"You wound me cruelly, Mr. Thornberry, but I can bear it," said Goldie meekly.

"Yes, I thought you could," said the heartless Oscar. "Look here; why did Atterton take that Mulkey girl home before this wine supper, if he didn't know it was wrong?"

"You are too cruel; I will not discuss it with you, sir," the other exclaimed.

"I wish," said Oscar icily, "that you'd quit saying '*sir*' to me; you're about ten years older than I am, doubtless, and six or eight years older than Peter, if *I'm* a judge."

"You are not a gentleman," said Goldie, with real anger. "You take advantage of my dependence to insult me. Not one other word will I speak to you." True to this resolve, she locked her meek lips, and proceeded to Mrs. Eden's house like a pale, injured spirit.

Having seen her to his cousin's gate, Oscar went home on a run. Stealing stealthily up to the room shared by Will, he found his brother sleeping profoundly. In order to wake him without disturbing the household, Oscar was driven to the severe expedient of a wet towel.

Will, starting up in righteous wrath, was silenced by

the first glimpse of Oscar's face. He sat upon the edge of the bed, staring.

"Get into your clothes, quick!" Oscar did not speak like a bookworm, but as one accustomed to command. Will began to dress before he stammered out his inquiry:

"What's up? house afire?"

"Worse," said Oscar, again making a gesture of caution. "Don't rouse the old folks. It would just kill 'em. *Peter's drunk.*"

"*Lord!*" exclaimed Will, dropping his shoe in amazed incredulity. "Did you see him, yourself?"

Oscar nodded brusquely.

Will's mind could not take in the astounding fact. "Did he tell you so, himself?"

Oscar picked up the shoe and handed it to his brother. "Put it on!" he ordered.

Will dressed as one in a dream. Then he exclaimed: "There's some mistake about this. It couldn't *be*, you know." His mind was riveted upon the image of the oldest brother as that image had grown and hardened in his experience; Peter, the proper; Peter, mentor and critic; Peter, the Thornberry who gave dignity and social value to his family.

Oscar explained in succinct whispers. "There was a hop to-night. After it, a wine-supper. Peter is lying on the well-curbing, in City Park, drunk as a dog. I couldn't wake him up. He's there alone. I brought that Pickens girl home. It was Atterton's doing. We can't leave him out there all night—he's too delicate. It might kill him. And we can't bring him here; that would kill grandmother. We'll get a carriage and drive him out to Cousin Winthrop's and let Atterton keep him till he has sobered up."

"There's no use taking him out there, if he's drunk," said Will. "It'll be all over town to-morrow, anyway. We might just as well carry him to the hotel. It's so late, nobody will see him but the night-boy." Will reached for his coat and vest. Oscar noticed that the tears were coursing down the other's face. Will made no attempt to brush them away.

"No," said Oscar, in the fixed tone of one who does not often prove obstinate, "we will take him to Atterton's. That's where the disgrace comes from; we'll take it home to him."

They slipped downstairs and went at once to the livery barn. Presently, the sound of wheels startled the night watchman of Core City. The horses were checked at the darkest corner of the little park. Oscar and Will strode through the dew-laden grass, unmindful of the path. They found Peter lying upon his back at the edge of the curbing. His mouth was wide open and his breathing was labored.

Oscar shook him roughly, but Peter only mumbled "Lemme 'lone," and snored on.

Will stared at the sorry sight and groaned. "I can't touch him!" he muttered.

"Yes, you can," said Oscar sternly. "Take him by the legs. You needn't be so careful, *he* won't wake up; he's drunk!" They bore the long, thin form to the carriage, and dumped it, a limp and senseless heap, upon the back seat. "Get in and hold him," said Oscar, "while I drive."

"No," Will exclaimed, "I won't hold him. I—I—don't want to touch *him*. He—er—he doesn't seem *human*, somehow."

"Oh, very well," Oscar retorted, "I'll hold him. Take the lines."

They drove rapidly away. There was a solemn hush in the open country. The hills of the Ozarks seemed peering through the misty vapor at the strange sight. The shadowy trees leaned toward the road inquiringly.

Once Oscar broke the silence: "This isn't an uncommon thing, Will. I was reading not long ago how many drunkards die every year—I forget how many tens of thousands. And every year, mind you! Why, a drunken man like this is one of the commonest sights in the world."

"But it's *Peter!*" groaned Will heartbrokenly.

"Yes, that's the difference," Oscar grimly acquiesced.

They said no more. When Winthrop Thornberry's country place was reached, Will opened the gate and led the horses through. They drove up before the silent mansion. There were no lights at any of the windows.

"Oscar," said Will, "don't you think——"

"No. Just tie the horses to that persimmon, will you? I'll wake 'em up!" Oscar trod heavily upon the porch and beat upon the door. The echoes had scarcely died away, when it was opened sharply, and Winthrop stood upon the threshold, fully dressed.

"Why! is that you, Oscar? I thought you couldn't come to-night," said the widower in a natural tone of voice. At the same time, he peered inquisitively at the livery carriage.

"I thought I couldn't," said Oscar abruptly. "Where's Atterton?"

"He hasn't come home; I thought he was going to stay all night with Peter."

Oscar was unprepared for this. "I was sure I would find Atterton at home." He hesitated. Then his voice grew steady. "And so I have brought Peter out to see *him*."

Will, having secured the horses, advanced with laggard feet. "Peter?" repeated the orchardman, "but where is he?"

"Oh, he's in the carriage," said Oscar bluntly. "He's drunk. We'll have to carry him in. We couldn't take him home, and I thought I'd better bring him to Atterton, as Atterton was the cause——"

"Now, Oscar!" said Will deprecatingly.

Winthrop lifted his hands above his head. "Drunk! Peter, drunk? Impossible!"

"Go back, daughter!" he added sharply, as Ethel, also fully dressed, appeared behind him in the hall. These two had been sitting in the library, reading aloud to each other, telling old tales, and softly singing, with the lights turned low. Ethel had done her utmost to drive away her father's despondency, and, to the extent of her feminine nature, had been a son to him. She recognized Oscar's face in the hall light, and the hard, even fierce, expression upon it filled her with alarm.

"But what is it?" she asked, pressing forward. "What has happened?"

"Cousin Winthrop," said Oscar, "can I bring him in the hall and lay him on that divan? I'll sit by him all night, and Will can take the carriage back to town. I don't want grandmother or grandfather ever to hear of this."

"Oh," cried Ethel, wringing her hands, "is Atterton hurt?"

"No," said Oscar, looking gravely into her frightened eyes, "but he has hurt my brother. You go on to your room, Ethel!"

Ethel was strangely subdued before this air of

reserved strength, and felt, more than ever, that she did not understand her cousin.

"Yes," said Winthrop, in great agitation, "bring him in. Oh, my God, Ethel, don't you understand that Atterton is breaking my heart? But you do understand, you do, honey——" Winthrop put his arm about Ethel, and sobbed aloud.

As in a flash, Ethel understood. Her arms went about her father's neck, but her eyes, shining with reproachful tears, were turned upon Oscar.

"Come on, Will," said Oscar shortly, as he started toward the carriage. He called back over his shoulder, "I couldn't take him home, I *couldn't*. I supposed Atterton was here; and where else could I go? When you've got a disgrace, you ought to keep it among your own folks. Take hold of him, Will."

Will, with shrinking distaste, grasped Peter by the limp legs. Peter stirred and murmured, "Anzhel!" The jolting over the hard ground served still farther to rouse the sluggish mind. "Whyn't you lemme shleep?" he complained, like a sick child. "Leggo me, I shay!" His tone was pitiful in the extreme. Had it not been Peter, the bearers might have laughed aloud; but as Oscar had said, that made the difference, and the whining entreaty excited only a sense of shame.

As they jarred the apparently boneless form in ascending the porch-steps, Peter opened his eyes and stared foolishly at the hall light. Ethel had fled, but Cousin Winthrop stood in sorrowful waiting. The limp heap was disposed upon the divan. Winthrop brought a pillow and quilt. As the burning cheek was laid upon the pillow, Peter was dully conscious of being once more in the lap of ease. "Oh!" he hiccoughed, "oh, anzhel, anzhel!" Then he knew no more.

The three men stood for a time in silence. Then Will said, "I had better take the carriage back."

"Yes," said Oscar.

Will departed without glancing at his unconscious brother.

"Now, Cousin Winthrop," said Oscar gravely, "you must go to bed and not bother about me. I'll just watch over him; I couldn't sleep if I were in the softest bed. I thought it was right to come out here, but if it was wrong, forgive me. And, anyway, I'm sorry about you."

"Don't be sorry about me, son," said Winthrop, wringing his hand, "you've got enough trouble of your own to think about. I reckon you've done for the best, though sometimes we can't see it, at the time. I hate it on Ethel's account, but it's justice to Atterton, and I wish he were here to get it. Good-night."

Winthrop retired to the library, where Ethel was awaiting him. He sank wearily into his easy-chair, and she sat upon the floor at his feet, with her skirts spread fan-like upon the rug. They said nothing. She leaned upon his knee, and stared into the dying coals of a little grate-fire. So this is what all their efforts at being cheerful had come to! Their exchange of happy reminiscences, their subdued duets, their readings of favorite morsels,—all ended in sorrow before the dying coals. How happy we could be, if it were not for other people!

Ethel's thoughts dwelt upon her cousin. How different he was from the studious, shy Oscar of her former knowledge! He could be rough, even masterful. Since the declaration of his love, he had been unconsciously forming a new image of himself in her mind. In his refusing, that afternoon, to go home with them, she had discovered an unexpected firmness. It is strange how, for many years, we may be convinced that we know a friend through and through, and one day discover a hidden vein in his inmost heart.

Winthrop went to sleep, resting in his easy-chair.

After awhile Ethel grew listless. She arose. It was two o'clock. She laid some sticks upon the coals and, kneeling down, watched the dying embers till they responded with a flashing smile. Still, her father did not wake.

Ethel stood under the shaded lamp and read a little without thought. Then she passed out into the hall.

Peter lay, as if dead, upon the divan, without sound or motion. His long form was draped with the quilt, and a handkerchief lay over his head. Oscar stood with his back to the divan, his hands locked before him, his head erect, and his eyes staring blankly at the window. He reminded Ethel of a sentinel of old, guarding the body of some fallen hero. The light was upon his face, and it shocked her with its pallor and stern grief.

An overwhelming sense of pity surged upward in her breast,—pity for her father, for herself, for Oscar. She approached him, wishing she might find some helpful, soothing word to say, but she could think of nothing; and Oscar, rigid and motionless, was unaware of her presence. How long she stood thus, she did not know. From the open library-door, came the ticking of the clock and the crackling of the little fire. The light sparkled upon her yellow hair, piling the gleaming coils against the shaded sheen of old-gold. The blue eyes, filled with melting tints, looked from the proud, yet humbled face.

She waited for him to look at her, thinking the light

of recognition in his eyes might prompt her to comfort him a little, and to relieve the painful tension of her own heart. But he did not turn her way, because the body of his brother lay between them. And so, at last, softer than she had come, she slipped away, with the cautious care of a culprit eluding detection; and Oscar, staring blankly at the uncurtained window, as if the blurred darkness typified disgrace, knew not that the tender eyes of a friend had shone upon him.

CHAPTER XIII

At so late an hour one could not think the choir was still practising its anthems, or rehearsing its wrongs; yet Goldie Pickens had not come home. Mrs. Eden grew uneasy. She feared, not that Goldie was unable to take care of herself, but that she might not preserve the credit of the family. She communicated this impression to Mary.

It must be admitted that both Mrs. Eden and Mary would like to have rid themselves of Goldie. Ever since the rainy night that Hodgins Thornberry left the stranger on the front porch, Uncle Groner had been a changed man. It is true he had never possessed a contented spirit, but he had shown his ill-will against life only by a grim determination to be pleased with nothing it contained; and he had not, until he passed under the musician's influence, taken up arms in actual warfare.

It was not so much on Uncle Groner's account, however, that Mrs. Eden hardened her heart. Though she and her daughter never discussed Peter's infatuation, it was a sore to family pride. When ten o'clock came and the organist had not appeared, the mind leaped to the inevitable conclusion that Goldie had gone to the hop.

"But there is no use for us to be blind," said Mrs. Eden, in an awed whisper. That the organist, after the practice of sacred songs, presumably in a devout state of mind, should betake herself to the carnal hall of Terpsichorean revelry, brought the hot blush of indignation to the hard-lined face. To the mind of Mrs. Eden, Goldie had carried the flag entrusted to her care as a Christian soldier over into the enemy's camp.

Eleven o'clock sounded. "*I am going to bed*," said Mrs. Eden, as if announcing the most fatal decision. Mary understood that "going to bed" in that frame of mind meant Goldie's going from the house on the morrow.

Mary was disturbed and restless, and for a long time lay upon a couch in her own room, staring into the darkness. She had blown out her lamp, for the coal-oil was even more offensive in odor than high in price, and it was not until the moonlight slipped into her room, that she felt called to the window. She was not wretched on account of Peter's defection. She realized that she had never loved that most proper of all cousins. But she had thought she might, perhaps, and this had been the one little romance in a life of toil. And so, she sat at the window with a fleecy shawl drawn about her, and gazed wistfully at the shadows of other days. With the Peter who had wounded her sensitive nature, she had nothing to do. Her mind leaped backward into a happy schoolgirl's past, and she saw herself on the haywagon, Peter always by her side, rolling, jolting, sliding, jarring over the hilly roads of Arkansas. They were in a play given by "home talent." They were graduated in the same class from the public school, and they had ridden on the same "pony," at the same plodding gait,—through Cæsar. It was all very pleasant to think about,—mildly sad, no doubt, in view of the unhappy ending; but, by force of mind, the conclusion could be held dimly in abeyance, and the

.....rted so many trains ...
scious of the flight of tim...
with fleeting glimpses of ...
reached that union statio...
Definite Conclusion, when...
vancing townward, was ...
carriage, gleaming in the ...
for its driver; and that dr...

Instantly Mary scented ...
peace would William Th...
projected through space. ...
Either the moonlight wa...
o'clock! Why was Will ir...
Why had Oscar brought ...
Where was Peter? Had ...
mystery? Suddenly it oc...
returning the carriage to tl...
side yard on his way home...
shorter way to Timothy T...
noticed that, for some reas...
the road leading past her m...
sprinkled with signal lan...

falls. She slipped cautiously downstairs, and went out
into the yard, drawing the shawl over her head. Walking around the hole which still gave the front walk a
character of its own, she stopped at the front gate, and
leaned her arms between the projecting pickets. She
did not have long to wait before a man's footsteps
sounded upon the air, and Will Thornberry passed
through a field of moonlight to plunge again into the
sea of gloom that surrounded Mary.

At first sight, Will thought the waiting maiden was
Goldie Pickens, and sheered off to the middle of the
road; but at Mary's whisper he came hurriedly to the
gate, glad and sorry in a breath.

Mary began at once with the main point. Her voice
sounded stern, even accusing; but that was only from
her determination to get at the truth. "Where is
Peter?"

"Let me come in," said Will, "and I can talk better."
This he said, not because he wished to reply more at
ease, but that he might evade her question altogether.
He entered the gate. "The moon is so bright to-night,
isn't it?" he observed. With Mary so near, his soul
was full of poetry; but there was no coal of fire upon
his lips.

"Will, I saw you driving back to town in a hired
carriage. And I was sitting at my window, when
Oscar brought Miss Goldie home. Now, that is all I
know; tell me the rest."

It flashed upon Will's mind that Mary had been sitting at her window to see Peter, when he should bring
the music-teacher back from choir-practice; and that
she would not have waited thus for hours unless in
love with him. A great bitterness surged through the
young man's soul. Never, by look or word, would he

betray his own heart to Mary, thinking she loved his brother, and that his brother loved her. But a recollection of Peter's drunken stupor,—the feel of his limp, damp flesh, the foulness of his reeking breath, the glimpse of his glazed eyes, and the foolish words that had escaped his feverish lips,—proved more than he could patiently endure. He was resolved that Peter's disgrace should be kept secret, if possible, so his indignation sought another vent.

"Why were you sitting at that window?" he asked accusingly. His voice came harsh and unnatural, full of meaning. His words were really not a question, but an accusation. And an accusation of what? Was it reasonable to attack Mary because she had desired a glimpse of her lover's face? Will's voice committed this offense, and Mary could find no excuse for him, since she had never suspected that she was loved by Peter's brother.

She understood precisely what his tone implied, and in her excited and supersensitive state, it came as an insult. She did not know whether to take the question at its literal worth, and reply with assumed indifference, or to let him see that she was deeply offended by his insinuation. The more she thought of it, the more grave seemed the other's affront, so it ended by her saying nothing. She turned her back upon him and started toward the house.

Will bitterly rued the luxury of self-expression. He hastened forward and overtook her near the door. "Mary!" he pleaded. "Mary!"

That was all he could say. Mary, her head erect, her form at its straightest, paused with no ill grace of common anger, but in the self-poise of an offended goddess. She waited to hear what he might say, but he had already delivered himself of the sum-total of his eloquence.

"Mary!" he repeated despairingly, seizing her hand in great agitation. Mary sought to draw coldly away, but his clasp was so convulsive that she was compelled to exert undignified force. She had not freed herself when the door opened, and Goldie Pickens looked out.

"What is the meaning of *this?*" Goldie demanded in a low, thrilling voice. "Mary Eden, it is past *two o'clock!*"

"I think, Miss Pickens," said Mary, trying to speak calmly, "that you are almost as good as a night-alarm."

The young man stood bewildered at this unexpected advent. Mary darted into the house and fled upstairs, leaving him with Goldie.

"Shall I close the door?" asked Goldie politely.

"Miss Goldie," said Will desperately, "Mary saw me drive by, and came out to ask what was the matter. I wouldn't tell her about Peter, and she doesn't understand, and was unkind to me; but if she understood, it would be different."

"Mr. William," said Goldie judiciously, "what I saw would not seem to bear out your statement that Mary was at all *unkind* to you. Good-night, sir."

Goldie sadly but firmly closed the door upon him, and betook herself to the repose of the innocent.

The next morning, on coming down to breakfast, the music-teacher announced to Mrs. Eden in a gentle but inflexible voice, "Mrs. Eden, I have decided to leave your house."

Mrs. Eden, taken aback at being thus forestalled, began in some confusion, "Well, Miss Goldie, I had already——"

"You will remember," Goldie interrupted, "that

when I came to board with you, it was with the understanding that I might terminate our relation at any moment. Indeed, you yourself made that a condition. I desire to terminate that relation to-day. Please put a little more sugar in my coffee than you did yesterday."

"Miss Goldie," said Mary, as she cut the steak, preparatory to serving, "in regard to what passed last night———"

"It is useless," said Goldie fixedly, "to try to dissuade me. It has become a matter of conscience with *me*, to depart; and when my *conscience* is involved, there is but one side to any question."

"Far be it from me, Miss Goldie," said Mrs. Eden, "to oppose your conscience, particularly when it prompts you to leave us, as a boarder. I shall always wish you well, but———"

"And I," said Goldie, "forgive everything."

"Miss Goldie," Mary politely inquired, "what have you to forgive?"

"Don't beg me to stay," cried Goldie, in distress; "it can do no good."

"We won't," Mary assured her. "Are you ready for your meat?"

"Let me add this before we move to a more cheerful theme," said Mrs. Eden earnestly. "I urge you, Miss Goldie, not to go to the hops so long as you lead the choir."

"Mrs. Eden," said Goldie quietly, "there are other things worse than dancing." She looked meekly at Mrs. Eden with her blue eye, cast a shaft at Mary from her black orb, and drooped her creamy lids in resignation.

Having packed her belongings, Goldie put on her

hat and sallied forth like a knight of olden times in quest of new adventures. She bent her slender feet in the direction of the home of genius and sensibility, and so, in due time, reached the door of the man most likely to take sides against the Thornberrys. Cousin Elizabeth responded to her timid ring, but Goldie made little of Cousin Elizabeth.

"Is this Mrs. McCormack?" she asked, rather coolly. "May I see Mr. Waldo McCormack on business? I am Miss Pickens."

Waldo McCormack heard the constrained voice from his literary retreat, and entered the room,—the front door opened directly into the parlor, with no red tape in the way of hallways. Mrs. McCormack hesitated whether to go or stay. Unfortunately the pale, thin woman with the great startled eyes had not yet discovered a secret back-door to her husband's mind, through which she might creep to find out what was going on in there. It usually happened that her course of action was not the one the literary light would have marked out for her.

Waldo's thin legs advanced toward the visitor with something like eagerness, and his massive head was energetic with welcome. "Miss Goldie!" he cried. "What a pleasure! Do be seated."

Goldie sat down and Waldo sat facing her. Mrs. McCormack hovered.

The music-teacher came to the point with childlike frankness and appealing plaintiveness. "Mr. McCormack, I want to come here to board. Oh, don't, don't refuse me! To live under the same roof with real genius would be the experience of my life. I am without a refuge,—cast into the street. Do not leave me shelterless."

"I thought," Mrs. McCormack ventured, "that you were boarding at Polly Eden's."

Goldie paid no attention to the wife. "To think that I might lodge near you, Mr. McCormack, as if I were in touch with an Emerson or a Plato—do not deny me! Please, please!" She clasped her little hands and looked up at him with seraphic meekness.

"Really, my dear young friend," said Waldo, with heavy deliberation, "this takes me so by surprise,— though I do not deny that your appreciative presence would be grateful to me and a blessing to my wife—you would no doubt be company to my wife——"

Goldie interrupted: "And you could read me one of your great works from the manuscript. What an event to boast of in my old age! Do not tell me you have no masterpieces in manuscript, for Mr. Timothy Thornberry told me you had *ever* so many, that you couldn't get printed."

"Who said that?" exclaimed Waldo, turning red, and stiffening.

Goldie, fearing that she had overshot the mark, in thus turning aside to give the captain a good turn, resumed hastily: "But the world is so unappreciative! If I, in my humble sphere, have found it so, how much more you, in your exalted plane. If I could only write one book! If Captain Thornberry was right, it merely proves that you are in the company of the truly great whom, Mr. McCormack, the world has never appreciated, while living."

Goldie's voice was so powerful in its feeling, and her face so religious in its exaltation, that Waldo instinctively murmured, "Amen!" Somewhat embarrassed at this display of piety, he said hastily, "Yes, you may come to us."

"But, Mr. McCormack," said his wife timidly, "the practising on the piano—for Miss Pickens will want to bring her piano—how can you meditate through the five-finger exercises?"

"Oh, Mrs. McCormack!" cried Goldie, in great distress, "do not tell me that you *object* to my coming!" She clasped her hands as if to ward off the blow.

"It is enough," said Waldo, frowning at his wife. "The music will have the power, perhaps, to soothe ah—er—my breast."

"Oh, joy!" Goldie exclaimed, giving Waldo a look of such affectionate gratitude that he felt toward her at once as a father, or elder brother, or cousin, or at least something near and precious. She went on with inspiring simplicity: "I hardly know whether or not to tell you why I have left Mrs. Eden's. Perhaps it would be best for me never to mention it as long as I live. But I am a woman, and we are not so magnanimous as you men. Poor, poor, dear Mrs. Eden! How my heart bleeds for her! Mr. McCormack, had any one told me —— But I must say no more."

"No, my child," said Waldo gently, "speak on, and do not think to surprise me; *I* know the Thornberrys."

"But do they," said Goldie, with a gasp. "What will you say when I tell you that last night—at two o'clock —hearing a stealthy sound on the stairs, I came out of my room—I heard something in the yard—I called for Mary at her room door—that door was open and Mary was gone—had not touched her bed the whole night. I hurried downstairs and opened the front door, for it was already ajar, and there stood Mary and William, holding each other's hands, and gazing into each other's eyes. When they found that I had discovered them, Mary broke away from her lover in violent agitation—she spoke a few biting, insulting words to me, and ran into the house to hide her blushes of—of—— What she said to me I shall never forget, but I can forgive; this morning I told her that I forgave everything, I said to Mary——" Here Goldie burst into dry sobs and hid her face in her handkerchief.

"If there is any truth in this," exclaimed Elizabeth, trembling violently, "you have distorted it, Miss Pickens."

"Mrs. McCormack," exclaimed Waldo severely, "do not insult my friends, if you please, in my own house. Turn your attacks upon me, Mrs. McCormack,—I can personally bear any insult. But when it comes to denouncing my friends, I beg to remind you, madam, that I am master here."

"And I will remind you," cried Elizabeth wildly, "that I am a Thornberry."

"That," said Waldo coldly, "I am never suffered to forget. This is not seemly. Enough. Miss Goldie has related what she saw; perhaps it can be satisfactorily explained,—to a Thornberry. As for me, I want no explanation, nor will I listen to any. I care nothing about it. I can not, Mrs. McCormack, disturb my mind, nor have others disturb it. Can I write poetry?" cried Waldo, with powerful appeal, "while my mind is distracted by the petty troubles of commonplace people?"

"Mr. McCormack," said Goldie, "I see, now, that it was very wrong for me to relate this dreadful story. If I have destroyed some noble idea in your brain as it lay there in the germ, what shall I do?"

"Do not give way to remorse, young friend," said Waldo, with grave magnanimity, "you did not realize the consequences. This subject must never be mentioned to me again, nor any other that causes my wife so far to forget herself. Elizabeth, show Miss Goldie that front room upstairs. Let her piano be placed against yonder wall. I shall retire to recompose my mind."

As sensitive as was Waldo McCormack, his mind was composed long before Peter's. Roused from drunken stupor to find himself at Winthrop's country home, the young man's distress was pitiable. His memory of the hop with its wine-supper aftermath, faded off into gray shadows that deepened to impenetrable black. At the country home, he saw no one but Winthrop, who gave the scanty information that he had been brought thither by his brothers. That was all Peter learned. Later, he could not summon the resolution to mention the disgraceful affair to Will or Oscar, but he understood Oscar's general bearing of stern disapproval, and Will's pathetic attitude of dazed awe.

He resented both. After all, one lapse from the path of sobriety was no criminal matter. His grandparents did not know the truth; his daily companions had not heard of it. Being no moralist for the morals' sake, Peter could not regard his conduct as a vital matter, save as it might affect Goldie. His getting drunk had merely shown himself unused to strong drink,—a virgin soil for champagne. He had taken part in the wine-supper as a man of the world,—say, as a prince. The excitement of Goldie's *"I love you"* had driven him from glass to glass. But what had happened after the world faded out of his eyes? Did Oscar and Will find him in the hall? Who took Goldie home? But above everything else, what did Goldie think of him now? Had he slain her love on the night of its confession?

He sought out Atterton Thornberry for comfort and advice, but Winthrop's son was beyond giving either. Goldie had done her work too well. The information that his father meditated disinheriting him, and that his favorite cousin, Mrs. Eden, was conniving with the widower to spy upon his actions, so far from making Atterton circumspect, drove him to reckless bravado. To a cautious and calculating spirit, Goldie's hints would have brought a far different result. But Atterton was not one to be guided by considerations of prudence.

"They are spying upon me, to see if I will be good," so ran his thoughts. "All right. I'll show 'em something! Who wants their rotten money?" Every time his mind was overwhelmed by the thought of Mrs. Eden's discussing the scheme with Goldie Pickens—which had been implied rather than expressed by that young lady's words—the young man felt an added pang of shame, and a fiercer impulse toward revolt. Why should Mrs. Eden lay bare such sacred family matters to aliens?

For several days following the hop, Atterton kept himself in a condition that offered no aid to Peter. All day he hung about the club-rooms where imported Missouri whisky was dealt out to the minority of the prohibition district. When he began to sober up, his brooding over fancied wrongs sent him after more drink. He wanted no doubt to linger in his father's mind as to his own determined plan of life. He scorned false pretenses. Let the property be made over to Mrs. Eden as soon as possible; let the time of spying and distrust come to an end; let himself be "proved,"—

to use their own word, with which Goldie had taunted him. And then, when all was ended, he would go out into the world and show himself independent of anybody's money.

At last Peter sought Goldie at Waldo McCormack's, not troubling himself to inquire why she had moved; nothing interested him except Goldie; the setting was immaterial. He called in the evening and found her sitting at the feet of Waldo McCormack. Mrs. McCormack was still hovering. Waldo was reading aloud.

"I have been wondering why you haven't come," said Goldie gravely. "But Cousin Waldo,—he lets me call him so,—is just starting on the eleventh chapter of his last book."

"Shall I go on?" Waldo interrupted, frowning at Peter, and fluttering the leaves impatiently.

"Oh, yes, *yes!*" cried Goldie eagerly. "Peter, I want to speak with you, but you can see this is no time for that. Come to-morrow at ten——"

"But I shall be in the bank," murmured Peter, heavy-hearted.

"Oh, very well," said Goldie, with quiet coldness.

"I'll come," said Peter quickly.

"Peter," ventured his Cousin Elizabeth, "how are Aunt Polly and Uncle Tim?"

"Good-evening, then, Peter," said Waldo, "unless you think you could be interested by beginning so far over in this work."

Peter departed very sad, as regarded Goldie, and yet not without an almost insensible lightening of the heart. After he had gone home, he wondered dully, as sometimes a wretched spirit may, what it was that had pleased him. Then he remembered Cousin Waldo's book, and his escape from hearing it. He smiled with a certain grimness.

The next morning, punctually at ten, the First National Bank of Core City saw not its Thornberry. Peter found Goldie alone in the parlor, idly sounding a key of her piano here and there. She did not rise from the stool, but held up her hand as soon as Peter had closed the door behind him. "Stay where you are," she said, in a low voice.

Peter remained like a culprit, holding his hat in a nervous grasp. "Goldie——" he said.

"Back!" cried Goldie dramatically. "Back, Peter!" He paused, as if rooted to the floor. "I can not forget that night, if you can," said Goldie severely.

"But Goldie—but won't you forgive me? I love you so—you can't imagine how much I love you—forgive me!"

"I am a Christian, I trust," said Goldie. "I have forgiven everybody, but, oh, Peter, I do not trust you, —after what took place that night. But I am going to give you an opportunity to redeem yourself."

"Thank you, darling. May I not take your dear hand?"

"No, Peter, do not touch me. Back, Peter! When you have shown that you are the man I still believe you may be—then—perhaps——"

"But *do* you love me, Goldie? Show that you forgive me, sweetheart."

"Can you speak so to me, after what happened in the park?" asked Goldie mournfully.

"Goldie," said Peter desperately, "what did happen?"

"I was so trusting," murmured Goldie, hiding her face with her hands. "You asked me to walk home through the park. When we came to the well, we sat down upon the curbing. I was so simple and unsuspecting! How could I know you were not yourself?"

"But what did I do?" faltered the other, a cold perspiration bedewing his solemn face.

Goldie looked up at him, then put her hands over her eyes. "We rested there upon the curbing," she answered, "and we talked about the moon. It was very bright. And you called me 'little wife,' but almost at once, you lay right down, and went fast asleep. You were drunk—oh, you were *drunk!*"

"O Lord!" groaned Peter, wringing his hands.

"I felt," said Goldie, as she hid her face, "that I, innocent and trusting, had been insulted. How could I ever look the world in the face after that? But," added Goldie, rising, meek heroism pictured upon her face, "I shall take up my life and its duties. I belong to you, but you must first prove yourself worthy. Peter, do not touch my hand. *You* are not worthy. *Think on these things!*"

"But what can I do?" Peter faltered.

"You may write to me," said Goldie. "I promise to read all you write. But do not come here for two weeks, two whole weeks. Thus I shall test your self-mastery. Ah, you won me, Peter, but lost yourself. Now go. You should be at the bank."

Peter realized the importance of a speedy return to his place of business, and made no longer delay. After all, affairs were not so bad as they might have been. He was to call in two weeks, and in the meantime he could pour out his soul upon paper. In running to town, he encountered a man hastening even more rapidly in the opposite direction. Peter hardly acknowledged the shrill greeting of the pedestrian. It was his cousin, George Nicodemus.

Nothing but a case of urgent necessity could have carried George Nicodemus thus hastily past the young Thornberry "in the bank," and to none other could necessity so naturally direct him as to Mrs. Polly Eden. He found that busy lady engaged in the laborious process of "making up bread," and as her baking was upon a large scale, the kneading was as much as she and Mary could well do.

"Come right in, Cousin George," called Mrs. Eden, as the little dried-up man of forty peered through the kitchen door. "We've got our hands in the dough, and I'm glad you came around to the back, for we've disconnected the front doorbell."

Mary added heartily, "Now that our boarder's gone, we don't have to get dinner unless we want to, Uncle Groner being away."

"Cousin Polly," said the little man anxiously, "I hate to bother you, but mother's had another spell—the worst one yet—and, oh, won't you come at once? She wants you, and I—and I can't do without you."

"Poor Cousin John Ann!" exclaimed Mrs. Eden, hastily scraping her hard hands with the back of the iron caseknife.

"I'll go on with the work," said Mary, hiding her weariness. In an incredibly short time, Mrs. Eden's apron had disappeared, and she was hurrying with Nicodemus along the street. Nicodemus was genuinely alarmed about his mother, but he could not help taking a sense of pleasure in Mrs. Eden's willingness to pass through town by his side. Since his eclipse in the state's prison, no Thornberry, with the exception of Hodgins, had cared to stand by his side in the pillory. He made the most of Hodgins' friendship, but he was aware that it did not furnish a step to respectability;

and it warmed his heart that Mrs. Eden should go with him as readily as she had with Winthrop, to nurse the lady who had called no Thornberry "cousin."

Mrs. Mulkey saw them pass. She called Gladys Lucile to the window. "Come here, daughter; I want you to look at that Mrs. Eden. Did you ever see a woman of a respectable family go as she does?"

Gladys Lucile understood that by "go," her mother did not refer to any specific movement of limbs, but to the garments that hid those aids to locomotion. She gazed in silence.

"Look at that hair," said Mrs. Mulkey. "Look at that skirt a-draggling like a wet feather! Why won't some women keep themselves neat?"

"We are obliged to excuse a great deal in creatures of her class," said her husband, with grave magnanimity. "As we say on the Continent, she belongs to the peasantry, the lower stratum. I wish, indeed, that her attire were the most reprehensible feature of the poor woman; but Miss Goldie Pickens has given me an insight into her character such as I could never have dreamed possible in a writer of religious poetry. I am sorry we ever stopped at the house of one so dissimulating; but I congratulate myself on the fact that I did not stay there long!"

Gladys Lucile, as usual, was silent; she returned to the book from which she had been called.

"She says nothing," her mother often remarked, "but she thinks a great deal."

In the meantime, the object of their criticism, happily unconscious that her hair was being looked at, passed on with hurried feet. George Nicodemus lived in the largest house on the east end. It was a green frame building trimmed in white, crowned by a square cupola painted a light yellow. About halfway between foundation and roof, a broad stripe of black cut the building half in two. It was a house with character, a house that readily claimed the most errant attention, and was known, not so much as "the Nicodemus house," as the "big green house," or "the house with the yellow cupola," albeit the feature thus designated was given the general pronunciation "cupilow."

Nicodemus conducted Mrs. Eden to the sick-room, and, having dismissed the nurse, installed his cousin in the chair at one side of the pillow, while he stood at the other. His mother, who was about seventy years old, lay white and spent, having passed through a season of severe suffering. Her hair lay about her like drifted snow. The sunken eyes were closed, and the thin form had the stillness of death. As George looked down upon the wasted frame, his face seemed to alter strangely. His forehead still beat backward to get under cover of his short black hair; his chin remained practically swallowed up in his throat; and his nose stood forth as sharp and keen as on the day of the funeral of Winthrop's wife. Moreover, his skin was just as dried and lean, and his form as insignificant. It was, then, no physical change that made itself manifest to Polly Eden. He seemed to have sloughed off that part of himself that had taken him to a place no Thornberry mentioned; and he stood by his mother's side with the undisguised love of a child.

When the old woman, at last, opened her eyes, they fell upon Mrs. Eden, and their look brightened. The lips moved, but the voice was not strong enough to be heard. It was strange what a difference it made to the pallid, wrinkled face, when the great brown and ever-young eyes opened. It was as if the soul within the aged body looked from the windows to say, "I am still here!"

"Don't try to say anything, mother," said George softly; "it only tires you. I can hear what you whisper." He sat upon the edge of the bed and put his ear to the thin lips. Then he nodded at Mrs. Eden. "She's mighty glad you came, Cousin Polly. She says if you'll stay with her to-night she'll be able to get along after that."

"Bless your heart, Cousin John Ann!" cried Mrs. Eden, rubbing the cold hand, "I'll stay as many nights as you need me."

Mrs. Nicodemus whispered.

"No, you're not, mother!" George protested. Then he explained to Mrs. Eden. "She says she's a troublesome old woman. But only the Lord knows what on earth I'd do without her. She's all I've got in the world."

Again the old mother whispered laboriously.

"Now, don't say that, mother!" cried the son, in distress. "You know I'm not ready to give you up. You've got to stay—you must stay till I make you proud of me. That's all I'm living for. Do you want to make it a failure?"

The bright eyes looked at him beseechingly and the lips fluttered with eagerness. "No, mother," he returned, "I am not doing it for God. I'm doing it for you. I broke your heart, and I mean to make you proud of me before you die. You wait. I'll show you!"

"Cousin George," said Mrs. Eden, "she is already proud of you. See how bravely you have taken up your life—this home you have built for your mother—the canning factory you own—the fruit-shipping you superintend—the apple-butter and cider industry. No man in Core City would be more missed than you; you have built up its business. And no son is a better son than you. And all those mines you are going to develop——"

"And you know, Cousin Polly," George interrupted eagerly, "that I paid back every penny of that money. . . . Nobody can say what I have now is gotten in a wrong way."

"Nobody!" cried Mrs. Eden.

"And yet," said George, "you know very well, Cousin Polly, that the Thornberrys give me the cold shoulder —all except Hodge; and Hodge, poor fellow, is no 'count. When Cousin Tim gave that supper to Cousin Waldo McCormack, was I invited? I bring money to Core City, and I give employment to men and women and young folks, what with paring and drying and canning, and 'stomping' on the apples to make apple-butter, and the like, to say nothing of the apple-screens, and the barreling. But, socially, I'm a dead man. But it's going to be different. I'm going to take my place in society. I'm going to make mother proud."

His mother whispered something.

"Cousin Polly," said George, with illuminated face, "lean over here; I want you to hear that." Mrs. Eden bent down to the almost motionless lips.

"I *am* proud of my boy," came the faint whisper.

"Did you hear it? I can remember the time when I thought never to hear those lips speak such words. When my wife had deserted me, and the court had given her our only child—little George—and nobody wanted to speak to me on the street. . . . But I came right back to the Thornberry nest, and I built up business; and I'm going to build up socially, you'll find."

When Mrs. Eden had waited upon the old lady with tender care, and the latter had fallen peacefully asleep, George beckoned his cousin from the room. "Let's sit here at the open window," he said. "I want to talk a little, and we can peep in at mother every minute or so. Pretty nice window-seat, eh, Cousin Polly? No expense spared to make everything comfortable. When they were painting the house I said, 'Go ahead, use all the paint the walls will hold,' and they did it, too. Did I understand you to say your boarder has left you?"

"Yes, she's gone to board at Cousin Waldo's."

No one ever thought of referring to the new boarding-place as "Elizabeth's."

"That young lady,—that Miss Goldie Pickens, now," said George meditatively, "she certainly makes a creditable impression. Now, I'm not religious, Cousin Polly, and don't know as I'll ever get to be, though likely as not; but do you know, looking at Miss Goldie's face—just the looking at it, is the same to me as—as—er—prayer."

"Are you acquainted with Miss Goldie, Cousin George?"

"I think I know her pretty well. I take it, she's about thirty years old; I'm forty, your own age, Cousin Polly, unless, maybe, you're a few months older'n me. Not but what you look older than that, for you do; but the world has used us both hard, though you not deserving it."

"Cousin George," said Mrs. Eden, in the voice of one resolved at any cost to do her duty, "I fear you've a mistaken view of Miss Goldie. Far be it from me to point out the faults of any one. But you speak as if you desired to know this music-teacher better."

"Know her better? Why! I desire to marry her;

and that's what I mean to do," cried George, with the charming hopefulness of the Thornberrys, handed down directly from his mother. "But as to her faults, I'd like to hear of them, if you please; the more faults she has, the more accessible does she prove. Now, Cousin Polly, you know I'm visibly handicapped, and I can't expect to marry perfection."

"I never dreamed that you expected to marry at all, after your great sorrow. Can't you leave marrying alone? Look how happy I am, since my dear one left me; for is he not waiting for me? Every day that passes brings us closer together. It's like marking off the calendar at school—life's just a school where we learn the primer and the elementaries of eternity. And besides, even if you are desiring to marry, have you a right? Your wife is living. Remember the scriptural law. And as to Miss Goldie,—she is not at all like a prayer—unless it be externally. But what she really is, I can not put into words, it is all so vague and insinuating. To call her a hypocrite or impostor or deceiver, is to make me coarse. It would seem that, to correctly describe her character, some words ought to be invented for the purpose; there may be some in the foreign languages."

George Nicodemus knelt, one knee upon the window-seat, and looked forth upon the world thoughtfully, his hands in his trousers pockets. He seemed smaller than ever; his straight hair was ruffled about his ears, and this, together with his projecting elbows and his beak-like nose, gave him the appearance of a bird about to fly forth in quest of prey.

"Cousin Polly," he said feelingly, "you are a good woman if there ever was one. Yes, life *is* a school; and what with me playing hookey, so to say, from the moral playgrounds, I can speak with knowledge of the house of correction; though as you know, Cousin Polly, I meant to pay back every cent of that money before it was found out, and had I been as wise as I was earnest in my speculations, and if people hadn't blown so much, there would never have been any smoke. Anyway, I paid for it with time and money, and now I put all that from me." Although it was a habit for him to say he had put his past behind him, he seemed to be always conscious of its looking over his shoulder to peep into the faces of his friends. He went on hastily:

"Enough of that. As to Miss Goldie,—well, I have no doubt she's all you think, for I know you, Cousin Polly, and I'll swear to any word you say. I'm sorry you can't find the English word for me to swear by, but I'll stand by any or all the languages, living or dead. The fact that she has faults is mighty encouraging to *me*. I'm not much afraid of Peter. He's younger than she is, and too good for her, and he hasn't but a very little money of his own. Marrying is the only way I can see to reinstate me in society. Just going with business men can't meet the problem. It takes women to make you respectable. You say she's not like a prayer, except external? Well, that's all about a prayer I know, anyhow. I'm always wondering what's inside of the man's heart that's praying, and if he's thinking of God he's talking to, or us he's talking at. Now, I ain't posted but a very little on the Bible, and I don't know as it covers my case or not. But when my first wife leaves me, keeps my only child till he dies, not letting me know when he dies, then ups and marries a Chicago stockman, such as she has done recent,—why, to be plain, Cousin Polly, I'm not going to Inspiration to find out if I'm free."

CHAPTER XIV

"I AIN'T got no excuses to make," Hodgins Thornberry told Mr. Mulkey, on returning from his camping-out. "You tell me Jim Coalwin wouldn't move your house for you. Well, that's for *him* to say. I'm willing to go ahead with it in the morning—not to-day, Mr. Mulkey, excuse *me*. I want to plan. That old rope has laid out in the wind and rain till I misdoubt but she'll bust when the strain comes. What I like to see is a rope that stands true when the strain comes. Some don't. Why, a rope is jest like a man! They is some that you can't put no dependencies in."

"Ah, very true," said Mr. Mulkey, in his deepest bass.

"I'll tell you how it is," said Hodgins, lazily inhaling from his cigarette, "if you'll buy a new rope, your business will soon be did."

"But," objected the other, "how do I know you'll move the house, even though I *do* furnish the machinery?"

"Well, that's so," rejoined the other, affably. "I don't know how it is,—I never had no energy a-tall, seemed like. Some has, but I ain't one of 'em. I'm going to give up this house-moving business, anyhow. Most of us fellows jest lays eround till the apple-crop comes due, and then we can make enough, what with the canning factory and the other institootions, to keep us through the year in a kinder concomitose state—I don't know as I get the word as it is in the standards, but I lays little claim to scholarship. My wife, she has made such a point of my finishing with your house, that it must be did; for when my wife makes a point of anything, she goes to digging with it. So if you'll buy that rope, senator, I'll give you my word, I'll do the job to-morrow, if I am spared."

"But how do I know you will keep your word? You broke it before."

"Well, that's so," Hodgins agreed, looking regretfully at the magisterial Mulkey. "I wish they was some way to convince you, but I reckon they ain't. All right, I'll bring my old rope to-morrow; but I ain't saying it'll stand the strain."

Much to Mr. Mulkey's surprise, Hodgins actually appeared the next morning at an early hour, with a wagonload of ancient contrivances, many of them patched, and others in need of patching. By noon, Hodgins had succeeded in collecting half a dozen good-natured fellows to assist in the operations. By three o'clock, the ropes were connected to the main-rope of the windlass, and a venerable white horse, the soul of gentleness and decrepitude, was hitched to the windlass.

It was a very warm afternoon in late June. The men were practically stripped to the waist, the sweat showed upon the horse's hinder parts even before he bent to his task, and the tongues of several dogs belonging to the party were airing themselves extensively. Gladys Lucile and her mother were in the house.

"They might's well stay in there's not," Hodgins had remarked; "they won't know when they're a-goin'." Mr. Mulkey, like a gloomy officer of the law, patrolled his premises, disapproving of the crowd of citizens momentarily swelling before the yard.

Waldo McCormack and Goldie Pickens came along the sidewalk, and, skirting the throng of spectators, stepped over some of the foundation-stones, and gained a cleared corner of the side yard. In crossing the stones, Waldo had held both of Goldie's hands. They often took walks together. The young lady continued, of course, to call the author "cousin." "Do you know," she said to him once, "you seem very near to me?"

It was not possible for the author to describe his feelings toward the shy music-teacher; but he had no desire to do so. It was a pleasure to him when Goldie came near, and he felt a lack of something when she went from his presence. There was a charm about her face and form and coyness and shrinking humility, that appealed to him as a poem or as a woman, he knew not which. Never for an instant did it enter his mind to be untrue to his wife,—in fact, he did not think of his wife while with Goldie. What had his wife to do with this sweet friendship? She could never have understood his exalted emotions on holding Goldie's supple hand.

On the present occasion, the author murmured, when he and Goldie stood apart from the vulgar herd: "I was wondering, Goldie, as I led you over the stones, what the philosophy might be of the joy I experienced when, in a purely physical sense, our beings were linked by our hands. These hands are nothing, they are no real part of the Ego. That delicate spirit which shrines itself in your—er—symmetrical form,—what has it to do with hands?"

"I understand you," said Goldie, "as far, at least, as one of my limited capacity am able to grasp your higher thoughts. I think an explanation is to be found in physical soul. There *is* a physical soul, do you not think? Our physical souls meet when our hands are clasped."

"It is a naïve idea," said Waldo McCormack thoughtfully. "Yes, physical soul. That is a definite concept."

A rude shout of laughter interrupted him, and he looked up angrily. Thus, in ordinary life, does the commonplace jar upon the sublime. Four of Hodgins Thornberry's men were in readiness to assist and guide the rollers—in case they rolled. The other two were watching to see if the house moved. Hodgins sat upon the ground under the framework of the windlass, preventing the rope from winding upon itself. The strain had at last come upon the old rope.

There was a moment of intense suspense. Hodgins cried excitedly, "Now, boys, either the house will move or the rope 'll bust." Hodgins, however, failed to take into account the fact that the strain came not only upon the rope, but upon the old white horse. The horse stood still. Hodgins held a long stick. He leaned over as far as he could, and hit at the horse's legs. He was barely able to reach the near hind leg. The horse held up that leg, out of range, and stood his ground. The spectators laughed again.

"I must go," said Waldo abruptly. "I find that such scenes deteriorate the sensitive stuffs of the creative faculties. I remember one year, following the street carnival, I could not think a thought, for weeks, that did not seem besprinkled with confetti."

Waldo was aware that George Nicodemus had approached them, and was looking for recognition, but the great head held itself like that of a lion which scorns the mouse its claws might crush.

"Cousin Waldo," said George, stiffening himself and pulling more of his neck above his collar, "how is the new book progressing?"

Waldo McCormack reddened in shame and anger. "I do not acknowledge the cousinship," he said shortly. "I bid you good-afternoon——" this to Goldie.

"Git ap, there!" cried Hodgins, chuckling. "Here! one of you boys come drive him, if you ain't too busy watching the house move."

"Jake," said one to the other, "*you* go."

The man addressed as Jake sat down as if he were the victim of a paralytic stroke.

When Waldo McCormack turned his back and started away on his long, thin legs, Goldie knew he would not turn around; she accordingly acted with promptitude,—her custom when people's backs were turned. She addressed Nicodemus with sweet cheeriness, for his warehouses and canning factories ever appealed to her poetic side.

"We meet again," said Goldie, almost archly.

Her tone and look were like balm to his sensitive spirit. She must know of his former enforced retirement from the free activities of life; nevertheless she always met him with apparent pleasure. "I have been wanting to see you ever since our last meeting," said Nicodemus, turning his beaked face upon her, as if with half an intention of taking a friendly peck. "Your music has delighted me,—and your spirituality. You have done a difficult thing, Miss Pickens; you have consolidated the choir marvelously, by making the most rampant of those who stood for concert pitch think you favored concert pitch, and by convincing those who had conscience for low 'c' that your conscience is lying *along*side of theirs."

Goldie darted a swift, startled look at the shrewd bird. Her heart suddenly stood still.

Before she could speak, he hastened on. "Oh, you know Bill Thornberry, don't you?"

"William? I have met him, sir," said Goldie, in a voice that slightly trembled.

"He had a fight a little while ago. I was coming through town—my mother's been sick a week, and I was staying with her—mighty fine old lady—I want you to know her, Miss Pickens."

"Thank you," said Goldie faintly. Without knowing why, she felt a little fear as this man kept his keen, deep-set eyes upon her face. Did he really understand her secret nature? Impossible! She rallied. "Fight! William looks so mild and peaceable!"

"He didn't look peaceable when I saw him! As I come up to Cousin Tim's grocery store,—all these Thornberrys are kin of mine,—my mother was one of 'em,—William—Bill, *I* call 'im,—was setting in front o' the door, same's an old hen. A young fellow—one of those Lee boys—steps up and says he, 'Bill——'—well, I disremember the exact words, but as how *you*, Miss Pickens, had seen him and Mary Eden a-courting in the yard at two o'clock at night, and as how it was all over the town from your telling it everywhere—and Lee, he wasn't meaning any particular harm in speaking to Bill, he had been drinking with Atterton Thornberry (another cousin of mine), and thought he was saying something smart. Well, when they picked up Lee, and carried him away, I told Bill the fellow was half-drunk, and Bill, he said he acted before he knew the other's condition. So it was patched up,—and so was Lee."

"How shocking!" cried Goldie.

"Yes," said George Nicodemus suavely. "Well,

I've known Mary Eden and her mother before her, from the infancy of both of 'em; I was raised with Polly, and I helped raise Mary, I might say, not that I claim I imparted any of her disposition. Miss Pickens, did you ever look through a canning factory? It's too early now to show it at work, but I'd like to explain it to as intelligent a lady as yourself. Let me show it to you some day."

"I should be charmed," said Goldie, with something like a blush.

"Why, thank you, hearty!" cried the other. "I'm a mighty lonely sort of a chap except for my mother,—not as old as I look, you see, so I don't feel like quitting the world just yet. I haven't got anybody to lean on,—did you ever study much on Christian Science? *I* haven't much; but if you have you'll know that I'm a free man. I haven't any family but my mother. My son he died, and so did my wife; she died *in science*, I may say. My 'mortal mind' tells me she's a-living som'ers as another man's wife, but I've cut off all my mortal mind as appertains to my matrimonial history. Have you seen any of our Arkinsaw hills hereabouts, Miss Pickens? We've got a series of splendid caves and springs within easy driving distance. Now, look a-here; how'd you like to drive out, some day, and view our natural resources?"

"Very much, indeed," said Goldie, still as in a dream.

An interruption occurred. The rope broke. It was necessary to tie the two parts together, but in order to do so, it had to be slacked from the windlass, and it could not be slacked unless the old white horse would back. This the horse refused to consider, perhaps reflecting, with his old horse-sense, that he had gained his ground with too much labor to retrace his steps.

hile Hodgins was battling with this difficulty,
s for weapons, and ill-digested thoughts for am-
tion, Atterton Thornberry espied Goldie. He had
 standing among the spectators, jeering at the
. He pushed through the crowd and came into
ard. The sight of Goldie had sobered him a
 deal, but he was not yet sober enough to be
et.

[ow'dy, Cousin George!" said Atterton to Nico-
s. Then he at once addressed Goldie with, "I've
ht a good deal about what you told me that night,
 Pickens, but my mind hasn't been exactly clear
 few days." He laughed recklessly. He was
ngly handsome, and the burning eyes, but for their
 glint, would have added a touch of winning
n.

/e had better not talk here," said Goldie hastily.
)h, I don't want to talk anywhere," said Atterton
y. He had never liked Goldie, and the deeper he
 under the influence of liquor, the deeper grew his
ion. "Is it the truth that Cousin Polly told you
ather means to disinherit me if—if I——"

f you are not a good boy?" Goldie helped him. "I
orry, sir, that you didn't heed my caution."

)h, thank you," Atterton laughed. "And they
pying on me to see if I'll suit my actions to their
, are they?"

 am sorry you have not done so," said Goldie.

terton thrust his hand into his pocket and tore
 a letter. "Here's a note from Cousin Polly
," he said, "asking me to come to see her." He
 to tear it up into small fragments. "I wish
 tell her," said Atterton, "that this is my answer."
ast the fragments upon the grass. "Go and tell

her, will you?—you are so interested in my affairs!" He laughed out loudly, and hurried away.

"Oh!" said Goldie, "Mr. Mulkey invited me here to watch the house-moving as a diversion, and it has resulted in mortification and insult. I had better go and isolate myself, for it seems I am always making trouble. What's the use of trying to do good in the world? What's the use of anything? I'm always misunderstood and persecuted."

"I make bold to say this, Miss Pickens," said Nicodemus, nodding his head violently,—"do not be offended; I make bold to say that never have I admired the qualities of a woman as I do yours,—not in the same way, I mean. And note this, Miss Pickens; I admire you because I understand you; others admire, but they do not understand. It seems to me that I can enter right into your mind, and watch your motives at play. Let us be friends. *I* understand you; who else does?"

"I do not understand myself," said Goldie, in a low voice. Again she felt that odd, vague sense of fear.

The rope was fastened together, the old horse was in motion; the strain had come once more upon cable, beast and—the public. Suddenly, there was a terrific report. The windlass was torn from its moorings. Bits of wood flew through the air, and cords and ropes whipped about Hodgins' head like living snakes.

Mrs. Mulkey rushed to the open window. "Are we moving?" she called excitedly.

"Oh, no, m'om," said Hodgins cheerfully; "we just busted some of the stobs loose."

At last, Mr. Mulkey's dignity succumbed to anger. "Look here, sir!" he cried, "I am paying you for this time and at an exorbitant rate. I can't afford to spend my money for trifling. It was not obtained by trifling, sir."

Hodgins laid down an iron-tipped stave he had picked up, and reached for his hat, which, in heat of battle, he had discarded. "Then move your old house, yourself," he said with unwonted spirit. "I may be a mule and I reckon I am; but nobody can't drive me a leg!"

Goldie went away from this popular spectacle, still confused. George Nicodemus had not spoken many words to her, yet every word, as she better realized upon reflection, had been most carefully weighed before its utterance. Why had he explained that he held himself free to marry again? Why did he wish to drive her out to the hills, and to show her his canning factory? He had told her plainly that he admired and understood her, and every word had shown that he did understand. In the most insinuating and delicate manner, he had conveyed the fact that he knew Mary to be innocent, that he knew Goldie had willfully traduced her; that he loved Mary as the innocent child he had seen reared from the cradle; yet, though Goldie had spread the false report over town, he still offered her his friendship.

Why? The reason was obvious enough to Goldie's keen perception. This man wanted to marry her. It gave her a vague terror,—this thought that anybody truly understood her nature. So used to dwelling in shadow, to moving in secret, to scheming queer double-turns for her daily bread, or for sympathy, she had thought to live her life thus, known only to herself; and not even to herself fully revealed. Of course, she would marry; but her husband would find her either a saint to be adored with awe, or an incomprehensible mystery of cold, unfeeling calculation. This George Nicodemus understood, and yet admired her. She had hitherto imagined, not without reason, that to gain the liking of people, she must hide the under-currents of her soul. There was no need to hide anything from this man; indeed, it was impossible to hide from him, because his nature intuitively apprehended hers. Yet he admired!

When Goldie reached home, she was still agitated. It was not fear alone that shook her, but a certain strange sense of exultation. It was nothing to her that this man who understood, yet admired, was dried up, little, hawk-faced, and coarse-haired; that he was twelve years her senior, and looked still older. Had he been as handsome as Atterton Thornberry, and as young, it would have been nothing to her, compared with a canning factory, warehouses, and a large mansion. Her first unhappy love, her only passion, had burnt away the materials which, in many hearts, are left for a second kindling; and the warm clasp of a man's hand did not stir her to a responsive thrill as did the cold touch of a dollar. However, her interest in the Thornberry who had once suffered eclipse, was not wholly of a pecuniary nature. It seemed that the one passionate dream of her later life was about to be fulfilled; that some one should know her as she was, and knowing, love.

As the days passed, Atterton Thornberry adhered, in his wild life, to the determination to make his father understand that there was no likelihood of submission. He told himself that he drank, and gambled, and consorted with vicious people, because he had been driven to it. In reality, his conduct was not much different from that he occasionally exhibited at Hot Springs, while "in business." But his conscience was freer.

"Give me another drink," he would say to "the boys," "I am driven to this. I'm a desperate man. I must drown my wrongs." When he had "drowned" them a little deeper, his sense of injury would take on a rich melancholy. "I might have been a better man, if people had left me alone. I am the victim of fate—destiny—kismet. The best friend I had in all the world has failed me. I tried to be a good sort of a chap, you know; I didn't do any one harm. But the flood—what is it Byron says?—the storm—no, the sands—'The last sands of life—where not a flower appears.' Another glass of that, boys, and let's play; let's stake high, and win all, or lose all."

One afternoon, as Atterton, half drunk, a quarter sober, and the remainder of his mind in a state of abeyance, walked down Main Street, he saw his father's carriage standing before the only extensive drygoods store of the town. As it was Saturday, he knew that his sister must be within. He looked through the door and saw not only Ethel, but Winthrop Thornberry. The young man had not seen them for two weeks, and, in a reckless sense of defiance, he was moved to face them and speak out his mind. A bench stood before the building, for the accommodation of those citizens who took their politics and tobacco on the sidewalks. Atterton sat down upon the bench with no defined intention of doing so, and found, much to his surprise, that he could not get up again. He looked at his legs to discover the trouble, but they appeared as usual. While he was pondering upon this mystery, Ethel came out upon the sidewalk and saw him. The bench was opposite the carriage, and, as she hastened from the door of the shop, she deflected her course to the foolish young man. As on all clear-weather Saturdays, the street was thronged with town and country folk, doing the week's shopping, or watching other people at work.

"Brother," said Ethel hastily, as her cheeks burned with shame, "please come home with us. You are breaking father's heart." The passers-by who had nothing else to do, and even those who had, stopped and stared in pleasurable curiosity, to find out a bit of news for kindred detained at home. However Atterton might act, and whatever Ethel might say, it would form unwritten "copy" for those unable to come to town.

Atterton tried to rise,—not that he meant to obey, but that his refusal might be more dignified and impressive. "'Tain't your fault, Eth," he murmured, as his legs failed him. "Go 'way, sis; I'm a wronged man, and the world's all against me,—all, ever' clod of it. Go 'long, dear; leave me to my fate."

Ethel was almost overwhelmed with shame from the staring of men and women who were resolved to lose no look or word. Naturally, she was unsympathetic toward the common and humble, but her brother's debauchery gave to her pride an air of unfeeling coldness that was not an inherent part of it. She lingered beside the bench, for love of father was stronger in her than thought of self.

"Please come, Atterton," she said, in a low voice, as she laid her hand upon his arm. "Father will forgive you."

Atterton, at that, shook her hand away. "Forgive!" he exclaimed bitterly; "maybe *he* will; but *I'll* not. Tell him so; never!"

Ethel hurried to the carriage. She was expecting

her father every moment, and she took the back seat, and stared straight before her, seeing neither friend nor stranger.

Peter Thornberry hurried out of the bank with a sheaf of papers in his hands, but Ethel did not see him as he passed.

Atterton was more observant. "'Lo, there, old fellow!" he said. "Come and sit by me. I'm a discouraged man. They're all against me, Pete."

Peter, heartily ashamed of his cousin, sped by without greeting. "Oh, Pete!" Atterton called. "Pete!" Peter heard him not. Ethel turned impatiently toward the building, but her father did not appear. Instead, Oscar Thornberry came forth. She hastily looked another way.

Oscar, thrilling with joy at the sight of Ethel, was starting toward her, when he espied Atterton. He took in the situation at a glance.

"'Lo, there, Osk!" said Atterton. "How's rest'urnt, eh, old fellow?"

"Let's go and see," said Oscar cheerily. "Come along."

"Can't come," said Atterton ruefully. "Somethin's matter with sidewalk—wobbles, you know."

Oscar put his arm about Atterton and drew him to his feet. "Lean on me," he commanded. "Come along."

"Bless your heart!" murmured Atterton as they labored away. "Youze good S'maritan. That preesh and Levite of a Pete Thornberry, he passh right by, he passh ri',—he passh, he passh——"

"You shut up!" said Oscar briefly, "or I'll jolt you one!"

They were across the street now, and presently vanished from the hungry eyes of Core City. The burning blushes of humiliation gradually died from the sister's cheeks. More like a princess than ever she looked, as with chin slightly lifted, eyes unseeing, and form rigid, she awaited her father's coming. There was no tremor of the lip for the staring loungers to note, no visible shrinking from the sting of disgrace which had laid its lash across her heart. But at sight of her father, who had issued from the shop, suspecting nothing, she felt a great wave of tenderness which threatened to dash a spray of sympathy into her eyes. She suddenly drooped her head, clasping her hands nervously over the lines.

"Well, honey," he said cheerfully, "time to go, I reckon."

He climbed into the front seat and glanced over at the screened-in restaurant. "I'll declare!" he said, smiling, "that boy Oscar has gone away at the busiest time of the day!"

Ethel, who knew that Oscar was even then piloting the unstable Atterton to a back room of the city hotel, pressed her lips closely together. Her bosom heaved convulsively.

"That Oscar Thornberry," Winthrop went on, in a tone of tolerant affection, "will never amount to anything on earth, hey, Ethel?—not in a restaurant, nohow!"

"I think," said Ethel suddenly, "that he's worth a great deal, wherever he is!"

When Oscar had disposed of Atterton, he returned to his place of business to find Mrs. Polly Eden waiting. A fleeting glance told him that Winthrop had driven his daughter away, but Mrs. Eden's troubled face soon banished Ethel from his mind.

"I'm looking for Atterton," she said hurriedly. "I wrote to him that I wanted to have a talk with him, but he didn't come. Some one told me that they saw you, a little while ago——"

"Oh, he's all right," said Oscar beguilingly. "I'll tell him, later on, that you want to see him."

"No, Oscar," said the other, seating herself for a minute upon one of the stools, "I know he is drunk; and I feel sure he won't come to me, because I fancy somebody has been making mischief. Where is he? I want to go and sit by him till he is sober."

"Cousin Polly, he's asleep now; *drunk* asleep. He won't get over it till about midnight, so it isn't to be thought of."

"Take me to him, dear. I will wait by his bedside. Mary is going to your house to stay all night. It's all arranged."

She rose, and Oscar, knowing her well, made no further objection. There was a brief colloquy with the landlord,—an old citizen of Core City,—then Mrs. Eden was installed in the back room of the hotel. It was a small room with an outside door, opening into the back yard, where the refuse-barrels of decaying vegetables stood. The air was close and damp and foul from the fumes of whisky. Atterton lay in heavy insensibility upon a single-bed, dingy in its furnishings. The washstand had its individualized odor of soap and hair-brush, and the little stand-table had another of tobacco-ashes and coal-oil.

"Poor boy!" murmured Mrs. Eden, looking down upon the flushed face. Oscar recalled how he had stood in Winthrop's hall, staring sternly at Peter in a like condition. The tears began to course down her hard-lined cheeks. "Oscar!" she exclaimed, with a sob, "we must save this boy. How bright and cheery he used to be! He was our flashing sunshine. We must save him."

"Maybe *you* can," said Oscar doubtfully. "*I* don't know anything about saving people. It always seems to me that people must be themselves."

"But Atterton is not himself. Look at him—mind and heart both deadened. Only the animal—that's all we see; that's all that drink leaves a man." Mrs. Eden was given an easy-chair, and she took up her watch. Oscar went back to his open-air restaurant, and tacked a notice upon the screen door: "Go ELSEWHERE." Then he returned to the hotel. He supplied Mrs. Eden with more books and magazines than she could have read in several days. He brought her a pillow to ease her shoulders, and the Arkansas *Gazette* to rest her mind. He wanted her to take supper with him in the dining-room, assuring her that Atterton would not wake up, and detailing, with zest, the bill of fare. Mrs. Eden would have nothing but a cup of strong coffee, black and fragrant. She was afraid to leave Atterton, lest he wake and flee. She read but little, and when the lamp was lighted, hovered long about the bed, looking, with little sighs and moans, at the handsome flushed face.

Oscar, who had taken the adjoining room, came in frequently, but he divined that Mrs. Eden preferred to be alone, and contented himself with letting her see that he was at hand, in case of need.

It was Atterton's custom to issue from the hotel about midnight, to spend the hours before morning in debauchery, and, thinking that force might be needed to restrain him, Oscar seated himself at his open window.

It began to rain. Not daring to trust himself with a book, lest he fail to hear the sounds of Atterton's awakening, the young restaurateur stared into the darkness, thinking about Ethel. He still hoped to win the proud hand of Winthrop's daughter, and hoping, he exulted in his memory of her aristocratic bearing. Oscar was not an egotist. His opinion of his own parts was humble enough; but he was a Thornberry; and he believed with a simple, whole-souled faith, beautiful in its purity, that a Thornberry was the equal of anybody in Arkansas,—that is, in the world. So he sat dreaming of the beautiful princess, spreading flowered thoughts for her feet to tread upon, clothing her regal form with gossamer fancies, and shutting out from her and him, with the golden bars of love, all sorrow, all disappointment. The rain gurgled in the rusty pipes and spattered upon the sills,—and he heard the murmuring streams of his summer castle. The decayed cabbage-leaves and the decaying onion-tops grew sodden in their barrels, but he smelled the roses of delight.

There was a stir in the next room, a movement soft and indefinite. Oscar started up violently, and snatched out his watch. It was nearly twelve; he had been stranded on a desert island two hours. He immediately took boat and put off from its gleaming sands, leaving Prospero to weave his magic spells without him. He slipped into the hall and looked into the adjoining room. Mrs. Polly Eden stood at the bedside. Atterton lay dressed as Peter had left him, but he was awake, and there were tears in his eyes. Oscar stared through his spectacles, not knowing what to make of this sight. Mrs. Eden was talking in a voice very low, very tender, very sweet. Oscar shook his head and went back to his room. He did not sit down, but stood at the window, hands in pockets, feeling uncomfortable. He did not understand the tears of men. He remained thus until a cautious knocking upon the wall signaled him to come. Almost hoping that Atterton was proving rebellious, and needed a strong hand, Oscar hurriedly obeyed the summons.

When he entered, Mrs. Eden sat in her easy-chair beside the bed, holding Atterton's hand.

Atterton's face showed the trace of tears, but his eyes were bright. "Oscar!" he cried impetuously, rising upon his elbow. "What do you think of this? See here, old fellow; I was a lost man,—stranded, hopeless, desperate. See what Cousin Polly has done,—the best woman that ever lived. I'm going to be a man! I say, Osk, do you know what it is to have the whole world look black to you, every clod of it, and of a sudden to have the sunlight break through the cloud?"

"No, I don't," said Oscar.

"Well, *I* do! Look here!" cried Atterton, whose mind was still slightly hazy. "I say, look here! That was a lie, you know, about Cousin Polly. She never made a confidante of that Pickens girl. The Pickens girl was eavesdropping, and then she pretended to me that Cousin Polly had told her all my most private affairs, don't you know; and that made me crazy."

Oscar now had something he could take hold of. "That Pickens girl," he cried vehemently, "is a devil-"—he checked himself, coloring painfully as Mrs. Eden's eyes opened wide, then added lamely—"-fish!"

"Oh, Oscar!" said Mrs. Eden reprovingly. "Why, *Oscar*, I didn't know you could do it!"

Oscar had been thinking of Peter's downfall, and the thought had carried him beyond himself. "Cousin Polly," he stammered, "I said that that Pickens is a devil-fish, and I'll stick to it."

It was about two o'clock before Oscar took Mrs. Eden to his grandfather's.

"I don't understand that kind of doing," Oscar remarked, as he held the umbrella over her head. The street was intensely dark, and they made their way slowly. "And, besides, Atterton says it was the Pickens girl that drove him to drinking. But, Cousin Polly, he did pretty bad at Hot Springs, before there *was* any Pickens girl."

Mrs. Eden sighed. "Oscar," she said, "we must keep patient. It's when you can't do anything yourself that God has His chance."

Speaking of God reminded Oscar that to-morrow was Sunday. "Well!" he said, in a comfortable voice. "It's *so* ra-a-ainy that I don't reckon any of us will be able to go to church in the morning!"

When they reached Timothy Thornberry's, Mrs. Eden, who knew the house as well as her own, went to the room where Mary lay asleep.

The next morning Mary woke as the sunlight streamed into the room, flooding the rag-carpet with a network of glorious cheer. As the house was perfectly still, she decided to slip downstairs and begin breakfast before her aunt appeared upon the world's stage. She accordingly dressed, but so weary was her mother from the night's vigil that there was no sound from the bed as the daughter left the room. She had, however, hardly gained the kitchen when a soft footstep caused her to turn, startled by the fear of meeting Peter alone. The man who entered the room was not Peter, but the old captain. He was in his stocking feet; his shirt gaped at the neck; his trousers hung, as it were, by a single thread, and his hair suggested that he had been tossed upon the back of some wild nightmare.

"Well, honey!" he exclaimed ruefully, "I didn't 'low to find company in my kitchen, and I'm pointedly glad I waited to put on one more garment before I come in. You might's well open the door, though, since you're on deck, and let in the fresh air." He began to make the fire, and as the kindling was wanting,—seemingly to his surprise,—he made a great show with some old newspapers.

Mary laughed and opened the door. The sunshine streamed through the side of the screened-in porch, but there were no chickens in sight; either because the Thornberry chickens stayed on their roosts unconscionably late, or because experience taught them to expect the Thornberrys to do so.

"Uncle Tim," said Mary, breathing the fresh air deeply, and letting the mellow glow crown her dark hair, "I wanted to do that myself. You ought never to do it with three strong men in the house."

"I don't hardly ever," said Timothy. "Peter,—of course, *he* don't make fires; he wouldn't know how. Oscar was up till two-thirty last night, and Will——" Timothy chuckled, and then said in a tone of exultant affection: "Mary, that boy, he jest loves to lie abed so bad that it warms my heart all over when I think of him snuggling up in his pillows."

"But," said Mary decidedly, "that is selfish of him."

"Now, don't you think that. That boy works as hard as any boy in town; but he don't work hard at getting up early, that's a fact. Is there any water in that bucket?"

Mary peered hopefully into the cedar bucket, but was obliged to shake her head. "But you ought not to go for it, Uncle Tim,—you aren't dressed."

Timothy chuckled. "The neighbors can jest take potluck with me at not lookin'!" he declared. As he returned, a far-away voice came faintly through the house: "Honey, go see what your Aunt Polly is a-sayin'!" cried Timothy. "I got a mighty pore stand of fire here; it ain't near a half-crop, and I dassent leave it."

The plaintive voice of the old lady was wafted to them in a continuous trickle of inaudible phrases. Mary followed it up, and learned that her aunt had forgotten to have meat bought the evening before. The meat-markets were not open on Sunday mornings, but Oscar drowsily announced through his bedroom-door that there was plenty of steak in his ice-chest at the restaurant.

The house was now astir. Old Mrs. Thornberry appeared in her black lace cap, tying on her apron as she crossed the hall. The captain went after the steak. Mrs. Eden began playing old familiar hymns on the squeaky organ in the front room, and as Timothy was long in returning, she was joined by one after another of the family. When the old gentleman at last reappeared, everybody was singing lustily, "Abide with Me," and the kitchen fire was breathing its last.

When they sat down to breakfast it was nine o'clock, and the chickens were straggling up toward the back door. Mary sat between her mother and great-aunt, thus avoiding the charge of partiality, and at the same time insuring herself against Peter's company. The boys looked strong and alert, and Will was, as usual, markedly handsome.

"Mary," said Oscar judiciously, "you look awful pretty this morning." Then, as Mary blushed with surprise, he added hastily: "Well, sometimes you don't, you know." All laughed except Peter, who considered laughing rather low, and Oscar, who felt he had made a blunder.

"Well," cried Mary gaily, "*you* never do, but I think just as much of you as if you did!"

"Honey," said Timothy, looking at his wife from over his spectacles, "this steak is mighty rare."

"You were so long coming," returned the other, "I thought maybe you'd forgot what you went for."

"Oh!" said Mrs. Eden, "you know it's fashionable to have your steak rare."

"Then pass mine up to Peter," drawled Will.

"Honey," said Mrs. Thornberry, looking at the captain fixedly, "seems to me ever since you come back they's been something on your mind."

"I met George Nicodemus," said the captain evasively. "His wife has married, and George wants to set out. Nobody ever knew what his son died of; how old was he, Polly?"

As there were two Pollys present, they answered as one voice, "Twelve."

"Yes," said Timothy, "I reckon he was too young to be *hung*. I can't think *what* the child could have died of. It looked like that child was a born rascal. I remember before the separation, George come to me one day and he says, 'Cousin Tim, what business would you advise me to raise my son up to?'—he called him 'Georgie.' I says, 'Pick out a trade where rascality is a virtue.' He said he'd make him a politician. Well, I told him it was *in* 'im all right. Yes, they ain't no question but what Nicodemus was born again; he was born anew in that poor little Georgie. Good thing he died, I reckon. Better off, as Groner says. Polly, when 're you looking for Groner to come back home?"

"Look here, Timothy," said his wife, "you can't fool me that away. Now, what was it George Nicodemus told you that makes you so cur'us this morning?"

There was a pause, then Timothy said bluntly: "If you must have it, I gather that Will, here, has been into a fight."

Will turned red and the others stared. Oscar, who alone knew of the occurrence, sought desperately to turn the subject, but it was in vain. As Will was the most peaceable of mortals, amazement grew with his silence.

"Since this unpleasant subject has come up," said Timothy, "I'd jest like you to tell me, William, that your Cousin George was a-lying."

"It wasn't no fight," said Will sulkily. "I didn't know the fellow was drunk. He just said something, and I didn't say a word to him. He just made a remark to me, and when they picked him up, they didn't have to take no stitches." Will saw Mary's eyes fixed upon him, and added hastily, "*Any* stitches; I meant not *any* stitches."

"*Stitches!*" echoed his grandmother, aghast.

Finding he made matters worse by harping upon the word, in his striving for grammatical form, Will relapsed into silence.

"But what was it about?" demanded Timothy.

tempt to divert the conversa
mischief-maker that ever live
for Atterton's making a fool

Peter started up, white to th
friend I have in the world, and
he cried, "and I will not hea
saying, he stalked from the ro

"Well!" ejaculated old M
trothed to that limb! Great f
to become of Peter? It ough
othy, you ought to stop it."

"If I was a character in a b
thy remarked drily, "but bei
Arkinsaw Thornberry, I reckon
liam, seeing we've made a mess
might as well have the thing co
Pickens girl say?"

"I shall not repeat it," Will d

"I believe I know," said Mary
"and I'm

hour; and Will knew that if the carriage were mentioned the facts about Peter's drunken orgy must be laid bare. Oscar also understood the slender support that kept the sword above the old people's heads, and the perspiration started to his brow. Mary observed their alarm, and was forced to the conviction that Will had some uneasy secret in his breast. She vaguely connected it with Peter's failing to bring Goldie home from the hop; but she could not imagine Peter drunk.

"Well, Mary," said her mother, "don't leave us there in your story."

Mary resumed slowly: "I saw Will in the street, and I wondered. As I was dressed, I thought I'd go downstairs and ask him why—if anything was the matter."

"I was out late that night," Will murmured.

"Yes," said Mary, "it was about one or two o'clock. I went into the yard, and we spoke a few words. Will said something to me that offended me, but I know he didn't mean to. I knew it even then, but I was excited and wouldn't think. He was sorry I misunderstood him, and wanted me to shake hands, I believe—wasn't that it?"

"I don't know," said Will stiffly.

"Anyway," said Mary, "he grabbed my hand to keep me from going into the house, and just then Miss Goldie opened the door, and looked out——"

"Good gracious!" whispered Mrs. Polly Thornberry.

"Yes, and she accused us of—of—oh, you know what she would think!"

"Mercy me!" cried Mrs. Polly Eden.

"It must of looked particular," old Timothy remarked.

"Now, Will," said Mary, turning her reddened face toward him, "was *that* what the fight was about?"

"There wasn't any fight."

"But whatever there *was*," cried Mary impatiently, "was it about *that?*"

"Yes, it was," returned Will, thus brought to bay. "That Pickens girl—*my future sister-in-law,*—she told all over town that she caught you and me making er—a—courting I mean, in the yard at night and—er——"

"But you explained, didn't you?" exclaimed Mary, redder than before.

"I didn't explain nothing. I just knocked 'im across the pavement and went on into the store."

There was profound silence about the table. Even Timothy's cooing over his coffee was inaudible. Presently the old gentleman spoke to his wife: "Honey, don't you feed this rare meat to Thomas Jefferson; I don't want that cat made wild."

Mrs. Eden smiled.

Mary looked anxiously from face to face. "But there has *never* been anything like that between us," she said eagerly. "Such a thing as love between Will and me was never mentioned,—*was* it, Will?"

"'Course it wasn't," said Will gruffly.

"I feel like I can't bear for such a story to go 'round," Mary went on miserably. "But how can it be stopped? I always thought of Will just as I did of Atterton, or Oscar, or—or as I do of Peter; we are not very closely related, but we always felt near. And that's the way Will always thought of me; *isn't it*, Will?"

Will reached for the bread, although supplied, and said nothing.

Mrs. Eden smiled again. So did Mrs. Thornberry.

"You always looked upon me as your poor little cousin who was always doing the wrong thing, *didn't* you, Will?"

Will mopped his brow and was mute.

Mary stared at him with accusing wrath upon her face, usually so mild. There were a few moments of painful tension, then Will said doggedly, "No, I didn't!"

"Oh, *Will!*" cried Mary accusingly.

"I've loved you all my life," cried Will, in a raised voice, "and I'm not going to say I haven't!"

"Oh, *Will!*" said Mary, this time with a sob.

"I don't care!" Will exclaimed. "The truth's what you must have, and that's it. I've always loved you, and I always will. But I never let you know it, because I thought you wouldn't like it. And I *must* say you seem to like it even less than I expected."

Mary rose and started from the room, her hands over her face. As she went out, they could hear her catch her breath. Will struck viciously at his meat.

"William," said Timothy reprovingly, "now see what you've done. If you had ever let me suspect the truth——"

"I didn't know it was customary," said Will stiffly, "for fellows to tell their grandfathers when they fall in love. Where's my hat? I have to go uptown." He rose, still very red.

"Will," said Timothy gently, "do you want the new straw? The new straw is in the china cupboard."

"Why, Timothy!" cried his wife, "where will you put that hat next?"

Will had already regretted his heated reference to grandfathers, and he understood the proffer of the new straw as an olive branch. It was not his disposition to make a display of his feelings, but he answered with sudden graciousness: "Yes, grandfather. I'll take the new straw."

As Will went out, Mrs. Eden followed him to look after her daughter. She gave the young man an affectionate pat on the shoulder. It cheered him somewhat.

"Oscar," said Timothy ruefully, "I reckon you'n me'll be the only ones to black our shoes together this mawnin'." (For once we render the word as all Thornberrys deliver it.)

"I reckon I'd better go over to the hotel and see Atterton safe out of town," Oscar replied. "Cousin Polly believes in his promises, but I'll believe in his going when I see him a-going."

Not long after, Mrs. Polly Eden came out on the back porch and found the captain seated alone on the steps, with the blacking-brush on the ground. "Do come out, Polly!" cried the old man. "I'm awful lonesome. I'll never get this other foot blacked without company."

Mrs. Eden gathered her skirts carefully and sat down upon the top step. "I must hurry home and get my Sunday dress," she said. But she didn't hurry.—Instead, she luxuriated in the delicious morning air with its odor of ripened June apples.

"Honey," said Timothy cautiously, "did you see Mary after she left the dinin'-room?"

Mrs. Eden nodded two or three times.

"Seemed pow'ful cut up," murmured Timothy.

"When I saw her," said Mrs. Eden—she looked carefully all about, then sank her voice to a whisper, "she was laughing!"

CHAPTER XV

Oscar found Atterton finishing his breakfast at the hotel. Winthrop's son grinned shamefacedly, but soon rallied.

"Well, Osk, here's the prodigal S.," he remarked. "Come to cheer me on my way, have you?"

"I mean to see that you get out of town," said Oscar, seating himself at the table.

"Say, old man," muttered Atterton, "you don't happen to know whether or not Gladys Lucile is posted up in my recent history, do you?"

"She may be *one* person who doesn't know about your drinking, and gambling, and shooting on the street, and the rest of it," returned Oscar unsympathetically, "but if so, she's in a class by herself."

"I know you're cruel only to be kind," remarked Atterton, with a short laugh. "Well, Gladys Lucile is the only one in the world for me, anyhow. But I've got to see Peter before I go out home. I'm going to give him a few pointers relative to one Miss G. Pickens."

"Good for you!" exclaimed Oscar, with more heartiness. "He left the table at home in a towering passion because I dropped a word against her. Maybe he'll listen to you. I think we'll find him at the post office. Come on, old fellow; you've the right stuff in you, after all."

Atterton laughed. "I know you think I'm going to cut off my own head," he cried gaily, "but I can say anything to old Pete."

Sunday morning offered diversion, from nine to eleven, by the opening of the mail; not because the citizens of Core City conspired with the postmaster for the manufacture of an excuse to be late to church, but because at nine o'clock the train brought the Sunday illustrated newspapers. The opening of the mail was usually an event, though business prevented, on weekdays, as large a representation of business men as was to be seen on Sunday, when nothing but religion called elsewhere.

On the Sunday in question, as on every first day of the week, a large crowd waited upon the sidewalk, while, within the post office, a long line of men, women, and children stretched from the door to the wicker window. Those who had keys hovered about the boxes, watching for the fall of a letter into a particular receptacle, and peering through the network at the postmaster's assistant, like birds waiting for crumbs. The men who were not smoking, were chewing, with proofs of evidence about their sturdy boots. Those who had no keys were obliged to stand in line, pressed like sandwiches between black and white, male and female, rich and poor.

Oscar saw Atterton lead Peter away from the common herd. They vanished in the rear of a drug store. Perhaps half an hour passed before Atterton reappeared alone. His step was somewhat hurried, and there was a flush upon his cheek.

He came to Oscar and said: "I'm going to walk out home. It'll do me good. Yes, I know the ground's wet, but I don't care."

"Did you talk to Peter?" Oscar asked, and for reply Atterton gave a long significant whistle.

"Did he like it?" Oscar insisted.

"Like it, you villain! why didn't you tell me the ass was engaged to that Pickens girl? Lord, how he did rear and charge!" (Atterton pronounced it "rah an' chahge.") "Well, he'll never speak to *me* again, Pete won't. But while I was about it, I made it plain. He heard something. I don't see how a little of it can help sticking to his brain. But bless yo' soul, Osk, that boy's *off*. He's crazy. He's got the Goldiemania. Well, when he fetches that music-teacher into the family, you can tell yo' Uncle At. good-by; he'll just go off som'ers, and found another dynasty."

Oscar did not tell Atterton that it was his intention to come out to the farm that evening. His visit was to be a fateful one, entirely devoted to Ethel. When he had seen the young man safely from the corporate limits, Oscar decided that he would go to church, as a fit and solemn preparation for his interview with Winthrop's daughter. Accordingly, he passed his restaurant with the air of a stranger, read its "Go ELSEWHERE," and said aloud: "All right, I'll do so."

From Ethel's plain declaration that she could never love him, an ordinary man, not a Thornberry, might well have supposed that the final interview with Ethel had already taken place. But Oscar meant to have another one,—if we may be permitted the solecism,—at about half-past seven that evening. As he sat under the Rev. Mr. Wells' sermon, hearing little of what the discursive gentleman said, but striving dutifully to hear all, he tingled with subdued excitement. His love for Ethel was so sincere and intense, in its quiet way, that he was appalled at the contemplation of a future without her. Indeed, he could not bring himself to admit the probability of such a barren prospect. As he said to himself: "What would be the use of me without

Ethel?" That appeared unanswerable. Goldie's meek face was to be seen in the loft, its blue eye upon the congregation, and its black eye next the choir. The choir, as was their wont, busily read the hymns during the sermon, fluttering the leaves and occasionally glancing at the minister, as if wondering why he did not dispense with exposition, and permit them to sing.

"But they's always this to be said," Hodgins Thornberry remarked to old Timothy after the service, as they stood in the churchyard,—"however long brother Wells may preach, an' however many verses they is to the solo, it has both got to end in nature, and after all *that* comes the Sunday dinner."

"Yes," said Timothy, winking at his wife, "and sometimes a mighty pore one."

To dinner came not Peter; and while Will took his accustomed seat, he had the startled, watchful air of a turkey, ready to dart away at a word. The others understood, and "Mary" was not mentioned; but there was such elaborate care taken in avoiding the only subject that could enter the old people's heads when they looked at Will,—and Oscar was so taken up with anticipations of his fast approaching visit to Ethel,— that, for the most part, silence reigned. Thomas Jefferson lay asleep upon the floor,—papers had been spread upon the couch to keep him off that vantage ground, for he was, as usual, "shedding." After Timothy had passed a few comments upon the sermon, no part of which had seemed to him exactly as it should have been, he held up a bit of cheese and called the cat.

Thomas Jefferson kept his nose between his hind legs, and did not even purr.

"Here, Tommy," called the old man, "Tommy! have *you* got dumb like the rest of us? Come here!"

Thomas Jefferson looked up sourly at being disturbed, shifted his green eyes at the old man, and snapped out an ungracious "Meh! meh!"

"Well!" cried Timothy, "what's got the matter? I reckon *you* ain't fell in love!"

That afternoon, Timothy went upstairs to his wife, who was reading her church paper. He bent over her, tugging at his white beard. "Honey," he whispered, "have you saw Osk?"

"Not since dinner. Mercy me, Tim? what has happened?"

The captain grew more impressive. "He has been a-bathin' himself for the past hour, a-splashin' and a bringin' and kerryin' water like a porpus. An' he come to me jest now, dressed up like a dook; an' he says he wants old Speckle for the evening." (Old Speckle was the horse that served on week-days in the delivery wagon.) "I reckon that's to keep his shoes shiny, for, naturally, he wouldn't want to take no particular person out behind old Speck. They ain't no two ways about it; he's goin out to Winthrop's, an' he's goin' to do some hard fightin'."

At about seven o'clock, Oscar came down from his room, dressed with elaborate care. Old Speckle was awaiting him at the gate, but between them stood Mrs. Thornberry, her black cap trembling at her own temerity.

"Oscar," she faltered, "would you wear this?" And she held up a perfect rosebud. Oscar blushed. "Maybe," said the old lady shyly, "it will bring you good luck."

"Pin it on, grandmother," said Oscar, solemnly bending down that the fragile hands might reach his lapel. Then he kissed her.

He drove slowly out of town, wondering how he would feel when he again viewed the familiar streets. Slowly, too, he wound his way among the hills. The sun went down, but it remained light and warm. The world was still all aglow with memories of the day so lately departed. The heat ceased to be oppressive. Flowers and fruits perfumed the air. Why should not love be inspired when all the Ozarks formed a setting for love?

At Winthrop's front gate, there stood, by happy chance, Winthrop himself. Oscar could hardly have come at a less auspicious time. Ethel was expecting, in about half an hour, one of her distinguished friends, a young man from no less pretentious a city than Fort Smith. This young man had been graduated from Arkansas University at Fayetteville; he had served as some sort of secretary in Washington; had been to Europe; and, above all, had passed six months in Boston. Winthrop appreciated the untowardness of Oscar's appearance, but, with the Thornberry weakness, had not the heart to turn the young fellow away. No, he would leave Ethel to manage the affair.

"Just come with me," said Winthrop gravely,—he was resolved not to encourage him,—"Ethel's in the flower-garden. She's getting some roses for the parlor. In fact—er—she's looking for company; very fine company, in fact."

Oscar followed Winthrop, calm in the certainty that nobody could have bathed more thoroughly, or dressed with more care, than he. They reached the flower-garden, adjoining the back yard. Ethel was among the rosebushes, dressed all in white, from hair-ribbon to slippers. She was snipping off the long stems with her *shears*, and the fallen blooms of red and pink and cream were all about her feet. Lest she tread upon the flowers, she did not look up, thinking she recognized the footsteps of her father and brother.

"Honey," said Winthrop, "Oscar is here."

Still under the delusion that Winthrop and Atterton had come to announce the unwelcome news, Ethel was forced to the conclusion that Oscar awaited her in the house. The shears snapped impatiently as she exclaimed:

"But what shall I do? Did you tell him I have an engagement. Mr. Johnson will think——"

"Ethel!" warned her father, as Oscar's face showed a pathetic attempt at cheerfulness, "Ethel!"

Ethel, still with head bent low among the roses, groaned half comically, half dismally. "Now, father," she exclaimed, "you know very well, and so does Atterton, that Oscar never knows how to leave. He can't go, even when he wants to. He has never learned how to get away."

"Well, Ethel," Oscar spoke up with some abruptness, "I'm not too old to learn, and I believe you're a pretty good teacher!"

Ethel dropped the shears and straightened herself in surprised discomfiture. She stared at her cousin, her face as white as his own.

There was a moment of strained silence, which Winthrop took advantage of to beat a hasty retreat. "It's between them," he reflected; "let 'em have it out!"

Ethel murmured confusedly as she sought to recover herself: "Father should not have brought you here, Oscar. I am very sorry for what you heard me say."

"After all," said Oscar, trying to speak with composure, "it is well enough for me to know just what you think."

... could find nothing t
forgive me!"

"Yes, of course; there's noth
paused, and seemed to stagger.
ence of absolute hopelessness.
want to tell you good-by."

She understood that his word
icance. "Do you mean that yo
Core City?"

"Yes, I am going to New Yo
time he had thought of such a pla
smile that showed no bitterness
just about enough to land me
I'll see the Battery where Was
to walk. And Central Park.
Street." Then he added hastily,
I really must go." He had sudd
words. It was upon his lips
would take pleasure in now show
learned how to "get away": but

"But won't you go in, and speak to father and brother?"

"Oh,—I'll write to 'em," said Oscar desperately. He hurried away. He still held his spectacles in his hand. Drawing near old Speckle, he put them on, and in so doing struck his hand against the rosebud upon his lapel. He unfastened it and threw it as far as he could; then, with wide staring eyes, went on, still white to the lips, still numbed and deadened. A new experience, indeed, for a Thornberry,—absolute hopelessness!

But not long could blank despair reign in Oscar's soul. Gradually above the chaos of desolated hopes, stole the timid light of reawakening possibilities. Oscar suddenly stopped short, turned off to one side, and presently sank upon his knees in the coarse Bermuda grass, looking for the rosebud. The first warm touch that had come to his frozen heart, was the memory of his grandmother's love. He was still looking, groping here and there remorsefully, when a light footstep startled him; then a white slippered foot came so near he could have touched it. But he did not look up.

"What is it, Oscar?" Ethel asked, her voice trembling with compassion.

"Just my rosebud. I lost it," said Oscar simply.

"Oh," cried Ethel, "do take this one!" and she tore a flower from her bosom.

"No," said Oscar, intent upon his search, "I want my own."

When he at last found it, he rose with a subdued "There!" of satisfaction, and gave Ethel but a fleeting glance before turning away. That fleeting glance caused him to look again. Large tears stood in Ethel's eyes. Her arms hung trembling at her side, and in one hand drooped the rejected flower.

"Ethel!" exclaimed the young man remorsefully, "you didn't understand. I never meant to refuse your flower; of course, I will take it. But the rosebud,—it was given me by the only woman in the world who loves me, and I'm going to keep it. It didn't bring luck, but it has made things seem easier since——"

"Listen, Oscar," said Ethel earnestly, "I don't want you to go to New York. That's too far away. But I *do* want you to leave Core City. And I want you to take Atterton with you, and watch over him and be his guardian, and have him in trust from me. I don't care for you as you wish,—I have never felt as you feel. But there's nobody higher in my esteem than my Cousin Oscar Thornberry, and—and, who was that woman you spoke of?"

"What woman? did I say anything about a woman? —oh, you mean grandmother!"

A sudden smile flashed over Ethel's face, and in its light the last shadow of her pride was dispelled. She extended her rounded arm. "Yes, take this rosebud," she said. "Now you have flowers from the *two* women who, in all the world, think most of you."

CHAPTER XVI

THAT Sunday had proved a period of violent stress of emotions to Peter Thornberry. The remarks dropped by Oscar, relative to Goldie Pickens, and the open accusations of Atterton, had not, indeed, opened the lover's eyes to the real nature of his fiancée. They had, as a matter of course, embittered him against Oscar, and enraged him against Atterton. Nevertheless, no matter how much we may be infatuated in a person or belief, adverse criticism, backed by solid argument, is not without its effect; we may persist in our devotion; but, in the one case, adherence descends to blindness, in the other, to prejudice. Peter told himself that he loved Goldie more than ever, because she had been maligned; at the same time, he was anxious to hear what she had to say in her own defense.

His passion for the organist was a strange mixture of idealized emotions. He had of her both a heart and a mind picture. In taking her image upon his perception, his love held a magic glass over the sensitive plate, correcting each imperfect line. She was an airy, spiritual, nebulous soul, fashioned as of fleecy clouds and twilight haze and moonlight softness. There was nothing sensuous about her, nothing that in the faintest degree breathed the warmth of human responsiveness. That was his mind picture.

The heart picture was quite different. It presented the music-teacher as a woman, with soft, splendid curves,—a woman with a throbbing breast, a deliciously rounded face that called for the caress of a man's hand, and lips that should find a woman's joy in the language of passion. It was his delight, in fancy, to combine these into a composite photograph, to merge the angel into the woman, the woman into the angel, to dream of her starlike purity trembling to divine warmth in his arms, and, at the same time, to think of her physical charms as etherealized to the elusiveness of the woodsprite.

No wonder Peter could insult his brother, and drive from him his one intimate friend, for such a miraculous creature as this,—a woman to desire and not to possess. Believing her misunderstood, brought him to the front in her defense. But that he might intelligently fight her cause, he sought an interview, to express his sympathy and confidence. She should tell him what to believe, and he would believe it. Ah, the charming confidence of love,—when one is young!

Goldie knew he was coming, for he had slipped a tiny note into her hand at church, as both sat in the choir. But the ragged slip of paper, torn from the page of a long-suffering hymnbook, hinted nothing of the real object of the visit. Goldie supposed him spurred on by blind devotion. Her government of Peter was severe, but wise. After two weeks of total abstinence, she had suffered him to call upon her twice a week. This Sunday made the third time within seven days. Goldie did not forbid his coming, but she was resolved that he should have but the tips of her fingers. As her duties, as church-organist, interfered with the conventional hours of society, Goldie had specified three as the hour, than which there are few less romantic in the course of the twenty-four; Peter, however, stood in no need of extraneous incitement to romance.

It happened that some time before three, Waldo McCormack felt impelled to read aloud that which he had last written on his newest book, and Goldie, apparently overjoyed at listening to the words of wisdom, seated herself in the middle of a tiger-skin, before the closed-up fireplace. She made a graceful picture as she looked demurely up into the author's face, one little foot, which had forgotten where it was, taking an airing, and both hands locked about her supple knee.

Elizabeth McCormack sat near her husband, as if by physical nearness she could ward off the magic influence of the girl on the tiger-skin. But when Waldo looked up, throwing back his leonine head to let his intellectual claws sink deep, it was always Goldie's meek, exalted face that gained his glowing eyes, and it was always Goldie who murmured, "Ah, how true!" or "Oh, how sad!"

The doorbell rang.

"Dear me!" said Goldie regretfully, "Peter has come. Pray remember the place, Cousin Waldo, I don't want to miss a single word. But I'm all in confusion. Will you help me to rise? May I have your hand?"

"Certainly, certainly!" cried the great man, with eagerness. He raised her up, and after she was safe upon her feet, her hand lingered a moment in his own; he was wildly, sweetly thrilled by his perception of "physical soul."

Then Goldie lifted her drooping lids and looked at him wistfully. "Good-by," she murmured, and walked out with a slow, noiseless tread.

sometimes act as boomerangs.
of conscience that made her
mapping out her conduct.

She had almost decided to
demus. He had proposed, an
own time to give him a final
passioned love, his youth and g
her, and his submission to her t
weigh the canning factory, the
houses, the shipping depots, and
cupola. Nevertheless, though al
the president of the Nicodemus
better or worse, she had not br
with Peter. There is always th
thing happening when the future
George Nicodemus might fail he
as had other prospective husband
from worldly considerations, the
Peter's warm and confiding devo
ful to the li..l

held up her hand; "Back, Peter!" she said with dignity.

"Forgive me," said Peter humbly. "I know this is one day extra, but I—but I couldn't help it, dear; I"—the words burst forth impetuously—"I love you so! You are so beautiful, and so pure, and—and good."

"Hush, dear heart," said Goldie softly, "do not call me good. Say only that I want to be good, and fall far short." Inwardly, she was laughing at him for being a fool, and yet it was laughter tinged with bitterness. For she realized that she was not good, as he meant the word, and would never be, since she scorned such "goodness." Yet, in a way, she felt inferior to the young man, because he idealized a quality which she could not desire. But she justified herself in that she was a woman who must wrest a livelihood from hard conditions. Of course, she might have been as he desired her, had she possessed wealth and ease. "To be good," she mused, with a slightly ironical lifting of the upper lip, "one must have time for it."

"*You* not good?" cried Peter vehemently. "You are all heaven in a woman. Why, pure angel, you are so far above me that you are entirely beyond the world of sense! You love me, yet shrink from my kisses,—may I not have one to-day?"

"No, no!" returned Goldie hastily. The few times Peter's burning lips had been pressed against hers, she had seemed to see the cruel ghost of her old lover mocking at her heart of stone,—that lover who could not marry her because both were poor.

"You see?" cried Peter, in mournful triumph. "You can not feel as coarser natures. That is why I regard you as all spirit. Do you remember—after those

I had been so base, so degraded.
very feet were the feet of an a
a moment upon the earth, befor
upper air. I didn't consider the
consider them at all as feet, yo
with an exalted look. "Or ratl
say it was because they were *you*

"And then," said Goldie, in a l
"I forgave you."

"Oh, yes!" Peter whispered.

"Peter, you are a dear boy," s
tire sincerity. Such devotion wo
calculating shrewdness.

After that Goldie played "The
ing him the exquisite pleasure of
When the music died away in a l
melody, her hand lingered upon
laid his hand upon it, and said:

"Sweetheart, I want to speak to
Goldie's

what did Mr. Oscar say? I'm prepared to hear anything; for since that night he had to take me home because you could not, he has hated me; he thinks I led you into temptation."

"How unjust!" cried Peter. "Does Oscar think that I'm not my own master?"

"But what did he say about me, this brother Oscar?" she asked softly.

"He says, and Atterton says, that you have told—have told around—that you saw my brother Will making love to Mary Eden in the front yard at two o'clock in the morning."

"Well?" said Goldie, drooping her lids.

"Of course, I know you didn't, dear love, for Will never had the least thought of Mary. And, of course, Mary was not in the yard at any such an hour. And if she *had* been, she is too discreet and innocent a girl to have been doing as rumor says."

"Oh, indeed!" returned Goldie, not very graciously. "And was there anything else? Pray let us hear the conclusion of the whole matter." She quoted the words, as many a wiser scholar quotes, with no use for the latter part of her text.

"And that," Peter went on desperately, realizing that he was alienating her, but impelled to speak the very worst, "that you eavesdropped at Cousin Polly Eden's kitchen-door, and then pretended to Atterton that Cousin Polly had confided in you his most sacred affairs."

"You believe all of this, I suppose?" snapped Goldie, every word clicking at the end of her tongue like broken icicles.

"You know I do not, I can not believe it," said Peter reproachfully. "But I speak of it that you may tell

what I told Mrs. Lee. I tho(u)
she hates all your family, bec
cated high 'c'. It was very,
to trust her, but, Peter, I must

"But what did you tell Mrs.

"I told her about catching (
love to each other, at two in t(
the house in which Mary *shou*
all *good* girls should have be
other," she added vaguely, bro(
sion by Peter's face.

"Making love!" echoed Pet
nothing for Mary, or for anyb
And Mary wouldn't have acted :

"They were holding each ot(
I opened the door they tore them
ran into the house and hid her bl(
if she didn't. Ask Mary, herse

Peter was silent.

"But," said Peter, bewildered, almost speechless, "Atterton has already asked her; and Cousin Polly thinks you must have overheard what she said."

Goldie laughed out. "She admits it, then?"

"But she says that you accidentally overheard something at the door."

"Peter," said Goldie, rising dramatically, "what does this mean? Do you believe in me?"

"Of course, I believe in you. And I also believe in Will, and Mary, and Cousin Polly. I am sure we will find a way to reconcile what you have said with what they say."

"You can not reconcile our several statements," said Goldie gravely, "because I speak the truth, and they do not!"

Peter's face grew red. "Don't say that, Goldie!" he exclaimed hastily. "The Thornberrys do not lie."

"Does that mean that I do?" came the fierce retort.

"Oh, Goldie, how could you say that!"

Goldie took a step nearer. "Are you trying to break off our engagement, Peter? Is that what you came here for?"

"Good Heavens, Goldie! Are you mad? It never entered my mind——"

"Not entered your mind? Then what is in your mind? You say Mary didn't make love to Will in the yard at midnight——"

"I do say it!" Peter cried hotly, "and I'll stake my life on it. I know Mary and I know Will."

"And do you pretend that Mrs. Eden told the truth when she said——"

"I know she told the truth," Peter interrupted

know what you are doing. (
am I?" He sank in a chai:
face.

"Peter," said Goldie, "wh
thought it for life. I realize,
live happily together. You dc
I, alas! understand you. So
My conscience tells me that 1
you are, I would have taken y
but," she added, unable to kee]
her tone, "I do not care to 1
relations."

Peter started up. "Just a lit
mered, "I thought you a lady.
grasp this."

"Peter," said the other, wi
know this is right. Your famil
could ever be. All is ended, P

"Goldie, Goldie!" he cried

manner, "go to your truth-loving relations. You never really cared for me. Farewell, Peter. If ever again——"

But the young man heard no more.

Goldie, with an emotion she seldom experienced, watched him hurrying away. His love had long been balm to her heart. She had seen it transformed to something like contempt. She would fain have soothed her calculating spirit longer with the solace of his devotion; but spite is never born dumb, and her dislike of Mary Eden, and, indeed, of the Thornberry connection, had found no uncertain voice. In accusing Peter's cousins of falsehood, she had driven him to the conviction that she herself was false. What blind faith in family rectitude! Goldie had imagined she could alienate her lover from his kindred, but in the attempt had brought upon herself his scorn.

He believed now that he understood her. But did he? Did she understand herself? She mused upon the sincere words her lips had spoken almost unconsciously,—

"There is no Goldie Pickens!"

She asked herself with something like a smile: "*Is* there a Goldie Pickens?" So long had she hidden her old self from the world, and so many different parts had she played, that sometimes she found herself wondering if there were any reality in any of them.

She heaved a dismal sigh. Well,—here was an end to youthful adoration, to the shining of eloquent young eyes, and the hot, impulsive words of passion. She had not meant to finish with Peter before taking up George; but, after all, it was best to have the episode brought to a close. As the wife of George Nicodemus, she would launch forth on the full tide of wealth, never again to teach the difference between a sharp and a flat. To George, she would be no angel, no mystery; yet it were better so, for angels carry no purses.

Goldie was sure she had acted wisely, but she was somewhat moody at the loss of Peter's respect. She would have avoided everybody at that hour, had it been possible; but the way to her chamber led through the drawing-room.

"Come in, come in," said Waldo McCormack, rubbing his hands, "and we will have the next chapter."

"I can not listen now," said Goldie wearily.

"*What* is it?" asked the other in amazement. His wide-opened eyes wrought upon her nerves.

"I said I didn't want to hear it," she replied, in a louder tone.

"Very well," gasped the author. "I thought as it was my own work I was offering to read, my very own——"

"I think it poor stuff!" cried Goldie hysterically. "I never understand half of what you read to me. I'm tired of having to sit and listen to you, when my nerves are half torn to pieces with giving music lessons; and for once, I will speak out. Why don't you read to your wife?"

Waldo was purple.

Elizabeth rushed to her husband's side, and put her arm about him protectingly. She glared wrathfully at Goldie.

"Miss Pickens!" she cried wildly. "What do you mean by treating Mr. McCormack this way? Don't you know he won't recover for a week after such an unwarranted insult? Is it your intention to disturb him so that he can't write any more, *ever?*"

"It wouldn't be much of a loss," snapped Goldie, venting her full heart upon friend and foe. "It's poor stuff, *I* say. Everybody knows it, but nobody has the courage to say so. But I have. I'm not afraid of the devil!"

"Merciful powers!" gasped Waldo. "Elizabeth, tell her to prepare to leave this house at once."

Goldie laughed. "Well, Cousin Waldo," she cried, "I've done one good deed to-day; I've made you put your arm about your wife, and that's better, for you, I assure you, than holding *my* hand! If you'll take a little more notice of her from now on, and treat her half as lovingly as you've treated *me,* I'll feel more like the angel you tell me I am. I might as well do a little missionary work, I suppose, on my way through this vale of tears!"

.... on the first da
the necessity of an evening m
an elaborate Sunday dinner
certain that in Core City th
from one o'clock till the next
was not missed from home a
red hills, dazed, tortured, abje
did not appear in the choir l
anthem progressed from pag
him not. Long after Timotl
into slumber, a wretched,
fugitive crept up the stair anc
entrancing dreams.

It was a homely apartment, l
several windows, all open t
breezes. In one bed lay Osca
the other side of the rag-carp
other bed inviting Peter. He
ing of the breath. On that
dream-ladders had rested, re

to stone, stared into the darkness, his chin cutting into his benumbed palm. The house was filled with the ticking of a hall-clock which groaned so dismally throughout its rusty machinery, whenever it struck, that one could hardly count the hour. Once a phantom form glided through the door and crouched in surprise at sight of Peter.

It was Thomas Jefferson. His air said plainly: "What! you, too, are looking for a mouse?"

"Come here, old fellow," said Peter softly. He straightened himself and felt violent pains up and down his thin frame. He had not thought of the time, but a faint lift in the gray air told him it was approaching dawn. He could not remember having ever petted the cat before, but now he took the resisting creature upon his knee. "Are you afraid of me, Jeff?" he said plaintively. "Don't be afraid. Why! I've made a specialty of cats. You ought to meet Miss Goldie!"

Perhaps Thomas Jefferson recognized the lonely kindliness in the tone; perhaps he smelled the Thornberry; at any rate, he put his paws upon Peter's breast and began to purr.

Morning came on. The clock struck six, which meant three-quarters past five. Peter rose to his feet, rubbed his long legs, and went down to the kitchen. He was making the fire when his grandfather entered, partially clad.

"What on earth?" cried the old man feebly.

"Let me do it, grandfather," said Peter. "I won't have a chance often. . . . I'm going away. . . . Grandfather, of all the fools Core City ever produced, I am Number One. But I know that Pickens girl now, for just what she is. . . . I owe all of you an apology."

alive!" she murmured.

"Yes, m'om," said Timothy
done with that Pickens gorl, b
her. He knows her like a book
has made him a new man. I
and he never peeped. He never
told him I *'hadn't brung'* in the
nothing. I believe he's done
quit trying to improve us; whic
haps our last days may be our b

"Timothy," said the old lad
that glass with my teeth in it, w

"Yes, honey, as soon as I find
ones."

Mrs. Thornberry climbed care
sympathetically, "Oh, where *can*

"It ain't so much a question o
returned the captain, "as where
found so many good places to ke
few days that

him by the relentless Mary, was still far from suspecting the truth.

When Will started forth for the grocery, Peter accompanied him, and as soon as they were upon the street, went at once to the point.

"Will, I want to borrow some money."

"All O. K.," said Will; "all I've got's yours."

"Thank you," returned Peter contritely. Among the many facts to which his eyes had been opened, the real worth of his brother stood prominent. "I'm going away, and I'll need something like a hundred dollars."

"All right. But, *man!* I'll be lonesome! Oscar and Atterton are going to pull out in a couple of days. Where are *you* going, Peter? What about the bank?"

"For one thing," said Peter desperately, "I'm going where I hope never to hear of that Pickens girl again. The rest is immaterial."

Will secretly exulted, but he was too wise to show any signs of triumph.

He observed simply enough: "Oscar is going to take Atterton to Little Rock to watch over him, to see that he keeps straight. Ethel is at the bottom of it. A young man was visiting her from Fort Smith—you know—Johnson—the fellow that lived six months in Boston. He was called, last spring, to be superintendent of schools in the capital, and now, all of a sudden, one of the teachers has upped and married, and it's a hard place to fill. He was telling Ethel all about it, so of course she thought at once of Osk, praised up his studying, and learning, and said how he had made up his mind to leave Core City, and branch out. The Boston fellow,—Johnson,—he was mighty interested, and wanted to see Osk right away; and the upshot of the matter is that Osk is going to Little Rock at once.

...... out of trouble,—don't s.
How do you think you'd like Lit
ground?"

"As well as any," said Pe
course, it would take away som
to be with the boys."

Then his tone grew more c
Will; I want to speak to you a
was told by that Pickens girl.
told her I knew it wasn't true;
posted on what everybody is say

"Now, Little Rock," said Wil
voice, and gazing at a distant gr
trying to count their smooth, slim
likely city. You know it's calle
Of course, there aren't many r
because the people have let the wee
The roses would be there if they
and the folks look out on those
sorter imagine they can see the b

niggers. But when I was in Little Rock, it did seem to me that the cotton business on Scott, between Markham and Second Street, beat the world. There's the Board of Trade on the corner, and the planters come from *everywhere*. Fort Smith,—none of our family would like that place, Pete; they're too busy there. It's confusing."

"You listen to me, Will," Peter interrupted in a determined voice. "That Pickens girl is telling all about town that you're in love with Mary Eden. I told her it wasn't true. But she says she caught you both in the yard at two in the morning, and you were holding Mary's hand; and when that Pickens girl opened the door, Mary broke from you and ran into the house."

"What form do you want that money in?" demanded Will.

"You never cared for Mary, did you, Will?" asked Peter, with sudden doubt.

Will stopped on the sidewalk. "I have loved her ever since I can remember," he answered, looking Peter in the eye. "But I thought you loved her yourself, and I could see all the time that she thought more of you than she did of me. I never was anything to her but a chummy sort of a cousin, and I never will be. And I never would have told how I felt, if she hadn't asked me plump at the breakfast table, yesterday, just after you had gone streakin' out of the house. She's heard what that Pickens girl has been telling, and she wanted to show 'em it wasn't true, and she just turned to me and *asked* me if I cared for her, expecting me to say 'no,' as a matter of course. I tried to get out of answering, but an answer she would have. And I wasn't going to lie about it to her, or you, or anybody living," cried Will, growing rather excited for one of his phlegmatic temperament. "It's something I'll never speak of as long as I live, if people will let me alone."

"There, there!" said Peter soothingly.

"She thought the sun rose and set just to accommodate you, Peter," said Will, recovering his slow soft drawl, "and if you hadn't gone to keeping company with that Pickens girl, she'd have been dead in love with you. But you saved her from the final leap. Anyway, she never thought anything of *me*, and she never will. She couldn't, you see, because I've grown up as a sort of brother to her. Cousin Polly Eden acts toward me as if I was her own son,—exactly. That's what I value. If people will just keep still, Mary and I can go on being the best friends in town. But as long as people up and ask me if I love her, I'll either knock 'em down, or tell the truth. And the truth is that I *do* love her, and will as long as I breathe the breath of life. Now, if this isn't plain——"

"It's perfectly plain," cried Peter,—"perfectly. I'll excuse you from illustrating it with a diagram. And now I'll hunt up Oscar and Atterton."

Peter's tone was light, but Will's words had sunk deep. It was, however, no time for self-pity. He had cast aside the possibility of Mary's love. He was as sure of it, as if Will had not spoken. But there remained something Peter could do, even yet. There comes a time when no act of ours can bring our hearts one step nearer their desire; but there is always a time when our help can stretch forth strong arms to the helplessness of others.

Peter found Oscar and Atterton in the screened-in restaurant. On the door the notice, "Go Elsewhere," still presented its inhospitable message. The young men were taking an inventory of the stock.

They were in gay spirits. Peter hastily explained that he was thinking of going with them. Goldie Pickens was not mentioned; but her influence was felt. In the language of the rainy-day Christians "she was there in the spirit."

"What!" cried Atterton, who had not for a moment harbored resentment toward Peter, "*you* going? How jolly! This is a regular exodus, hey, Pete? Osk, don't forget to put down that chafing-dish. And don't list any of those Greek and Latin books that you've got all mixed up in the cooking utensils. Why, yes, Pete, this will be known in the history of Core City as the Hegira of the Thornberrys. It's great! We'll be the Three Guardsmen of Arkinsaw. I guess I'll put up a shingle and practise law in earnest. And you, Pete, will you apply for a bank-directorship?"

"I think, maybe, I can get something to do in a bank," said Peter modestly.

"Osk has his job," said Atterton, perching upon the margin of the counter and swinging his legs; "he's to be a school-teacher."

Oscar nodded. "I've lots of information," he said, "and I hope to utilize it. I ought to have specialized; I'm afraid I've covered too much ground. Perhaps next year, if I don't like teaching, I'll take up journalism. If I don't like that, I can drop it."

"I've heard journalism is pretty hard to let go of," said Atterton, "but it's a good thing. I guess I'll go in for society, and work that for all it's worth as a stepping-stone to politics. By the time I'm in Congress, Pete ought to own the first national bank, and you, Osk, will be editor-in-chief of the biggest daily in Arkinsaw. Poor Bill! doesn't it seem a pity to leave him here to grub in that grocery store! Why, it's a perfect shame!

...is way, we'll just naturally hav...

"As for me," remaked Oscar ...
every penny I have laid by in day...

"And as for me," said Peter, "...
I can borrow."

For a moment, Atterton looke...
then he said: "All right, then, I'll...
fellows find out which one can ...
piece of dough, and I'll lend the ...
his equal to it, and I'll take the...
will make the whole thing like ...
know."

In spite of Peter's humiliation,...
cheered by such an inexhaustible...
Oscar, for a rejected lover, appe...
posed. Atterton, in fact, was not...
he was of lip. He had thought...
Gladys Lucile since his disgracef...
his acquaintance with her had n...
point that he felt it wise to ask fo...

house of "Senator" Mulkey, and on both occasions was told that Gladys Lucile was indisposed. Atterton haunted the neighborhood, but the family remained close at home. The only signs of activity to be seen were occasioned by the stone-masons putting the old foundation back under the house, which had not yet been moved.

The last day came, and Atterton went once more, and was once more told that Gladys Lucile could not see him. He supposed, of course, that she knew about his past dissipation; but in spite of this conviction, he persevered.

"I'm sorry she's sick, Colonel Mulkey," he said to the erect, magisterial form in the doorway, "but won't you please say that I am going away,—possibly forever,—and that if it is not too great an inconvenience,—I don't feel that I can go without saying good-by."

"Sir," said Mulkey gravely but kindly, "I feel sure it will do no good to deliver your message."

"Then I will take a look at your father, if I may," said Atterton desperately.

"Surely," replied the other. Atterton entered.

Old Mr. Munkey and Mrs. Mulkey sat in the room through which pervaded a gentle insistence of turpentine and camphor. The fleshy lady was kindly sympathetic over Atterton's departure, but it was evident that both she and her husband were laboring under a strong restraint. The old gentleman was not so hampered.

"I rejoice to be with you, again," he cried. "Do you remember our little chat about my caloric some time since?"

It was an excessively warm afternoon, and Atterton sat mopping his brow while Mrs. Mulkey fanned vio-

"Oh,—yes," said Atterton
that—er—I have been so—sc
you ever think of a long tube

The old man set his brigh
face. "A tube projecting th
inquired.

"Yes,—with you breathing

"Do you think that feasibl
doubtfully. "Do you think I
of it?" He had a high opin
ment.

"Mr. Mulkey," said Attert
as to the other's name, "I wil
advisement." He turned to M
turned to the room.

"Mr. Thornberry," said the
ter, I regret to say, is too indis

"Mr. Mulkey," said Attert
indisposition is prompted by a

fied words, expressed her pleasure at the manly attitude you have assumed."

Atterton flushed. "Then——" He checked himself. He rose. "I will not conceal from you," he turned to Mrs. Mulkey, then to Mr. Munkey, and then to him, "that I have formed for Miss Gladys Lucile an attachment,—I mean I love her," he went on, in a firmer tone. "I have no intention of telling her so yet; it is my purpose to first prove myself, then ask for her hand. But I do want to see her and—and I don't feel that I can go away until I do, because—well,—I just love her, you know,—and——" He sat down again, quite helpless to depart.

"Sir," said Mulkey. He paused. The tears showed in his eyes. He was extremely agitated. "Sir——" he began again.

"Sylvester!" murmured his wife.

"No," cried Mulkey, "I will speak out! I will make a clean breast of it to this noble young man. Sir, you have suffered, and you will be able to sympathize with one who has preserved a discreditable secret—in brief——" Mulkey clasped his hands nervously and looked at Atterton as for aid.

Perhaps the young man's eyes gave it. The other continued: "For years, sir, my wife and I have kept a secret from Gladys Lucile. All her life she has thought us rich, whereas we have only with the utmost toil been able to present an aristocratic front to the world. We have kept servants—when they would work for us,—here in Core City they are not obtainable,—but Gladys Lucile has had her every wish gratified. We have held an elevated place in society; no one, *no* one, sir, has lived better than we. I have had my law-office, but that was merely for effect; my

I ply my trade at night. As s
Lucile has retired, I bring fo
sit far into the night, making sl
always sleep till the noon-hour.
convenience to me. I ship my
in Chicago, who disposes of the
do finished work,—none better

"Why not open a shop, here
bewildered.

Mr. Mulkey was too surpri
speak. While he stood starir
Gladys Lucile glided into the
but as beautiful as ever.

She went swiftly to her fa
about him. She looked at Att
my father's voice I have guess
you."

"I have already told him," s
bly.

that is all. So you mustn't dream that I refused to see you because I was too proud to have a—shoemaker for my father."

Atterton was speechless, and the venerable member of the family, thinking no doubt that this was a time for general confession, cried out, "And my name is Munkey!" This, however, was lost on the young man, whose mind could not take in so much at once grand burst of light.

Mr. Mulkey, still rigidly erect, and apparently unconscious of the arm about his waist, continued with labored dignity: "Sir, you know me now for what I am,—not a lawyer, not a man in high state, and church, and society, not a colonel, not a senator—though I did run for Congress on the—er—hum!—on the—er—the—the Prohibition ticket—when I was but a boy,—but a boy, sir. You know me for what I am, a shoemaker. If I have worn another front, I conceived it to be nobody's affair. If I have crowned my life with dignity and appeared to the vulgar crowd as an aristocrat, it was not so much for my own pleasure—although it was—er—hum!—it was pleasant; but all this was done for my daughter's sake. My wife and I have lived for her, and her happiness is our only thought in life." Here Mr. Mulkey turned to Gladys Lucile and, bending down, laid his cheek against the glossy hair.

Mrs. Mulkey, overcome at this sign of giving way, hurried to her husband, exclaiming: "Sylvester! What's the matter? Aren't we just as we were before? And can't we go on just as we have in the past?"

"No!" cried Gladys Lucile, "you can not. For now I know that you two have been slaves that I might be a princess. I have done nothing all my life, and you

What I can't understand is, wl
I had done the work he has, I
house steps. I hear my train v
Give me that hand, Mr. Mulk
honors it above that of any se
Mrs. Mulkey." The fleshy lad
blindly, for her tears were fal

Atterton turned next to the
get up!" cried Winthrop's so1
the arms of his chair.

"I *will* get up!" cried the
honor you, young man. Sylv
you are gone. Take my bless
to brighten my days, sir."

"Bless your heart!" cried A
he faced Gladys Lucile.

"I'm not going to say anytl
with a whimsical smile playing c
though there was a tender mc
eves. "except to ask if I

Gladys Lucile was laughing and blushing, and half crying, too, for she had never anticipated such a declaration.

But she bravely held out her hand and answered so that even old Mr. Munkey could catch the words: "I'll answer every time you write!"

Atterton left the house on a run. He knew the engineer would try to hold the train till he arrived, but he wouldn't have missed a farewell word to the loved ones, had he, as a result, been obliged to walk all the way to Little Rock.

As he jumped Timothy Thornberry's fence, he beheld old Mrs. Polly Thornberry standing in the doorway.

"I knew you'd remember your old cousin!" she cried, her lace cap trembling with laudable pride. "But you haven't a moment,—Oscar and Peter went to the depot long ago, and even Timothy has gone—I do hope he won't get to talking on the road and forget! Now, good-by! You don't have to kiss an old woman, —just take both my hands——"

Atterton lifted her off her feet in a hurried embrace. "I'd like to see the man that could keep me from it!" he cried.

After he had left the yard, the old lady, eagerly following, called after him to stop "just a minute." He obeyed, and Mrs. Thornberry, having reached the front gate, picked up an old shoe. "This is what I threw after Oscar and Peter," she said valiantly, "and I'm going to throw it after you!" She exerted all her feeble strength, and got it quite over the picket fence.

Atterton pounced upon it. "And I'm going to carry it with me," he cried, laughing, "and keep it for our mascot!"

... ... The engine
and long, and the young m
"Old Jake,—he's getting n
burst into the drawing-roo1
a manuscript to his wife.

Elizabeth, while listening
away the tears, for she k
away, and it had been the
had been kept isolated fro:
worlds, however, would she
pect that her mind was not
work, for this reading alo
favor.

Atterton, who made nothi
people, carried such a whi
that the leaves of the mai
directions.

"Oh, Atterton!" cried E
able any longer to keep ba
come! the others forgot me

gave her a parting squeeze, then stopped at Waldo's chair.

"Well, good-by, old man!" he cried, patting the author upon his back. "Luck to you! Turn us out a masterpiece, and make the family famous!"

It is very doubtful if anybody had ever patted Waldo McCormack upon the shoulder, but certainly no one had since he could remember. But man, not being a machine, is a creature of inconsistency, and in an odd way, the great McCormack was pleased.

"Atterton," he said, "I wish you well, sir. I am glad you came. I honor your little visit. I'm afraid I've been a little distant with the boys,—it is a fault of a sensitive mind. I am sorry. I shall remember this with pleasure. Elizabeth and I will rearrange the leaves you have scattered hither and yon."

Atterton laughed boyishly. "All right—be good to yourself,—so long! I'm afraid that train will burst its whistle!"

When he was gone Waldo looked at his wife pensively. "Do you know," he said, "I like that scapegrace!"

Elizabeth rejoiced that the startling *"so long!"* had been thus received, and turned hastily away, that he might not see her pleasure and her tears.

At Mrs. Wullens's, Mrs. Polly Eden came to the door for the farewell kiss. "I owe everything to you," said Atterton, "at least what I don't owe to other people."

"I like a compliment like that," said Mrs. Eden, smiling. "It doesn't make one feel too responsible. Good-by, boy. Remember, I believe in you."

"That ought to keep me straight!" Atterton declared, "and it will, too. Don't you work yourself with you, anyhow?"

Peter, and Winthrop, a
Marietta, and Oscar, and M
dozen other minor relatives
of neighbors, crowded the pl

As Atterton ran up, he
"Hurrah for the slow trains (

The engineer grinned. I
inately mixed in the genera
Ethel, who contrived to stay
adverse conditions.

"All ready?" shouted th
thrust from the elbow of Wii

"Where's grandfather?" ci
told him good-by; for he sa
keeps store."

"Here!" shouted the eng
"climb that freight-car and :
old gentleman a-coming."

An excited burst rose fr-

Hodgins witnessed her advent with a frown of disapproval, and, crossing over to the buggy in which his favorite cousin remained, said to him in a low voice: "Say, did you drive that Pickens girl up here just now?"

"I reckon you saw me," was the defiant retort.

"Then I want you to tell me what you *mean* by having her a-buggy-ridin' with *you*."

George bent over the wheel and said slowly, "I— mean—business!"

"Then I want to say to you *now*, that any man that brings that Pickens girl into *our* fambly, after all the mischief she's did, and the more she's tried to do, I say, he'll never have *my* friendship."

"I have swore," said Nicodemus, "to make my mother proud of me before she dies, and nothing won't make a man respectable but a woman's society. I 'low to keep 'em living separate, and mother'll think her the pink of perfection. And the Thornberrys, excepting you and Cousin Polly, have been cold to me ever since I went that time into—retirement. And now I purpose to warm 'em up. I'll set that 'Pickens girl,' as you call her, on my side; and the rest of you fellows can simply wrastle and scrimmage for yourselves!"

Hodgins Thornberry gripped his cigarette so viciously that it was bitten half in two. He aided the pulverized tobacco out of his mouth by means of a hastily extended tongue. "I want to ask you *now*," he said, "if you have come to the p'int."

"We ain't talked nothing to-day," George Nicodemus replied, "but the canning factory. You can't melt your mourners on the bench till you've warmed 'em up. Nobody has much religion on a cold stomach.

"Mr. Peter," cooed the
"Cousin George has told m(
'Cousin George,'—that you
ever."

Peter grasped the railing of
"I want to tell you before
gently, "that I forgive you.
Mr. Peter. The silver co
bowl——"

Peter, pale and erect, turne
"The golden bowl is bro
Goldie. "The silver cord is
Peter!"

At this point, old Timothy
spirit aside with little cerem(
loudly, "I *have did* all you wan
to all that you ast saw to."

"Good-by, grandfather," sai
ing the other's hand; then he es

the three guardsmen of fortune were standing upon the platform, fluttering their handkerchiefs.

"When I look at those young fellows," said Timothy, in a voice that slightly trembled, "I see 'em as I know they're going to be a few years from now. You'n me'll be dead, Winthrop, like enough, and possibly *I'll* be in heaven. But I was just saying to myself, as old Jake let out that good-by whistle, that it's very seldom the same train carried away from as little a town as Core City, a bank-president, an editor of a great daily, and an Arkinsaw senator."

"Well, Cousin Tim," interposed Hodgins, "while you're feelin' so good, you and Winthrop come with me; I want to show you-all something."

The two Thornberrys followed him who had once been a house-mover. From a secluded nook of the platform, Hodgins pointed at a rapidly vanishing buggy.

"Nick is a-drivin' of it," he said, in a growling undertone, "and that Pickens girl is a-sittin' in it, an' the two of 'um, as Nick was jest a-forewarnin' me, is soon to be man an' wife!"

Timothy glared after the beak-nosed Nicodemus, then turned quietly to the rich orchardman. "Winthrop, God made man in his own image; but he never guaranteed the picture against fadin'!"

seem that the play must e
as this story must—becaus
is always somebody left
Oscar, and Atterton were
Timothy and his wife.]
old, and older friends have
the cords of our hearts a
"These, at least, will draw
bling hands and to brighte
was doubly lonesome to the
as they sat on the steps of t
their eyes toward the barn
yard offers no fit setting to
like old birds who have seer

They were sitting thus one
The captain had just come
Will at the grocery, to await

"Timothy," said Mrs. Pc
hungry?"

Timothy knew

came out here on the steps and sat down. I don't want to do anything. Looks like they ain't any *use*, you know."

"Kinder despondent, like," Timothy nodded. "All right, don't you do anything." He went in the house to telephone, and returned, striking his match on the weather-boarding as he came. He sat down slowly. "I got a letter here from 'um, if I ain't lost it," he said, groping in one pocket after another, "and I got a piece of news, too. And then I got something to say."

"Let's have the letter first," said the old lady. "Here it is in your hip-pocket. I reckon you never put a letter there in your life before, did you, Tim?"

"I dun'no," remarked the captain, "I've put 'um 'most everywhere, I reckon. And now I ain't got my specs, so the letter won't do me no good. I left 'um at the store."

Mrs. Thornberry sighed. "Then tell your news, and 'say something,' " she remarked with subtle irony.

"Groner has come home. I see him in the hack when it passed the store, about an hour ago."

"Oh, Tim! and Polly is out in the country! and like enough, Mary is off somewhere. How did he look?"

"Well, you know, honey, every time he stays to Pine Bluff a spell, he comes home mighty improved. He never goes there till he's too dissatisfied to live here another day; and when he gets to Pine Bluff, what with his daughter-in-law in the house with him, and the organ in his church, and the dust in the air, he gets mighty bidable."

"But they's an organ here in *our* church, Tim."

"Yes, but Groner never goes to it, unless there's a funeral, so it don't play no toons on *his* conscience. La, there comes Mary, now! Bless her heart!"

least I'll get this evening. down."

"Oh, I can't, I can't. Oh, *anything* you can lend us for came at four, but mother and while ago. He hasn't had any up everything on the place. bear."

"And as cross, too, I reckor "I see he looked lots more en through town; the visit has do he's an angel in heaven, he'll m a meal."

"My dear," said his wife repr no eating in heaven."

"Then Groner's not going the of my dream last night. I mus down a little while."

"Oh, I can't, I *can't!*" said hands. "I hoped you had some

down. She tore it open, remarking as she did so: "No, Aunt Polly; we have watermelon preserves of our own. Uncle Groner makes a disturbance when he sees 'em. He says he doesn't eat rinds, raw nor cooked." Mary laughed and read:

"Dear Grandpeople:—We are all right. I was surprised to meet Mr. Wullens to-day. He is going to move here, and he is glad I am here, so I can go on teaching him to read. He is very much interested in it on account of his wife, and so am I. Love to all. Your loving grandson,
"OSCAR T.
"P. S. I am no great hand at letter writing."

There was a minute's pause, then Timothy remarked: "I'm glad he told us all the *news!* Now I reckon if he hadn't studied Latin and Greek and history, he couldn't of been so descriptive!"

Mrs. Thornberry said: "You quit making fun of my Oscar. He's busy and that's why he didn't say more. The others didn't write a-tall."

The captain, fearing Mary would go, began hastily: "But I was going to tell you my dream; I thought I died and went to heaven,—of course,—and St. Peter, he says, 'Can you sing?' I explained I wasn't no vocalist. He says, 'Nobody can't get in here that can't sing, or ain't got a substitoot for 'em.' I told him just to call on my church-choir and they'd do my singing for me. I explained that the congregation ain't expected to sing down here, we let the choir take the music and own it, and *we* dassn't meddle with it. He says, 'All right,' very obliging, and went in to hunt my substitoot and was gone a good while, an' come back, an' he says, 'Well, I'm mighty sorry, but none of them choir fellows got in, I reckon!'"

Timothy looked solemnly at Mary from over his pipe.

"And little credit t(
"*You* do the best you l
will be left unfinished.'

The captain chuckled
Now, you listen to me.
Peter come and had a t
and Will,—now, don't g

Mary was on her fe
pulling her sunbonnet f(

"Peter had just been
tioned you,—and Willi
was projectin' about, a
and tells him that he lo
always will,—he *thinks*
that's a part of it, you kr
never tell you as long's
and wormwood to you,
as much as you cared fo
down anybody that brun

Mary laughed out and
me to endanger *my* life

"Timothy!" cried his wife, "I'm amazed at you. You're teasing Mary to death. Shame on you!"

Just then a blue sunbonnet appeared over the top of the barn gate. "Oh!" cried Mary, her voice rather tremulous, "there's mother, looking for me!" She gathered her skirts in her hand, and sped away like a deer.

Every Saturday night the band gave an evening concert in the city park. On one such night in August, Mary Eden and her mother, according to the custom of Core City, walked downtown, peeped into the stores, and mingled with friends on the sidewalks, till Timothy Thornberry locked up his store.

Will had already come out of the building, and hearing Mrs. Eden say that she was tired, he offered to escort mother and daughter to their cottage. Having arrived there, he asked Mary to return with him, to hear the concert. There was a look of determination upon Will's face, and a ring of decision in his voice, as if he had come to a conclusion of some importance.

As they walked to town, the moon cast their shadows before them. A silence fell upon both, painful and difficult to remove. They joined the stream of pleasure-seekers who, from eight to ten, circled about the central square of straggling trees and the creaking pump.

The band was provided by home talent, and there was but one cornet to carry the air,—a thin, slender thread of melody which wound its feeble way through the midst of an overshadowing forest of drums, trombones, and tubas.

"What are they playing?" Mary asked. She had not been listening, for her mind was busy.

Mary did not answer.

They walked up one block next. Suddenly, Will said: ' of life we have death—is th pointed to a buggy which h; blaring and booming of the Nicodemus and Goldie Picke

"What do you mean, Will? the application?"

"I don't know that there : Will. "Somehow, when I sa of that old saying, and when said it. I hear they are soo: Cousin George!"

They went around to the ne the margin of a vacant lot. ; vance. Practically, they were

"Mary, there's something] about. You know what you ; and what I ---- ' "

'way off somewhere in a foreign country, all by myself. For there's no pleasure in living here—or any other place—if I can't meet you, and be with you just as in old times,—good old days, past and gone."

Mary did not reply.

"You know what I mean, Mary, and I'd never have owned up to what I did feel about you—if you hadn't asked me. And—and you aren't going to be displeased with me about it, are you? You aren't going to make company of *me,* are you? I am just Will, you know, a plain, easy-going business man, not ambitious of anything except your friendship. Why, Lord! Did I ever think *I* was good enough for you? It never entered my head! I don't know anything, except to be honest, and stand up for my friends behind their backs, and feel like I ought to be religious, even if I'm not. Greek's no more to me than rabbit-tracks, and history very little better. What I'm now, that's all you'll ever find in me. I put it to you this way, so you'll understand that I never had a thought of anything—*anything* between you and me being serious, you know. Because I *was* never good enough. Nor anybody else, I reckon. Now, I don't want to seem to want to *appear*—to seem to want to be——"

Will left this sentence as hopeless, and offered a substitute: "Aren't you going to drive all that from your memory forever?"

"I can't," said Mary quietly.

Will sighed. "I'm sorry," he muttered.

"But I don't *want* to forget it," said Mary. "I—I like to think about it."

Will pondered this saying, but could make nothing of it.

"Will," said Mary desperately, flashing her eyes into

...do, too!" cried Mary, l...
half sobbing, all at the sam...
soon as you told me—that m...
heart had opened up—and ...
into it,—it had always bee...
thought there was another f...
locket, you know,—but it ...
time——"

"Oh, Mary!"

"It was *your* face, Will,–...
And after you spoke, and t...
you, I know it was that way ...
I've carried that face—*your* ...
of my mother's."

Well, they are on the open ...
first kiss now, no first embra...
there, walking to the music ...
hearts supplying the melody ...
and all manner of wind and st...
moon is bright; the earth is ...
from the rich odors of the gr...
world; and the blue hills of th...

Dorothy Canfield's
Gunhild

Gunhild, a peasant who has been in Kansas, seems half goddess and half child and plays an important part in the experiences of a little group of American tourists. The love story has some unexpected turns. There is considerable humor. ($1.50.)

New York Sun—"It is pleasant and charming. . . . Gunhild's beauty, simplicity, goodness, reverence and powers of imagination are well described and indicated. . . . A well-written story. It is fresh and readable and it conveys many impressions that will move and entertain."

Nation—"A vividly depicted Norwegian setting. . . . So well written as to leave one distinctly impressed . . . the finest and most vital of the characters, Aunt Nancy. . . . Gunhild, born in Kansas, and still hungering for the sunny vastness of the prairies, is finely portrayed, convincing in her beauty and simple nobility."

Chicago Record-Herald—"Original . . . the clever sketch of a group of well-defined characters under unusual circumstances . . . absorbing action is balanced by keen humor . . . a most commendable first novel . . . by turns poetic, tense and amusing."

Miss Cleghorn's
A Turnpike Lady

A tale of Beartown, Vermont, 1768-1796. 12mo. $1.25.

The story of the daily doings of a typical pre-Revolutionary family in a Vermont village, with the romance of Naomi, the Turnpike Lady.

Times Review—"It does not gloss over the poverty, amounting almost to squalor, and the rude, rough life of the time . . . and against it the characters of the men, women and children show all the more strongly for the contrast, by reason of their capacity for self-sacrifice, their affection and tenderness, and their touches of homely poetic or romantic feeling."

Life—"A bit of Revolutionary realism as opposed to Revolutionary romance. One has sometimes wondered how the other half lived in '76, the half that was not present at the battle of Monmouth and did not attend Sir William Howe's ball at Philadelphia. 'A Turnpike Lady' is a modest but not uninteresting answer."

Chicago Tribune—"Notable for its reality . . . this humorous study of the eternal feminine nature."

Outlook—"Really worth having. The reader closes the book with the hope that he may meet the author again."

HENRY HOLT AND COMPANY
PUBLISHERS   **NEW YORK**

...heart starts out on
author has caught the spirit of th
story gracefully and with skill. H
. . . Not a great book, but it is
with a very pretty wit and much ro

Chicago Evening Post—"The story
inine characters cleverly differentiat
such a charming rascal as one might

Chicago Record-Herald—"For light
turesque values, is to be warmly reco
ful story, and one that carries the w
from commonplace, everyday difficulti

Harrison Rh
The Flight

The story opens in and near Londo
rester, through tragic experience, com
only bring sorrow or death to wom
coast of Florida. Although he finds
the Eden of the title, for he finds there
death, a rude chivalry—and the shado

The Bookman—"There is a grim i
tragedy that grips the attention at on
the lighter mood that dominates the
the idyllic charm of the Florida episode,
relief. There is no question that M
portray people and incidents in a wa
them."

Chicago Record-Herald—"A strong
reading and full of promise. . . . Th

Boston Transcript—"Exceptionally
little known section, the watery desert
mosphere to a significant plot."

WILLIAM DE MORGAN'S SOMEHOW GOOD

After years of separation from his wife, the hero, during a complete suspension of memory and loss of identity, accidentally finds shelter in her home. This situation seems very simple, but the developments are far from simple, and form a story of complicated motives and experiences which holds the reader closely.

An almost grown-up daughter, ignorant of the situation, heightens the tension of the plot, and furnishes her share of two charming stories of young love.

"Somehow Good" is, in the unanimous opinion of the publishers' readers, an advance upon anything of Mr. De Morgan's yet publisht. $1.75.

WILLIAM DE MORGAN'S ALICE-FOR-SHORT

The story of a London waif, a friendly artist, his friends and family, with some decidedly dramatic happenings. Sixth printing. $1.75.

"'Joseph Vance' was far and away the best novel of the year, and of many years. . . . Mr. De Morgan's second novel . . . proves to be no less remarkable, and equally productive of almost unalloyed delight. . . . The reader . . . is hereby warned that if he skims 'Alice-for-Short' it will be to his own serious loss. . . . A remarkable example of the art of fiction at its noblest."—*Dial*.

"Really worth reading and praising . . . will be hailed as a masterpiece. If any writer of the present era is read a half century hence, a quarter century, or even a decade, that writer is William De Morgan."—*Boston Transcript*.

WILLIAM DE MORGAN'S JOSEPH VANCE

A novel of life near London in the 50's. Sixth printing. $1.75.

"The book of the last decade; the best thing in fiction since Mr. Meredith and Mr. Hardy; must take its place, by virtue of its tenderness and pathos, its wit and humor, its love of human kind, and its virile characterization, as the first great English novel that has appeared in the twentieth century."—Lewis Melville in *New York Times Saturday Review*.

"A perfect piece of writing."—*New York Tribune*.

∗∗∗ If the reader will send his name and address, the publishers will send, from time to time, information regarding their new books.

HENRY HOLT AND COMPANY
PUBLISHERS   NEW YORK

craftsmanship. Very certainly
book, if it had not been already

MAY SINCLAI

A story of a London poet

" In all our new fiction I have
' The Divine Fire.' "—MARY MOS

"A full-length study of the pe
curiously interesting environmer
excites one's admiration. . . . M
being of absorbing interest from

" I find her book the most rem
—OWEN SEAMAN in *Punch* (Londo

MAY SINCLAIR'S THE T

" Maintains a clinging grip upor
acknowledge the author's genius."

MAY SINCLAIR'S SUPER:

"Makes one wonder if in futu
may not be recognized as a new Ja

MAY SINCLAIR'S AUDRE

" It ranks high in originality, in
tinct creation."—*Times Review.*

MRS. E. L. VOYNICH'S THE GADFLY

An intense romance of the Italian rising against the Austrians early in the nineteenth century. Twenty-first printing. $1.25.

"One of the most powerful novels of the decade."—*New York Tribune.*

ANTHONY HOPE'S THE PRISONER OF ZENDA

Being the history of three months in the life of an English gentleman. Illustrated by C. D. Gibson. Fifty-first printing. $1.50.

ANTHONY HOPE'S RUPERT OF HENTZAU

A sequel to "The Prisoner of Zenda." Illustrated by C. D. Gibson. Twenty-first printing. $1.50.

These stirring romances established a new vogue in fiction and are among the most widely-read novels. Each has been successfully dramatized.

C. N. AND A. M. WILLIAMSON'S THE LIGHTNING CONDUCTOR

New illustrated edition. Twenty-first printing. $1.50.

A humorous love story of a beautiful American and a gallant Englishman who stoops to conquer. Two almost human automobiles play prominent parts. There are picturesque scenes in Provence, Spain and Italy.

"Altogether the best automobile story of which we have knowledge, and might serve almost as a guide-book for highway travel from Paris to Sicily."
—*Atlantic Monthly.*

C. N. AND A. M. WILLIAMSON'S THE PRINCESS PASSES

Illustrated by Edward Penfield. Eighth printing. $1.50.

"The authors have duplicated their success with 'The Lightning Conductor.' . . . Unusually absorbing."—*Boston Transcript.*

D. D. WELLS' HER LADYSHIP'S ELEPHANT

This humorous Anglo-American tale made an instantaneous hit. Eighteenth printing. $1.25.

"He is probably funny because he cannot help it. . . . Must consent to be regarded as a benefactor of his kind without responsibility."—*The Nation.*

∴ If the reader will send his name and address, the publishers will send, from time to time, information regarding their new books.

HENRY HOLT AND COMPANY
PUBLISHERS   (x-'07)   NEW YORK

Journal of a Russian Prisoner' from photographs. $1.50 net, by

"Holds a tremendous human interest and a delightfully feminine abandon."—

"This surprisingly outspoken volume only by an extraordinarily able woman politics and also had actual experience ii *Record Herald.*

W. F. JOHNSON'S FOUR CENT
CANA

With 16 illustrations and 6 colored $3.97.

"The most thorough and comprehensive *Nation.*

JOHN L. GIVENS' MAKIN

The author was recently with t $1.50 net; by mail $1.62.

Some seventy-five leading newspaj best detailed account of the busines manufacturing organization of a metr be invaluable to those entering up revelation to the general reader.

THE OPEN ROAD   THE

Compiled by E. V. Lucas. Full gi each (cloth) $1.50; (leather) $2.50.

Pretty anthologies of prose and American authors, respectively for wa

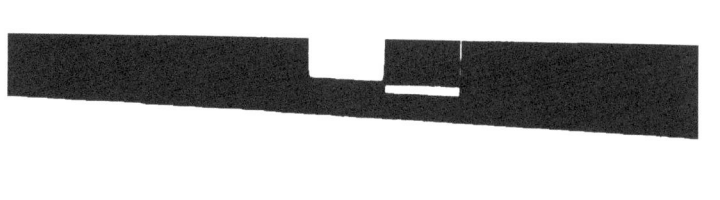

CPSIA information can be obtained
at www.ICGtesting.com
Printed in the USA
BVHW010645191122
652343BV00003B/16